the FOUNDERS' revolution

the
FOUNDERS'
revolution

The FORGOTTEN *History and Principles*
of the Declaration of Independence

Michael S. Law

NEW YORK

NASHVILLE • MELBOURNE • VANCOUVER

the FOUNDERS' revolution
The FORGOTTEN *History and Principles of the Declaration of Independence*

Published in New York, New York, by Morgan James Publishing. Morgan James is a trademark of Morgan James, LLC. www.MorganJamesPublishing.com

The Morgan James Speakers Group can bring authors to your live event. For more information or to book an event visit The Morgan James Speakers Group at www.TheMorganJamesSpeakersGroup.com.

ISBN 978-1-68350-585-3 paperback
ISBN 978-1-68350-586-0 eBook
Library of Congress Control Number: 2017907515

Cover Design by:
Rachel Lopez
www.r2cdesign.com

Interior Design by:
Bonnie Bushman
The Whole Caboodle Graphic Design

In an effort to support local communities, raise awareness and funds, Morgan James Publishing donates a percentage of all book sales for the life of each book to Habitat for Humanity Peninsula and Greater Williamsburg.

Get involved today! Visit
www.MorganJamesBuilds.com

To my wife, Kaori, and my children, Joseph, Satomi, and Kenji, for whom I struggle for liberty. To the Founders and their vision of liberty, which cost them many years of struggle and much blood.

Contents

Founders and Foundations   ix
Key Events in the Advance toward Independence   xii

Chapter 1   The Course of Human Events   1
Chapter 2   Unalienable Rights and the Proper Role of Government   18
Chapter 3   The Charges: Abuses of Executive Power   47
Chapter 4   The Charges: Abuses of Legislative Power   90
Chapter 5   The Charges: Abuses of War Power   121
Chapter 6   Reconciliation Attempts   134
Chapter 7   Separation and the Appeal to Heaven   140

Appendices   155
              The Magna Carta   157
              The English Bill of Rights of 1689   169
              The Declaration of Independence   177
Bibliography   183
About the Author   196
End Notes   197

Founders and Foundations

Today we hear from speeches, news outlets, social media, articles, and books a great deal of political turmoil and rhetoric surrounding government policies. And more and more of this discussion centers around what is thought to be constitutional and what is not. I have always wondered what America's Founders would have thought about what has been done to the nation they spent so many years shaping. Certainly they had their own issues, rhetoric, and political turmoil. They did not always agree with one another. In fact, they often voiced disagreements with each other's perspective on a handful of issues. However, they found unity around the Declaration of Independence and the United States Constitution.

On the Declaration of Independence, the Continental Congress voted unanimously in the affirmative with each state having one vote, even though each state had multiple representatives. The signers of the Declaration unified the nation to a common cause in time of war. That cause was not just America's but all humanity's, which is one reason the principles stated in the Declaration are universal and unchanging.

The Founders used specific wording, which their generation understood well and even today's students of their words can grasp fairly easily. They were masters of the English language as well as master statesmen. Take Patrick Henry, for example. He said, "I know not what course others may take, but as for me, give me liberty or give me death!" Then there is the schoolteacher turned spy, Nathan Hale, who, just before being hanged by the British for being a spy, stated, "I regret that I have but one life to give for my country." Then there is the story of John Paul Jones, America's first navy hero. While in the midst of his own sinking ship, one of his men called for quarter—surrender. The British captain they were fighting against was willing to give quarter to them, but Jones refused. He declared he had not called for quarter and told the British captain that he still intended to fight on, saying, "I have not yet begun to fight!" These words, even today, are inspirational and can help unify a nation to embrace a common cause—the cause of liberty.

Unfortunately, an increasing number of Americans have not even read the Declaration of Independence or the US Constitution, much less any of our other founding documents. They have read about them in textbooks and heard teachers and others talk about them, but they have not read them for themselves. How can Americans understand what they have not read? And among those who have read even just one of our founding documents, many do not understand the historical context in which they were framed, so they lack much that would help them understand the claims made, the truths set forth, and the principles articulated. My purpose, therefore, is make clear what the Founders intended when they used the wording they did and to liken their words, concepts, and charges to some of today's policies and rhetoric. I have drawn from many of the literary works that the Founders used in developing their initial documents. Some of these works are John Locke's *Second Treatise of Government*, the *Federalist*, and even the Founders' own words about the founding documents they drafted and approved. I cannot stress enough the importance of truly understanding America's foundational documents. James Madison said, "The advancement and diffusion of knowledge is the only guardian of true liberty." Understanding these documents is vital to the preservation of liberty in our country.

Writing this book has been a work of the heart. Few things are nearer and dearer to me than the words that have been chiseled into me—the words of the Declaration of Independence and the US Constitution and those of an inspired generation known as the founding generation. I hope you will *feel* those words as I have felt them. I also hope *The Founder's Revolution* does justice to those Founders who have received little to none in recent years.

—Michael S. Law

Key Events in the
Advance toward Independence

1215	Magna Carta (Great Charter)
1606	First Charter of Virginia
1609	Second Charter of Virginia
1611	Third Charter of Virginia
1620	William Bradford and Puritans arrive in New England, Mayflower Compact
1629	Charter of Massachusetts Bay
1630	John Winthrop and other Puritans arrive in Massachusetts
1632	Charter of Maryland
1639	Fundamental Orders of 1639 (Connecticut)
1642–1649	English civil war, king removed, Oliver Cromwell made protectorate of British Commonwealth
1660	Navigation Acts—only British ships allowed to carry British goods

1662	Charter of Connecticut
1663 (March)	Charter of Carolina (includes North and South Carolina and Georgia)
1663 (July)	Charter of Rhode Island and Providence Plantations
1681	Charter of Pennsylvania
1689	English Bill of Rights, English monarchy restored under William and Mary
1696	Navigation Acts renewed
1701	Charter of Delaware
1732	Charter of Georgia
1754–1763	French and Indian War, colonists raise own armies to support England
1763	Royal Proclamation, prohibits colonists from settling west of Appalachian mountains
1764 (April)	Currency Act, requires only hard currency in transactions
1764 (September)	Sugar Act, taxes sugar and tea
1765 (March)	Stamp Act, taxes legal documents, etc.
1765	Quartering Act, requires giving food and housing to soldiers
1766	Act repealing the Stamp Act
1766	Declaratory Act, makes all laws of colonies void, grants Parliament full legislative power
1767	Townsend Act, levies new taxes and heavy customs regulations
1767	New York Suspending Act, suspends colonial government in New York to force compliance with the Quartering Act
1770	Boston Massacre, eleven killed or injured
1773	Boston Tea Party, colonial protest against the Townsend Act
1774 (March)	Boston Port Act, closes Boston to commerce
1774 (May)	Administration of Justice Act, protects soldiers from colonial trials

1774 (May)	Massachusetts Government Act, all colonial government officers must be appointed by the king
1774 (June)	Quartering Act, reinstituted and expanded
1774 (September)	First Continental Congress
1774 (October)	Quebec Act, grants Parliament full legislative powers
1775 (April)	Battle of Lexington and Concord, the Revolutionary War begins
1775 (July)	Olive Branch Petition, the colonies attempt to reconcile with England
1775 (August)	The king rejects the petition and declares war on the colonies
1775 (December)	Royal Proclamation, Parliament declares war on the colonies
1776	Declaration of Independence, drafted and published
1781 (March)	Articles of Confederation
1781 (October)	General Cornwallis surrenders ending the Revolutionary War
1787	Constitutional Convention

Chapter 1

The Course of Human Events

WHEN in the Course of human Events, it becomes necessary for one People to dissolve the Political Bands which have connected them to another, and to assume among the Powers of the Earth, the separate and equal Station to which the Laws of Nature and of Nature's God entitle them, a decent Respect to the Opinions of Mankind requires that they should declare the causes which impel them to the Separation.

The Political Connections

In the summer of 1776, Thomas Jefferson, Benjamin Franklin, Robert Livingston, and Roger Sherman were appointed to a committee to draft a declaration of independence that would provide the justification for the American colonies to break away from Great Britain. The task for drafting the Declaration fell to Jefferson. And what we know today as the Declaration of

Independence is largely Jefferson's work, having undergone some revisions by the committee and America's then sitting Congress.

In the Declaration of Independence, Thomas Jefferson begins with the justification for the separation of the American colonies from British rule. What is this "Course of human Events" that required the people to "dissolve the Political Bands" to a nation that they cherished so much? What would drive a people strongly enough that they would willingly jeopardize their lives and livelihood to revolt? What is the "Station" to which people are entitled? What are these "Laws of Nature?" Why would Jefferson, whom experts describe as a deist[1] at best and an atheist at worst, claim that "Nature's God" gave the people that "equal Station" to which they were entitled? Justification was vital to their fellow countrymen and to others who may desire to follow in their footsteps. Thus, as we will see, Jefferson makes the case for separation.

First, the political bands to which Jefferson referred were the ones that tied the colonies to England. Jefferson and the rest of the Founders possessed these bands—namely, the rights they enjoyed as Englishmen and the form of government that guaranteed their rights and their protection under the English constitution. The Founders, indeed all the American colonists, held these rights in high esteem. Despite the officials in office failing to observe the written constitution, the Founders sought to reconcile their many disputes with the mother country by working through the system England provided. In order to understand the "Course of human Events" and why the Founders recognized the need to declare independence, we must first understand what rights the British government failed to observe and where the system failed.

Some of the first rights that England's king recognized came most prominently under the Magna Carta, or the Great Charter. After a variety of King John's abuses toward the common people, the nobles, the clergy, and, in short, all people living under him, his subjects forced him to accept the Great Charter in 1215. Later, the Charter underwent various revisions. This document was the real beginning to defining the rights and liberties of Englishmen living under the crown. However, as I will explain in the next chapter, the crown's recognition of rights as found in the Magna Carta and in any other documents that human beings produce are only a recognition of some of the rights bestowed upon all humanity by their Creator.

Many of the rights and limits on government that the subjects of the king demanded of him are recognizable under America's Constitution today. While listing all of the demands in the Magna Carter is excessive, I will cite some similarities with our Constitution as well as enough to demonstrate some reasons for America's colonists to push for separation from England.

First, the Magna Carta stated, "the English Church shall be free, and shall have her rights entire, and her liberties inviolate."[2] This is similar to our Constitution's first amendment affirming freedom of religion. Furthermore, the Charter informed the king, "We have granted to all freemen of our kingdom, *for us and our heirs forever*, all the underwritten liberties, *to be had and held by them and their heirs, of us and our heirs forever.*"[3] Of course, the Founders and the rest of the Americans, with few exceptions, would be included as descendants or heirs of "freemen of our kingdom."

The Magna Carta also guaranteed the right to property and freedom against illegal seizure: "Neither we nor our bailiffs will seize any land or rent for any debt, as long as the chattels of the debtor are sufficient to repay the debt." This is similar to the Takings Clause in the US Constitution's Fifth Amendment, which says no citizen can have his property taken for public use without receiving just compensation for it.

The Charter also guaranteed no taxation without representation and taxing within certain limits: "No scutage (tax) … shall be imposed on our kingdom, unless by common counsel of our kingdom … and for these there shall not be levied more than a reasonable aid." Until the change under the Sixteenth Amendment, the US Constitution prohibited a direct tax by the federal government, except in proportion to population, thereby keeping taxes more reasonable.

Another right stipulated in the Charter prohibited the king from forcing a change of venue into a court in a different country—country being in another community.[4] Similarly, under the US Constitution under Article III and reinforced under the Sixth Amendment, all trials must be held in the state or district in which the crime is committed, not out of state or country.

4 | the FOUNDERS' revolution

In addition, the Charter granted the right to "common counsel," similar to the right to an attorney. It also granted that any summons or appearance in court would be "for a fixed date … and a fixed place," and all letters must "specify the reason of the summons."[5] This is similar to the Constitution's requirement that citizens can request a writ of *habeas corpus* so that we might know the reasons for being detained or what alleged crime we committed.

The Charter also specified that "A freeman shall not be amerced (punished) for a slight offense, except in accordance with the degree of the offense … and none of the aforesaid amercements shall be imposed except by the oath of honest men of the neighborhood." In other words, the Charter prohibited excessive punishments as well as punishments imposed by anyone except a jury of one's peers. The Eighth Amendment of our Constitution also prohibits excessive bail and fines and cruel and unusual punishments.

The Magna Carta also contained provisions against the government seizing property without providing the proper payment: "No constable or other bailiff of ours shall take corn or other provisions from anyone without immediately tendering money therefor." Again, the right to property was preserved. And if and when property was illegally seized, it had to be restored.[6] Here again, the Constitution's Fifth Amendment prohibits seizure of property "for public use, without just compensation."

These are just a few of the rights guaranteed to Englishmen in the Magna Carta. And this occurred about 275 years before Christopher Columbus discovered America in 1492. It would be another one-hundred-plus years after Columbus, in 1607 at Jamestown, Virginia, before England had its first permanent settlement on the American continent. The first document of record regarding any political bands created on the American continent is the Mayflower Compact. It is important to understand how and why William Bradford and the rest of the pilgrims came to America and settled in Massachusetts. It is also vitally important to understand the political bands they created upon their arrival and why those bands evolved into the form they did.

The Magna Carta guaranteed certain rights to all Englishmen, including the lowest citizens. Among these rights, the clergy demanded that the king not incorporate his authority with that of the church. The clergy were to determine what was best for the church and its members in its sphere of influence and authority. Through the Great Charter, the English acquired freedom of religion and a separation of the state from the church. The crown was not to involve itself in the church's affairs.

However, when it came to William Bradford and the Puritans, both the crown under King James I and the church infringed on the rights guaranteed Puritan Englishmen by the Magna Carta. Bradford wrote of the problems they faced while in England in his book *History of Plymouth Plantations*. He and his fellow Puritans were "hunted and persecuted on every side, so as their former afflictions were but flea-bitings in comparison of these which now came upon them. For they were taken and clapt up in prison, others had their houses beset and watched night and day, and hardly escaped their [the church's] hands."[7]

Because of these ongoing persecutions and violations of guaranteed rights, the Puritans decided they needed to flee to Holland so they could enjoy the liberties and freedom of religion that they sought. Even as they worked toward that goal and planned to board a ship for Holland, the captain betrayed them and sent them back to town where their persons and property were "rifled and ransacked" and many of them were sent to prison for several months.[8] Finally, many of them were able to settle in Holland for a time.

Nevertheless, after a few years in Holland, they realized they would be unable to worship as they chose because of the customs and traditions of the Dutch. So they chose to move once again. They considered New Guinea, India, and several other places but eventually settled on Virginia and ended up in New England.

Once they decided to settle in America, they sought religious freedom from King James I, under whose reign they would once again live. However, just as the king denied them freedom of religion before, he denied them again, though not completely: "Some of the chief of the company doubted not to obtain their suit of the king for liberty in religion, and to have it confirmed under the king's broad seal, according to their desires … but it proved all in vain. Yet thus far they prevailed, in sounding his majesty's mind, that he would connive at them and not molest them, provided they carried themselves peaceably."[9]

Bradford also recognized the problem of acquiring the king's broad seal. He realized that none could guarantee that the king would not change his mind. The

Puritans could do nothing that would truly guarantee their liberties under the king. Nor did they have a guarantee that any future monarch would honor the previous monarch's agreement. As Bradford stated, "There was no security in this promise intimated, there would be no great certainty in a further confirmation of the same; for if afterwards there should be a purpose or desire to wrong them, though they had a seal as broad as the house floor, it would not serve the turn; for there would be means anew found to recall or reverse it."[10] Here we see that the Puritans trusted the king to do what history has shown kings always do— whatever is in their own best interest with little concern for the interests and rights of their subjects. A king's concern is typically not for his subjects but only for himself.

Despite these misgivings, the Puritans were still determined to plant themselves in another place so they could live peaceably and according to the liberty they knew was their right. They trusted in God to assist them in their endeavors and believed that their actions were in line with his will.

Thus, William Bradford and the rest of his company set out to America to pursue an opportunity to worship their God and free themselves, as much as possible, from the oppressions of the crown. God continued to test their faith as they departed from England. While most people know that the Puritans traveled the Atlantic Ocean aboard the Mayflower, the lesser-known ship, Speedwell, departed England with them and carried another half of their congregation. On the journey, the Speedwell began to leak and it could not be stopped. Bradford and his compatriots decided it would be unsafe to continue to press on toward America, so both ships turned back.[11] Despite yet another obstacle, after both ships returned to England, the Puritans split up into two parties with one returning to London and the rest continuing their voyage to the New World.

The charter they received was for Virginia and not for New England. A charter for Massachusetts Bay would eventually be established in 1629. However, divine Providence surely played a role in landing them in New England. It was late enough in the season that when they arrived, they needed to quickly find a place to settle and begin to build out of the wilderness their "shining city on a hill." Having arrived at Cape Cod on November 11, 1620 and knowing that the place was New England rather than Virginia, some "strangers amongst" the party recognized that their charter was for Virginia. These "strangers" were those not of the faith of Bradford and the main portion of the colonists. These "strangers" were determined "that when they came ashore they would use their own liberty; for none had power to command them, the patent they had being for Virginia, and not for New England, which belonged to another government, with which the Virginia Company had nothing to do."[12] Even though this was technically correct, Bradford and the rest of the company feared what the resulting "liberty" would be for those who were neither of their faith nor of the same common desires for the colonists' success, if given the complete liberty to do as they pleased. So William Bradford, John Carver, and the rest of the party established a new charter—one in which all agreed to participate.

This was the beginning of government established by the people rather than one established at the whim of one person, including that of a monarch. It also implied a better way than anarchy or no government at all. These individuals created a document that they called the Mayflower Compact, after the name of the ship on which they sailed for America and on which they signed the document. The Mayflower Compact is word for word as follows:

In the name of God, Amen. We whose names are underwritten, the loyal subjects of our dread sovereign Lord, King James, by the grace of God, of Great Britain, France and Ireland king, defender of the faith, etc., having undertaken, for the glory of God, and advancement of the Christian faith, and honor of our king and country, a voyage to plant the first colony in the Northern parts of Virginia, do by these presents solemnly and mutually in the presence of God, and one of another, covenant and combine ourselves together into a civil body politic, for our better ordering and preservation and furtherance of the ends aforesaid; and by virtue hereof to enact, constitute, and frame such just and equal laws, ordinances, acts, constitutions, and offices, from time to time, as shall be thought most meet and convenient for the general good of the colony, unto which we promise all due submission and obedience. In witness whereof we have hereunder subscribed our names at Cape-Cod the 11 of November, in the year of the reign of our sovereign lord, King

James, of England, France, and Ireland the eighteenth, and of Scotland the fifty-fourth. Anno Domini 1620.[13]

This was not a constitution or even a creation of government. What this succeeded in accomplishing was to construct an agreement that everyone would work together to form a government that would meet the needs of everyone involved.

Numerous points made in the compact contribute to laying the foundation of good government established by the people. First, by mutual agreement, they combined themselves into "one body politic." They all agreed to form a government.

Next, they declared to what purpose they formed government—for their mutual preservation and to create order. Otherwise, there would be chaos and anarchy. Anarchy is not conducive to prosperity, and these men and women understood the need for an ordered government. The purpose of government, therefore, was for the preservation of each individual as well as the means to that end, namely, their liberty and property.

They concluded the compact with the procedures by which they would accomplish the stated purposes. The people would create the government and order it in such a way that the laws would be equal and just towards all of them. They could alter the offices and laws from time to time, as they saw fit, for the good of all. In addition, they all agreed to submit to the government that they would form.

Finally, they stated that their purpose for colonizing the "Northern parts of Virginia" was "for the glory of God and advancement of the Christian faith." The reason for their departure from England, Holland, and the rest of the Old World was so they could more freely practice their religion according to the dictates of their own consciences. The Old World did not offer them those opportunities, while the Puritans believed that the New World would, and this despite the adversities they would surely suffer settling in an untamed wilderness.

Of course, William Bradford and the rest of his people were not the only ones searching for a new beginning in the New World. Later, more Puritans would arrive in Massachusetts. Many of these Puritans had remained in England, believing that reform from within the Anglican church and the country they loved was still possible. Eventually, however, they too realized that England had little to offer by way of freedom of religion. In fact, they found that some other liberties the Magna Carta guaranteed were not theirs to enjoy either.

After departing England, John Winthrop, a leader of many of these Puritans, declared one of the reasons for their departure while still aboard the ship Arbella in 1630.

> For we must consider that we shall be as a city upon a hill. The eyes of all people are upon us. So that if we shall deal falsely with our God in this work we have undertaken, and so cause Him to withdraw His present help from us, we shall be made a story and a by-word through the world. ... But if our hearts shall turn away, so that we will not obey, but shall be seduced, and worship other Gods, our pleasure and profits, and serve them; it is propounded unto us this day, we shall surely perish out of the good land whither we pass over this vast sea to possess it. Therefore, let us choose life, that we and our seed may live, by obeying His voice and cleaving to Him, for He is our life and our prosperity.[14]

The Puritans sought religious liberty. Moreover, their intent was to display the blessings and freedoms that liberty bestows upon all who partake of it. This light would act as a beacon for the world concerning liberty, and it included spreading the gospel of Jesus Christ.

Later Roger Williams came to the New World pursuing religious freedom, which led to the founding of Rhode Island and Providence Plantations. Yet another seeker of liberty, George Calvert, founded Maryland on behalf of Roman Catholics who sought freedom of religion because of the oppressions of the king of England and persecutions from Virginians. Thomas Hooker led many Puritans to found Connecticut for their own version of Puritanism and religious freedom. William Penn aided the Quakers in their quest for religious freedom, immigrating to Pennsylvania. Many people of the Old World sought religious freedom and other liberties because of the numerous oppressions under which they lived. Unfortunately, the freedoms they enjoyed would be short-lived.

In the case of Virginia, relatively little was different concerning the rights that colonists expected to possess. Both Queen Elizabeth and King James I sought to colonize the New World in the late sixteenth century. The only proviso was that "the territories and districts so granted, be not previously occupied or possessed by the *subjects of any other Christian prince or State.*"[15] In 1606 when Thomas Gates and his associates received their letters of patent (that is, charter) granting them the right to settle, the patent included the same previously mentioned provision and, most importantly, the provision "that the colonists and their children should enjoy the same liberties as if they had remained, or were born, within the realm."[16] One of the purposes of this charter was to propagate the "Christian Religion to such People, as yet live in Darkness and miserable Ignorance of the true Knowledge and Worship of God, and may in time bring the Infidels and Savages, living in those parts, to human Civility."[17] Here we see that the desire to spread Christianity played a major role in colonizing the New World, in this case, Virginia.

Maryland, established by George Calvert, received its first immigrants from England in 1632. They were Roman Catholic. The historian David Ramsay stated, "Calvert their leader purchased the right of the Aborigines, and with their consent took possession of a town, which he called St. Mary's." Furthermore, Ramsay noted that Calvert strived to cultivate a friendship with the natives. This was especially important since so many Catholics, unhappy with their native lands, immigrated to Maryland.[18] Cultivating a friendship with the natives helped provide Maryland with peace and safety. Furthermore, Maryland became one of the first colonies to guarantee religious freedom to all individuals and groups, including non-Catholics.

William Bradford and the first group of Puritans arrived in America toward the end of 1620. They left under the reign of James I of the House of Stuart, whose government allowed the persecution of the Puritans to the point that they fled to Holland and later to America. By 1630, Charles I, son of James I, ruled England. It was at this time that John Winthrop and his group left England for America.

England entered a tumultuous period after that. By 1642, England was in civil war because of the oppressions of the absolute monarch, Charles I, which ended in 1649 with Charles I's beheading. From 1649, under Oliver Cromwell—the protectorate of the British Commonwealth, as England called him—until Cromwell died in 1658, Puritans greatly assisted in the government of England. After Cromwell's death, his son led the commonwealth until 1660 when the House of Stuart returned to the throne under Charles II, who ruled until 1685. Charles II's son, James II, believed to be Catholic, ruled until 1688 when Parliament engineered the Glorious Revolution, ousting James II, who fled to France.

It was during this tumultuous period that most of the rest of the colonies formed and when the reigning king granted charters to the colonies. Beginning with Connecticut, Thomas Hooker and other English settlers moved from Massachusetts to what would become Connecticut in 1636 in part because of religious freedom. Hooker recognized that the Puritans, the sect that he was part of, were prohibiting freemen from voting who were not of the Puritan religion. Disagreeing with this, Hooker and others moved to Connecticut. Hooker is known as the "Father of Connecticut," and he was a Puritan minister. Soon after arriving in Connecticut, Hooker and the other settlers formed their own government, known as the Fundamental Orders of 1639. This was a representative government of the people agreed to by all.[19]

By 1662, King Charles II granted a charter that allowed for self-government. One of its expressed purposes was this:

> Our said People Inhabitants there, may be so religiously, peaceably and civilly governed, as their good Life and orderly Conversation may win and invite the Natives of the Country to the Knowledge and Obedience of the only true GOD, and the Saviour of Mankind, and the Christian Faith, which in Our Royal Intentions, and the adventurers free Possession, is the only and principal End of this Plantation.[20]

Here we see again the religious underpinnings in the charter.

Rhode Island received its charter in the following year, 1663. The settling of Rhode Island began because of religious persecution by Puritans in Massachusetts who clearly had forgotten their own persecution in England. Massachusetts exiled Roger Williams in 1636, and he moved to Rhode Island. When settling Providence, Rhode Island, Williams purchased land from the Narragansett Indians. In the creation of Rhode Island, Williams founded it on the principle "that every man who submits peaceably to the civil authority may worship God according to the dictates of his own conscience, without molestation."[21] Thus, the persecution of Williams led to the formation of a colony of religious tolerance and freedom.

In 1663, the crown granted Carolina a charter that was entrusted to a group of nobles because of their "Being excited with a laudable and pious zeal for the propagation of the Christian faith."[22] The charter of Carolina included in its territory North and South Carolina and Georgia. Later these three separated into independent colonies. Initially, the king granted the charter to those with zeal to propagate Christianity. Furthermore, the charter, like the others, granted full governmental authority to Carolina.

In 1681, Pennsylvania received its charter, which was given to William Penn, a Quaker. He departed England with a group of fellow Quakers. Ramsay points out that despite the grant from the king, "Mr. Penn did not think himself invested with the right of the soil, till he had purchased it from the native proprietors."[23] One difference with Pennsylvania and the rest of the previously mentioned colonies is that the charter granted no express stipulation of Pennsylvanians being British subjects. However, like the others, it did grant the right of self-government, and because the colonists were Englishmen, they still had the liberties granted by the Magna Carta.

These historical details provide the context and reasons for understanding why so many Englishmen left for the New World and why they sought for grants of land and for the right to govern themselves. By so doing, they could truly enjoy their rights as Englishmen, including their right to worship according to the dictates of their consciences.

After England's tumultuous period and once Parliament restored the crown in 1689 under William and Mary, Parliament presented the throne with a new Bill of Rights—the English Bill of Rights of 1689. This document first provided the grievances perpetrated by King James II and then set out the prerequisites for William and Mary to ascend to the throne. These prerequisites provided the remedies for the grievances. Among the rights guaranteed by the English Bill of Rights was the right of Parliament to give its consent to the king before he could suspend laws, execute them, or dispense with any of them. In addition, the king could not tax without Parliament's consent; the king's subjects had the right to petition the king; the king could not raise and keep a standing army in times of peace; the king's subjects had the right to keep arms for their defense; the election of members of Parliament was to be free; freedom of speech and debate were to be allowed in Parliament; no excessive bail or fines, nor cruel and unusual punishments could be inflicted; and no fines or forfeitures were permitted before conviction.[24] As I will demonstrate, Parliament and King George III violated the English Bill of Rights, as well as many of the rights guaranteed under the Magna Carta, which forced the American colonies to declare their independence from England. Moreover, the US Constitution derived many similar rights found in its Bill of Rights from this English Bill of Rights document.

This history of many of the colonies shows the course upon which America and the people of this land were set. These human events led them to the New World to create their own destinies and live according to the dictates of their conscience. Despite the persecutions they endured and the freedom they sought, they still maintained ties to their mother country, Great Britain. Eventually, however, the Hand of Providence set separate courses for the colonies in America and their motherland. The violation of the rights guaranteed by the Magna Carta, the English Bill of Rights of 1689, and, more particularly, the violation of the "Laws of Nature," which laws nature's God prohibits all governments from violating, required the eventual separation of the colonies from England.

The Laws of Nature

The Founders relied on the moral laws of nature as their foundational justification for separating themselves from the "Political Bands" of Great Britain and joining the world of nations as a "separate and equal Station." In order to understand the natural laws to which Thomas Jefferson referred, you need to understand the philosophies of one of the most vital, influential books from which Jefferson derived many of the concepts articulated in the Declaration and from which many of the ideas of government developed. I am referring to John Locke's *Second Treatise of Government.*

Even though the concept of the laws of nature, or natural law, did not originate with John Locke, his *Second Treatise* and his philosophy of natural law are vital to the discussion. Jefferson derived from Locke most of the foundational ideas expressed in the Declaration to the point that Jefferson used similar and even exact wording from Locke and his treatise. In reality, no philosopher, no one man, nor collective of men can lay claim to the ideas of natural moral laws. The ideas come from "Nature's God," as Jefferson wrote. However, Aristotle, Cicero, Thomas Hobbes, and others were among the first philosophers to articulate natural law and its implications.

Cicero wrote about natural law, which he described as "true law," in his *De Republica,* book I:

> True law is right reason, consonant with nature, spread through all people. It is constant and eternal; it summons to duty by its orders, it deters from crime by its prohibitions. Its orders and prohibitions to good people are never given in vain; but it does not move the wicked by these orders or prohibitions. It is wrong to pass laws obviating this law; it is not permitted to abrogate any of it; it cannot be totally repealed. We cannot be released from this law by the senate or the people, and it needs no exegete or interpreter. ... There will not be one law at Rome and another at Athens, one now and another later; but all nations at all times will be bound by this one eternal and unchangeable law, and god will be the one common master and general (so to speak) of all people. He is the author, expounder, and mover of this law; and the person who does not obey it will be in exile from himself. Insofar as he scorns his nature as a human being, by this very fact he will pay the greatest penalty, even if he escapes all the other things that are generally recognized as punishments.[25]

According to Cicero, the natural law is God-given law, impossible to change. And it must be followed by all individuals and governments. Violating this law will incur punishment—a punishment established by the law's divine Author. The natural moral law needs no interpretation for it is simple to understand and easily comprehended by most rational people.

John Locke explained what this law is when he wrote:

> To understand political power right, and derive it from its original, we must consider, what state all men are naturally in, and that is, a state of perfect freedom to order their actions, and dispose of their possessions and persons, as they think fit, within the bounds of the law of nature, without asking leave, or depending upon the will of any other man.
>
> But though this be a state of liberty, yet it is not a state of license: though man in that state have an uncontrollable liberty to dispose of his person or possessions, yet he has not liberty to destroy himself, or so much as any creature in his possession, but where some nobler use than its bare preservation calls for it. The state of nature has a law of nature to govern it, which obliges every one: and reason, which is that law, teaches all mankind, who will but consult it, that being all equal and independent, no one ought to harm another in his life, health, liberty, or possessions.[26]

The law of nature, or the state of liberty, that comes naturally to every human being does not permit one to act however one desires. The violation of another's life, liberty, or property is a violation of natural law and the consequences are equal to the violation. In addition to the natural rights for self, Locke also concluded, "When his own preservation comes not in competition, ought he, as much as he can, to preserve the rest of mankind."[27] Not only does each individual have the right to act as one wills, as long as it does not violate the same right to act of others, but each individual has the responsibility to defend the same natural rights of humankind when others wrongfully choose to violate another's liberty to act.

Another vital concept, coupled with the laws of nature, is the state of war. Understanding this is paramount to understanding how Jefferson correctly justified a separation from Great Britain. Thomas Hobbes believed that, in this state of nature, "they [man] are in that condition which is called war, and such a war, as is of every man against every man."[28] In a state of war, human beings take the lives, liberty, and property of other human beings. Hobbes thought that humanity existed naturally in a state of war.

Locke, on the other hand, described humanity's natural condition differently. First, he agreed that it is the responsibility of each person to protect his own life, liberty, and property, and each person has a responsibility to "as much as he can, preserve the rest of mankind." So for Locke, the state of war is conceived this way:

[H]e who attempts to get another man into his absolute power, does thereby put himself into a state of war with him; it being to be understood as a declaration of a design upon his life: for I have reason to conclude, that he who would get me into his power without my consent, would use me as he pleased when he had got me there, and destroy me too when he had a fancy to it; for nobody can desire to have me in his absolute power, unless it be to compel me by force to that which is against the right of my freedom, i.e. make me a slave. To be free from such force is the only security of my preservation; and reason bids me look on him, as an enemy to my preservation, who would take away that freedom which is the fence to it; so that he who makes an attempt to enslave me, thereby puts himself into a state of war with me.

This makes it lawful for a man to kill a thief, who has not in the least hurt him, nor declared any design upon his life, any farther than, by the use of force, so to get him in his power, as to take away his money, or what he pleases, from him; because using force, where he has no right, to get me into his power, let his pretense be what it will, I have no reason to suppose, that he, who would take away my liberty, would not, when he had me in his power, take away everything else. And therefore it is lawful for me to treat him as one who has put himself into a state of war with me, i.e. kill him if I can; for to that hazard does he justly expose himself, whoever introduces a state of war, and is aggressor in it.[29]

In other words, for Locke, if another individual *attempts* to violate the laws of nature, he has created a state of war on the individual level. War is a state of violence between two opposing sides. In this example, the opposing sides would be the thief and his victim, the outcome of which the opposing sides decide by the injury or death of either party and by the loss of the liberty or property of either party. The victim would be justified and the thief condemned in whatever outcome occurs.

Otherwise, the natural state is a state of liberty. This is where Locke differs from Hobbes. Hobbes believed that men, without some kind of a contract for peace, existed in a perpetual state of war; whereas Locke believed that a state of war existed only when there was an attempt to violate the state of nature or natural law.

The Founders believed that King George and Parliament violated the "Laws of Nature and of Nature's God," as well as the rights guaranteed to British subjects in the Magna Carta and the Bill of Rights of 1689. Therefore, this placed the American colonists into a state of war with their mother country, which required their separation from it. Jefferson later detailed in the Declaration of Independence the violations of the colonists' rights, reasoning and providing proof, declaring to the world how Great Britain violated the rights of her own subjects. The Founders trusted that the opinion of humanity and the understanding of natural law would provide the decent respect needed "to assume among the powers of the earth, the separate and equal station" to which they were entitled by "Nature's God."

Therefore, rather than simply fighting for their separation, the Founders decided that the world needed to be provided the arguments justifying separation, along with the evidence of the abuses that had been perpetrated against them. In consequence, the Declaration of Independence provided a case for humanity, a declaration of the rights of all humankind, not just the rights of citizens of what would become the United States of America.

Chapter 2

Unalienable Rights and the Proper Role of Government

We hold these truths to be self-evident, that all men are created equal, that they are endowed by their Creator with certain unalienable Rights, that among these are Life, Liberty and the pursuit of Happiness. That to secure these rights, Governments are instituted among Men, deriving their just powers from the consent of the governed,—That whenever any Form of Government becomes destructive to these ends, it is the Right of the People to alter or to abolish it, and to institute new Government, laying its foundation on such principles and organizing its powers in such form, as to them shall seem most likely to effect their Safety and Happiness. Prudence, indeed, will dictate that Governments long established should not be changed for light and transient causes; and accordingly all experience hath shown that mankind are more disposed to suffer, while evils are sufferable, than to right themselves by abolishing the forms to which they are accustomed. But when a long train of abuses and usurpations, pursuing invariably the same Object evinces a design to reduce them under absolute Despotism, it is their right, it is their duty, to throw off such Government, and to provide new Guards for their future security.—Such has been the patient sufferance of these Colonies; and such is now the necessity which constrains them to alter their former Systems of Government. The history of the present King of Great Britain is a history of repeated injuries and usurpations, all having in direct object the establishment of an absolute Tyranny over these States. To prove this, let Facts be submitted to a candid world.

T he second clause in the Declaration of Independence is one of the most important in the document. It provides the ideas of the purpose of government and the reason for throwing off a government that either neglects or refuses to fulfill the responsibilities for which men created it. It is in this paragraph that Jefferson described the reason for the creation of government, its purposes, the rights of the people who live under it, and when it is appropriate for the people to change the form of their government. Building on John Locke's philosophy, Jefferson begins to provide the foundation for the separation of the American colonies from Great Britain.

Self-Evident Truths

One of the first words mentioned, "truths," is tremendously important in understanding the Declaration and the concepts found in it, in the US Constitution, and in many of the other ideas that developed during the Founding Era. One must first recognize that with regard to principles, truth exists, and because of its nature, the truth of principles is absolute and cannot change. If the truth of principles changes, then that truth cannot have been true in the first place. For example, consider the principle that one human being should not murder another human for any reason, including for financial gain, power, or to hide other misdeeds. This principle is true, absolute, and immutable. It has been true since the first recorded incident with Cain and Abel and is still true today. So when Jefferson uses the word "truths," he is not expressing just his point of view. Rather, he is speaking about truths that never change and apply to all people everywhere—in other words, truths that are forever absolute, forever universal.

Jefferson also refers to such truths as self-evident. These are truths that need no further evidence to justify them. For example, "I exist" is self-evident. I cannot speak the words without existing, and I cannot deny my existence without affirming it. Mathematical truths are also self-evident. If I understand what the number 1 means and what adding means, then 1 plus 1 must equal 2. Some other statements are self-evident because they are true by definition: "All bachelors are unmarried men" and "All circles are round" are two such examples.

One truth that Jefferson will point to is that each individual possesses the right to exist and to maintain that existence—this is the right to life. As I mentioned earlier, John Locke described the natural law of existence. Each person, in order to continue his or her own existence, must be free to maintain that life by acquiring the items necessary to maintain that existence. In other words, one must acquire property, such as food and water, protection from the elements, and so on in order to continue living. Without those basic forms of property, existence would be impossible. In this natural state, each individual has the right to life, the liberty or freedom to maintain that life, and the property or the acquisition of the items required to maintain life. As Locke stated, despite being in "a state of perfect liberty," we are not in "a state of license." The violation of another's rights violates the natural moral law. In addition, this natural state of freedom is not a state that guarantees freedom from want. No guarantee exists that each person will be free from wanting the necessities required to maintain life. However, one is free to do what it takes to acquire the property needed to maintain their life as long as the acquisition does not infringe on the rights of others to do similarly. The right to life, then, is the most basic truth that Jefferson describes.

The truth that one exists and has a right to maintain that existence is in nature everywhere. Every animal naturally works towards maintaining its existence by the acquisition of food, shelter, and defending itself from predators or others of its own species that may do it harm. This is a naturally occurring state. Humanity is not different in this respect.

According to Jefferson, *self-evident* means that if an individual can recognize and reason about anything, then that person, without any prompting, will recognize that he or she must act to maintain their existence by the acquisition of property through his or her free will to pursue that maintenance.

All Are Created Equal

The first truth that Jefferson mentioned, "that all men are created equal," is not controversial nor was it controversial in Jefferson's mind. The equality to which Jefferson referred is the equality found in the state of nature. This equality is the right found in the "Laws of Nature" or the right to life, liberty, and the disposal or use of one's property as one sees fit. Nature's God granted this equality to every individual or, in other words, each individual is "endowed by their Creator."

However, some people have argued that Jefferson did not actually mean "all men" but only white men, that he did not include men of color (or even women). *After all, Jefferson owned slaves, which proves that he referred to only white men and not men of color*, some claim. However, Jefferson's own writings and actions debunk this misinterpretation. I will mention just a few examples from his writings and actions that prove Jefferson meant exactly what he wrote in the Declaration. This includes a section of the rough draft that the Founders amended out of the final copy of the Declaration. (A later chapter discusses this section.) In addition, so there can be no doubts about many of the rest of the Founders and where they stood on the issue of slavery, I will include evidence from some of their writings and actions.

To start, Edmund S. Morgan, a noted historian, professor at Harvard, and author of many historical books covering America's colonial beginning through the Revolutionary Era, including the book *American Freedom, American Slavery*, wrote: "The men who came together to found the independent United States, dedicated to freedom and equality, either held slaves or were willing to join hands with those who did. None of them felt entirely comfortable about the fact, but neither did they feel responsible for it. Most of them had inherited both their slaves and their attachment to freedom from an earlier generation, and they knew that the two were not unconnected."[30] As I will demonstrate later, by the time the Founders inherited their slaves, the English crown had already thrust slavery upon them and laws were in place that either prevented manumission altogether or prevented the manumission of slaves without providing for their financial support.

According to Morgan, Jefferson observed that slavery had a detrimental effect on the master-slave relationship. It created a feeling of despotism on the part of the master and submission on the part of the slave. The worst passions would tend to surface in the masters. But when it came to at least some of the American Founders, such as George Mason, George Washington, James Madison, and other Virginians:

> Whatever their complicity in the preservation of slavery, cannot otherwise by any stretch of the imagination be called depraved. ... They grew up under the conditions that Jefferson described, yet they displayed none of the boisterous passions, none of the lineaments of wrath, and certainly none of the disposition for tyranny that those conditions were supposed to induce. Jefferson himself, whatever his shortcomings, was the greatest champion of liberty this country has ever had.[31]

The foremost Founder, the president of the Constitutional Convention and the Father of our country, George Washington, opposed slavery even though he owned slaves. Washington's actions toward his black slaves and all black free persons testify to this point. He participated on a Fairfax County committee in 1774 that passed the Fairfax County Resolves of 1774, part of which stated, "Resolved that it is the Opinion of this Meeting, that during our present Difficulties and Distress, no Slaves ought to be imported into any of the British Colonies on this Continent; and we take this Opportunity of declaring our most earnest Wishes to see an entire Stop for ever put to such a wicked cruel and unnatural Trade."[32] Washington played a role on the committee that created the resolution and continued to work toward an end to slavery. And this even though he owned slaves.

Washington disliked the whole slavery system. In a letter to Robert Lewis, he wrote: "On this estate [Mount Vernon] I have more working Negroes, by a full half, than can be employed to any advantage. … But to sell the overplus I cannot, because I am principled against this kind of traffic in human species. To hire them out is almost as bad, because they could not be disposed of in families to any advantage, and to disperse of the families I have an aversion."[33] Washington valued families, including the families of his slaves, and although he sold slaves previously, it sickened him. He learned to despise the slave trade. He stated later that he hated "selling Negroes, as you would do cattle in the market."[34] He also portrayed his disgust with the system by keeping the families of his slaves together, which led him to owning too many slaves and thereby decreasing his profits, and by refusing to engage in buying and selling slaves. He regarded slaves as human beings, not some secondary or inferior species.

Washington acted no differently with other people of his same color as with those of another color. Two examples prove this point. Edward A. Johnson, a former slave who became an attorney and New York's first black legislator and wrote the first textbook by a black author to be approved by North Carolina, wrote about the two examples in his textbook. The first described the account of Primus Hall, a black servant of Colonel Pickering of Massachusetts. Washington often visited Pickering. On one occasion, Washington determined to sleep in Pickering's tent in which the servant and Pickering typically slept. The servant made the straw and provided the blankets for himself and Washington. Washington inquired of the servant's bed, and the servant informed him that there were enough blankets for the three of them. After falling asleep, Washington awoke and found Primus sleeping on a box. After chastising Primus for giving up his blanket to him, Washington ordered him to lie down with him because his blanket was large enough for both of them, otherwise he would sit up while Primus would have to lie down. Primus complied with Washington's demands.[35] In this clear example, Washington recognized Primus Hall, a Negro servant of Colonel Pickering, to be his equal and treated him with the respect of any other human being.

Here is the other example that Johnson documents:

Washington is said to have been out walking one day in company with some distinguished gentlemen, and during the walk, he met an old colored man who very politely tipped his hat and spoke to the General. Washington in turn took off his hat to the colored man, on seeing which, one of the company in a jesting manner inquired of the General if he usually took off his hat to Negroes. Whereupon Washington replied: "Politeness is cheap, and I never allow any one to be more polite to me than I to him."[36]

Washington showed respect to those who respected him, regardless of the color of their skin. The situation also showed his courteousness and politeness to others.

Washington freed his slaves in his will, which Virginia law allowed. This had not always been the case. In 1692, Virginia designed its laws to prevent any manumission of slaves without support from their former owners or without a way to provide for their own support.[37] Later, in 1723, Virginia banned any manumission of slaves by any private citizen. Only the legislature possessed the ability to free slaves until 1782 when it created an act that permitted the manumission of slaves in a will, which is the act that allowed Washington to free his slaves upon his death.[38] Virginia prevented this occurrence to happen again shortly thereafter, which left Thomas Jefferson without a chance to follow Washington's example.[39]

Many of the colonies, including Virginia, tried to abolish slavery in their legislative bodies before the Revolutionary War. Benjamin Franklin attested to this in a letter to Reverend Dean Woodward, who lived in London, in 1773. Franklin stated that even Virginia petitioned the king to prevent more importation of slaves into the colony, but it was to no avail.[40] Other colonies tried to do similarly.

Massachusetts was another colony that tried to abolish slavery. In 1718 a committee for raising revenue reported that "the importation of white servants be encouraged, and that the importation of black servants be discouraged." Part of the reasoning indicated was that the ownership of blacks kept out white laborers who owned themselves, which diminished "the true capital of the community."[41]

Jefferson, too, wanted to prevent more importation of slaves. King George III, however, disagreed with the colonists on the slavery issue and continued the importation. In the original draft of the Declaration, Jefferson wrote concerning the king's tyranny on the subject: "He [King George III] has waged cruel war against human nature itself, violating its most sacred rights of life and liberty in the persons of a distant people who never offended him, captivating and carrying them into slavery. ... Determined to keep open a market where men should be bought and sold, he has prostituted his negative for suppressing every legislative attempt to prohibit or restrain this execrable commerce."[42] Jefferson, like Washington, owned slaves but loathed the practice.

Like Washington, Jefferson treated his slaves with respect. Captain Edmund Bacon, one of Jefferson's overseers, detailed how Jefferson treated his slaves. Bacon stated that Jefferson rarely allowed whipping, even when the slave deserved it. For example, one slave stole nails and hid them. Once discovered, Jefferson verbally chastised him, telling him to "Go and don't do so any more." Jefferson even allowed his slaves to work extra for spending money.[43] Even though Jefferson owned slaves, he treated them with respect.

Thomas Jefferson, slave owner and despiser of the practice, writer of the Declaration of Independence, acted, as much as he could, on his principles. Some critics perceive him as a hypocrite. However, Jefferson's actions provide proof to the contrary. First, after Jefferson became a member of Virginia's legislature in 1769, he "made one effort in that body for the permission of the emancipation of slaves, which was rejected."[44] Then, of course, the previously mentioned original draft of the Declaration of Independence provided proof contrary to the charge of hypocrisy. And then in 1807, Jefferson signed an act prohibiting the importation of slaves into the United States, which took effect in 1808[45] and accorded with Article I, Section 9 of the US Constitution.

Few people described Jefferson's lack of hypocrisy better than John Quincy Adams. Adams gave a speech on the sixty-fifth anniversary of the signing of the Declaration. Part of his argument is as follows:

> The inconsistency of the institution of domestic slavery with the principles of the Declaration of Independence was seen and lamented by all the southern patriots of the Revolution; by no one with deeper

and more unalterable conviction than by the author of the Declaration himself [Jefferson]. No charge of insincerity or hypocrisy can be fairly laid to their charge. Never from their lips was heard one syllable of attempt to justify the institution of slavery. They universally considered it as a reproach fastened upon them by the unnatural step-mother country [Great Britain] and they saw that before the principles of the Declaration of Independence, slavery, in common with every other mode of oppression, was destined sooner or later to be banished from the earth. Such was the undoubting conviction of Jefferson to his dying day.[46]

Jefferson proved by his actions and words what he really believed about slavery. He worked within the Constitution's timeframe and methods to end slavery— an act that fit with what he had sought to do in the colony of Virginia many years earlier.

Abraham Lincoln, the Great Emancipator, understood the principles Jefferson defined in the Declaration of Independence and acted upon. Before his election to the presidency, Lincoln spoke about the principles of Jefferson and tried to convince others to return to those principles. In 1858, Lincoln spoke in Lewistown, Illinois about this matter. One of the principles established the truth that the Founders designed a system, not for property-owning, rich, white men, but for all humanity. Lincoln said that Jefferson

established these great self-evident truths that when in the distant future some man, some faction, some interest, should set upon the doctrine that none but rich men, or none but white men, were entitled to life, liberty and the pursuit of happiness, their posterity might look up again to the Declaration of Independence and take courage to renew the battle which their fathers began. ... Now, my countrymen, if you have been taught doctrines conflicting with the great landmarks of the Declaration of Independence; if you have listened to suggestions which would take away from its grandeur and mutilate the fair symmetry of its proportions; if you have been inclined to believe that all men are not created equal in those inalienable rights enumerated by our charter of liberty; let me entreat you to come back. … [C]ome back to the truths that are in the Declaration of Independence.[47]

Lincoln fully comprehended the principles of Jefferson. He believed that everyone needed to follow these principles. And the failure to comprehend and follow them led to the Civil War of the 1860s.

Jefferson defined the principles of the Revolution and the principles of America in the Declaration of Independence. In addition, he played a vital role in abolishing slavery in 1808 and assisted John Quincy Adams, Abraham Lincoln, and other abolitionists in ending slavery.

James Madison, the Father of the Constitution, similarly despised slavery and created the governmental means to secure the emancipation of slaves. Madison stated in Federalist No. 42:

> It were doubtless to be wished, that the power of prohibiting the importation of slaves had not been postponed until the year 1808, or rather that it had been suffered to have immediate operation. … It ought to be considered as a great point gained in favor of humanity, that a period of twenty years may terminate forever, within these States, a traffic which has so long and so loudly upbraided the barbarism of modern policy; that within that period, it will receive a considerable discouragement from the federal government, and may be totally abolished, by a concurrence of the few States which continue the unnatural traffic, in the prohibitory example which has been given by so great a majority of the Union.[48]

Madison found slavery "barbaric" and wished to see it end. However, he also understood the need to create a unified nation. Thus, the Constitution provided the means to continue slavery for twenty years until 1808, after which Congress could abolish slavery or regulate it by whatever means it chose to use. The Constitution also provided the means to limit the representation of the southern states. This means is known as the Three-fifths Compromise.

The Three-Fifths Compromise

In the Constitution, the Three-fifths Compromise reads, "Representatives and direct Taxes shall be apportioned among the several States which may be included within this Union, according to their respective Numbers, which shall be determined by adding to the whole Number of free Persons, including those bound to Service for a Term of Years, and excluding Indians not taxed, three fifths of all other Persons."

Some may view the Three-fifths Compromise as proving that the Founders thought that slaves were inferior. Were the Founders racist? Did they really not believe in human rights for all? Did they consider a slave to be only three-fifths of a person? The Founders' words and actions will bring to light who they really were and what they believed.

Madison and the Constitution's designers recognized the evils of slavery. Even though the Founders allowed the question of slavery to be resolved later, they actually pioneered the end of slavery in numerous ways. First, the Constitution provided for each state to have representatives in the House of Representatives as determined by the number of residents in that state. In order to limit the number of representatives and therefore the legislative power of slave-holding states, the Constitution limited the number to three-fifths of the total slave population. So every fifteen slaves counted amounted to nine residents. This effectively limited the power of slave states in Congress, particularly the southern states.

Second, the Founders limited the amount of time that the South had to acquire slaves outside of the US. After that time expired, which was in 1808, Congress possessed full authority to regulate or even abolish slavery.

The fact is that the Founders who were from predominately pro-slavery states and even those who owned slaves recognized the evils of slavery, worked hard to end slavery by constitutional means, and freed their slaves when possible. The Founders designed the Constitution as a means to end slavery.

Although the Constitution provided twenty years, until 1808, for the continuance of slavery, any of the states could take their own action against slavery. Many states abolished slavery within their borders. "Pennsylvania passed a gradual emancipation resolution in 1780, Rhode Island in 1784.

The state of New York formed a manumission society in 1785, and New York abolished slavery in 1799."[49] In Massachusetts, one slave, Felix Holbrook, along with other slaves, presented a petition for freedom and grants of land to the state legislature in 1773. The legislature passed the abolition act in 1774. However, governors Hutchinson and Gage (governors appointed by the British crown) refused to sign the act.[50] It is clear that the Founding generation pressed towards abolition even before the Constitution became the supreme law of the land.

In fact, many states allowed free blacks to vote before the Constitution's ratification and even before the several states ratified the Articles of Confederation. New Hampshire, Massachusetts, New York, New Jersey, and the southern state of North Carolina allowed free blacks to vote before the ratification of the Articles of Confederation.[51] After 1776, Maryland, another slave state, allowed all free men over twenty-one who held a certain amount of property to vote. And they voted so much that "complaints were made that the free negroes, at one time, controlled the elections in Baltimore."[52] Pennsylvania also allowed all free men, regardless of color, to vote in 1701.[53] These states obviously recognized free blacks as citizens and allowed them to vote along with white men.

When the Constitutional Convention convened in 1787, the Founders discovered a number of problematic items on the issue of slavery. They solved one problem by allowing slavery to continue for twenty years. (The other two problems were representation and taxation.) Once they determined to allow the importation of slaves, the problem of taxing them as imports arose. Roger Sherman of Connecticut disliked the idea because it implied that slaves were property.[54] In addition to the problem of taxation, the idea of slaves as property or as persons caused another problem—representation in the House of Representatives.

The idea of whether to count slaves as property or as persons became the focus of the slavery issue at the Convention. Ironically, the northern states wished to exclude slaves for the purposes of representation, which appeared as if they thought of slaves as property and not persons. The South, on the other hand, wished to count slaves for the purposes of representation because the southern states would acquire more power in the House, despite the fact that they regarded slaves as property. Gouverneur Morris, a delegate from Pennsylvania, summed up the conflict best:

> Upon what principle is it that the slaves shall be computed in the representation? Are they men? Then make them citizens and let them vote! The admission of slaves into the representation ... comes to this: that the inhabitant of Georgia and South Carolina who goes to the coast of Africa and—in defiance of the most sacred laws of humanity—tears away his fellow creatures ... and damns them to the most cruel bondage, shall have more votes in a government instituted for protection of the rights of mankind than the citizen of Pennsylvania or New Jersey who views with a laudable horror so nefarious a practice.[55]

In actuality, the northern states demanded the emancipation of slaves. That is, the North demanded that Congress not count slaves for the purpose of representation and believed slaves to be human beings.

One other delegate to the Convention who refused to sign the final document argued against the document because, in part, of the slavery issue. Luther Martin of Maryland argued in a letter to his legislature regarding the Convention that the anti-slavery Founders tried to reason with the southern states that slaves were human beings, not property: "If they [slaves] were to be taken into account as 'property,'... entitled to the high privilege of conferring consequence and power in the government to its possessors rather than any other property—[that is], why should slaves, as 'property,' be taken into account rather than horses, cattle, mules, or any other species?"[56] Luther and the other anti-slavery Founders' clearly argued that slaves were human beings and should not be owned as if they were mere property.

The Founders addressed this problem with the Three-Fifth's Compromise. Article I, Section 2, described the compromise. "Representation ... shall be apportioned among the several States ... according to their respective Numbers, which shall be determined by adding to the whole Number of free Persons, including ... three fifths of all other Persons." Some people think that this phrase means that slaves were only three-fifths of a person. However, Thomas West of the Claremont Institute correctly sees otherwise.

[T]he Constitution allowed Southern States to count three-fifths of their slaves toward the population that would determine numbers of representatives in the federal legislature. This clause is often singled out today as a sign of black dehumanization: they are only three-fifths human. But the provision applied to slaves, not blacks. That meant that free blacks–and there were many, North as well as South–counted the same as whites.[57]

Later in his essay, West stated that the Founders chose to limit the strength of the southern states by only counting three-fifths of the slave population rather than the total population, which he considered wise.[58] In other words, the wording of the Three-fifths Compromise and the historical context in which it emerged shows that the Founders and many others of their generation regarded blacks as human beings. The Founders chose to count only three-fifths of the total population of slaves in order to limit the political power of states that permitted slavery. If the Founders thought of black people as less than human, why did they count free blacks as full human beings?

Another way to look at this is with the Senate. It takes two-thirds of the Senate to convict a president in a trial. Does this mean that each state is only two-thirds of a state or each senator is only two-thirds of a senator? The logic is ridiculous. And yet it's the same logic that infers that counting three-fifths of the total number of slaves means that slaves were considered as three-fifths human. The logic is flawed, and the inferred conclusion is false.

However, this is not to say that all of the Founders disapproved of slavery. Some of them fought to maintain slavery, including Daniel of St. Thomas Jenifer and James McHenry of Maryland; John Blair of Virginia; William Few of Georgia; and Charles Pinckney and Charles Cotesworth Pinckney of South Carolina. Though they fought to maintain slavery, it is interesting to note how some of them acted after the Constitutional Convention.

Daniel of St. Thomas Jenifer owned slaves, which he bought, sold, and hired out, until his death. In his will, however, he declared the manumission of his slaves, which he demanded happen six years after his death. He owned approximately fifteen slaves at the time of his passing.[59] Even though he supported slavery, in the end he freed his slaves.

James McHenry also owned approximately ten slaves, which he never freed. However, he made an insightful statement regarding Benjamin Banneker, a black mathematician and astronomer. McHenry stated, "I consider this negro as a fresh proof that the powers of the mind are disconnected with the color of his skin."[60] Although McHenry was a slave-holder, apparently he was not a racist.

William Few of Georgia represented the constituents of his state well. He owned four slaves when he moved from Pennsylvania to Georgia in 1758.[61] Though he often failed to attend the Convention, he signed the final document. After moving to New York in 1799, he counseled the governor of New York regarding the slave trade in that state:

> Is there one person of understanding and reflection among you who will not admit that every consideration of justice, humanity, and safety, forbids that any more Negroes should be brought into your state? … and in violation of law and every principle of policy and expediency they are carrying on that diabolical and injurious traffic, and hastening those evils in their nature most dreadful, which seems to demand every exertion to retard or prevent it.[62]

Though he owned slaves early on in his life, Few recognized his error and corrected it.

Many of the Founders who played a vital role in the Constitutional Convention resided in Virginia. Most resided in the northern states, while the rest resided in either Virginia, which had the highest population of slaves,[63] or Maryland. Slavery defined the life of John Blair, another signer and Virginian. Blair meticulously chronicled his dealings with his slaves. He chronicled their health (which doctors treated which slaves), the legal actions brought against his slaves and the slaves of others, the births and baptisms of his slaves, and so much more. He seemed particularly interested in his slaves' health and well-being.[64] Though he owned slaves and never emancipated them, he voted on the side of his anti-slavery delegation in the Convention despite his own views.[65]

Most of the Founders, as well as most of the other well-known patriots of the Founding Era, opposed slavery and worked towards its end. Many of them, such as Franklin, Washington, and Jefferson, strove to end the horrendous practice even before the Constitutional Convention occurred. The Founders believed that blacks were human beings and not partial human beings or subhuman. Thus, the Constitution provided for all free *persons* and three-fifths of the total of all other *persons* counted for the purpose of representation. The fact that many states granted citizenship to free blacks and allowed them to vote, including slave states such as Maryland and North Carolina, provides further evidence of this fact.

The Three-fifths Compromise was about limiting slavery and limiting the representation of slave states. It had nothing to do with advocating or supporting the inferiority of slaves.

Benjamin Franklin, another well-known Founder and signer of the Declaration of Independence and the Constitution, along with Benjamin Rush, another signer of the Declaration, formed America's first abolitionist society.[66] Franklin believed that America must emancipate its slaves. Along with their emancipation, Franklin believed that they should be educated, as outlined by the abolitionist society. He believed that society as a whole should provide freed slaves with the skills needed for employment as well as given employment. He also urged that the children of freed slaves be educated "for their future situation in life."[67] Franklin proved to be one of the foremost abolitionists of his time.

Samuel Adams, best known as the Father of the Revolution, also opposed slavery. Adams opposed it so much that when his wife, Elizabeth, received a slave as a gift, he immediately told her: "A slave cannot live in my house. If she comes she must be free."[68] Later, during the ratification process, while others lamented the twenty years of continued slave trade, Adams "rejoiced that a door was now to be opened, for the annihilation of this odious, abhorrent practice, in a certain time."[69] Adams, like other anti-slavery Founders, worked toward the end of oppression and tyranny in all its forms.

While I could produce many other examples of this kind, particularly regarding Jefferson, I have provided more than enough to show that the Founders were opposed to slavery and believed what Jefferson wrote in the Declaration of Independence—that "all men are created equal" regardless of color, sex, or any other distinction. They believed that all human beings had the right to "life, liberty and property."

God-Given Unalienable Rights

Jefferson next mentioned in the Declaration "That they [all men] are endowed by their Creator with certain unalienable Rights." This statement is of paramount importance for various reasons. First, if the Creator endowed men with certain unalienable rights, then only the Creator has the authority to repeal those rights. If, on the other hand, government endows or gives the rights listed, then government can also remove those rights. The truth stated by Jefferson that the rights listed "are endowed by the Creator" served to eliminate government's ability to claim a right to infringe on its citizens' rights. The unalienable rights are a gift or an endowment provided by the Creator of humankind. These rights are unalienable. In other words, they cannot be justly surrendered, transferred, violated, or removed. The Creator has granted them to each and every human being. Therefore, no government should infringe upon these rights or act in a manner that would cause an individual to surrender his or her rights in whole or in part.

Locke, in discussing the power of government, particularly the legislative body, wrote regarding its power over the natural law: "The law of nature stands as an eternal rule to all men, legislators as well as others. The rules that they make for other men's actions, must, as well as their own and other men's actions, be conformable to the law of nature, i.e. to the will of God, of which that is a declaration, and the fundamental law of nature being the preservation of mankind, *no human sanction can be good, or valid against it.*"[70]

William Blackstone, though he came later than the Founding Era, agreed with Jefferson and Locke in his *Commentaries on the Laws of England*:

> Those rights then which God and nature have established, and are therefore called natural rights, such as are life and liberty, need not the aid of human laws to be more effectually invested in every man than they are; neither do they receive any additional strength when declared by the municipal laws to be inviolable. On the contrary, no human legislature has power to abridge or destroy them, unless the owner shall himself commit some act that amounts to a forfeiture.[71]

In other words, unless a citizen violates the right of his fellow citizen, laws cannot infringe upon the rights of the citizenry but only upon the rights of the violator.

The rights Jefferson listed are not the only unalienable rights endowed by the Creator. They are, as Jefferson stated, "among these" rights that the Creator has given. However, we will focus our attention on those he listed, which are "life, liberty and the pursuit of happiness," or life, liberty, and property. Even though Jefferson did not mention property, it will become clear that property is what he and the rest of the Founders had in mind when they used the term *happiness*.

As previously mentioned, Jefferson and many of the other Founders held John Locke in high esteem. In fact, Jefferson wrote in a letter to another signer, Benjamin Rush, that Locke was among "the three greatest men the world had ever produced."[72] It is no wonder that Jefferson used the works of Locke to the extent that he did, particularly concerning the Declaration of Independence.

Locke wrote about the "Ends of Political Society and Government," stating: "The great and chief end therefore, of men's uniting into commonwealths, and putting themselves under government, is the preservation of their property. To which in the state of nature there are many things wanting."[73] Life and liberty are included in the protection of natural property rights. Individuals uniting themselves under government would allow them to focus on the acquisition of property for the preservation of their lives and liberties. In the state of nature, human beings will find it more difficult to protect their unalienable rights than they would by uniting with others to form government to fulfill that purpose. Without the means to preserve life and liberty, that is, without property, it is impossible to maintain either life or liberty. Human beings without property in any form, whether the property is food, clothing, shelter, weapons for protection, or any other possession, is nothing, or shortly will become nothing.

One other Founder, George Mason, who is most credited for the Virginia constitution and declaration of rights, wrote in Virginia's declaration words nearly resembling the Declaration's. And Virginia's declaration of rights was actually drafted and adopted *before* the Declaration of Independence was. Mason wrote: "SECTION I. That all men are by nature equally free and independent and *have certain inherent rights*, of which, when they enter into a state of society, they cannot, by any compact, deprive or divest their posterity; namely, *the enjoyment of life and liberty, with the means of acquiring and possessing property, and pursuing and obtaining happiness and safety.*"[74]

John Adams, who was one of the foremost in persuading the Continental Congress to declare the colonies independent from England, wrote when he drafted Massachusetts' Constitution and declaration of rights: "All men are born free and equal, and *have certain natural, essential, and unalienable rights; among which may be reckoned the right of enjoying and defending their lives and liberties; that of acquiring, possessing, and protecting property;* in fine, that of seeking and obtaining their safety and happiness."[75] Elsewhere Adams wrote about the necessity of property and its protection and from where the unalienable right comes: "The moment the idea is admitted into society, that property is not as sacred as the laws of God, and that there is not a force of law and public justice to protect it, anarchy and tyranny commence. … *Property must be secured, or liberty cannot exist.*"[76] One must protect the use of his or her property, whether by force of arms or use of one's body, in order to protect liberty. Without external property or property of self, there is no liberty.

In October 1765, in opposition to the Stamp Act (see chapter 3), Samuel Adams authored a resolution in the Massachusetts House of Representatives, which stated, "There are certain essential rights of the British Constitution of government, which are founded in the law of God and nature, and are the common rights of mankind," adding that "no law of society, can, consistent with the law of God and nature," take away those rights and "that no man can justly take the property of another without his consent."[77]

In another one of his writings, Jefferson said, "A right to property is founded in our natural wants, in the means with which we are endowed to satisfy these wants, and the right to what we acquire by those means without violating the similar rights of other sensible beings."[78]

For the Founders, the "pursuit of happiness," among other unalienable rights, included owning property.

The Purpose of Government

Returning to Locke, he contended that the purpose of government, or the "uniting into commonwealths" or forming government, is the protection of property and the other unalienable rights. Locke further said:

> Though in the state of nature he hath such a right (to life, liberty and property), yet the enjoyment of it is very uncertain, and constantly exposed to the invasion of others: for all being kings as much as he, every man his equal, and the greater part no strict observers of equity and justice, the enjoyment of the property he has in this state is very unsafe, very unsecure. This makes him willing to quit a condition, which, however free, is full of fears and continual dangers: and it is not without reason, that he seeks out, and is willing to join in society with others, who are already united, or have a mind to unite, for the mutual preservation of their lives, liberties and estates, which I call by the general name, property.[79]

Rather than wasting time and energy in defending one's property, a person can join with others who are of the same mind. Together they can protect one another in their use and enjoyment of their own property, lives, and liberties. Through the government they create, they will be protected. Individually they may be unable to protect themselves, for none of them individually can be everywhere, particularly when their property becomes large and expansive because of their diligence at laboring to acquire and develop it. The purpose of government is to protect those rights and do so by the consent of the governed.

Throughout Locke's writings, he used the terms of *consent* or *common consent* or *consent of society* numerous times. The consent of the governed is an important aspect of the Declaration of Independence, the Founders' quest for liberty, and for liberty to continue for generations.

Locke wrote about the beginnings of political society declaring that "when any number of men have, by the *consent of every individual*, made a community, they have thereby made that community one body, with a power to act as one body." That body acts by the "consent of the majority."[80] Locke added "that men are naturally free" and that governments "had their beginning laid on that foundation, and were made by the consent of the people."[81] Jefferson affirmed it this way in the Declaration: "Governments are instituted among Men, deriving their just powers from the consent of the governed."

The Magna Carta prohibited taxation without representation and prohibited punishment except in the country of the accused by a jury of his peers. The dependence on common consent is clear in the Magna Carta. The 1689 English Bill of Rights also prohibited taxation and property seizure without the consent of Parliament. In other words, British law under the Magna Carta and the English Bill of Rights required the consent of society, or common consent, as a natural part of government.

Jefferson then described what happens when government fails to follow the principles of proper government by protecting life, liberty, and property: "It is the right of the people to alter or abolish it" and to create a new government that will follow these principles. The people are the sovereign authority of government. When government usurps authority and betrays the principles upon which the people created it, tyranny reigns. Consequently, the sovereign people have the right to alter or abolish such a government and replace it with a new government. In this Jefferson recognized the principles Locke taught.

Locke described government, particularly the supreme power of government found in the legislative branch, as only a fiduciary power to act for certain ends, those ends being the protection of the natural rights of man. A fiduciary power is a power entrusted in government and none other. However, as Locke said:

There remains still in the people a supreme power to remove or alter the legislative, when they find the legislative act contrary to the trust reposed in them: for all power given with trust for the attaining an end, being limited by that end, whenever that end is manifestly neglected, or opposed, the trust must necessarily be forfeited, and the power devolve into the hands of those that gave it, who may place it anew where they shall think best for their safety and security. And thus the community perpetually retains a supreme power of saving themselves from the attempts and designs of any body, even of their legislators, whenever they shall be so foolish, or so wicked, as to lay and carry on designs against the liberties and properties of the subject: for no man or society of men, having a power to deliver up their preservation, or consequently the means of it, to the absolute will and arbitrary dominion of another; whenever anyone shall go about to bring them into such a slavish condition, they will always have a right to preserve, what they have not a power to part with; and to rid themselves of those, who invade this fundamental, sacred, and unalterable law of self-preservation, for which they entered into society.[82]

Notice how similar the wording is to the words of Jefferson. Jefferson agreed with Locke that the government's purpose is to protect the rights of the people, and the people are the ones who have the sovereign authority to remove or alter their government as they think best for their safety and security.

One of the most difficult, yet simplest methods or tests for determining whether government has usurped authority and is trampling the natural laws and the authority of the sovereign, the people, is to ask one question: If this government did not exist, would you have the right to act the way this government is acting? For example, if one neighbor enters another's estate and removes property without permission, can the violated neighbor use force to retrieve the property that his neighbor removed? Could he search the property of his neighbor to determine if his property was on his neighbor's property or person? If there were witnesses testifying to that effect or if he was the witness himself, then yes, the person violated would have the right to take these steps to retrieve his stolen property. However, when government exceeds those boundaries, it is as Locke said, a usurpation of authority in which government places itself into a state of war, similar to one individual placing himself into a state of war when that person uses force to steal property, to enslave, or to try to take the life of another. "I say, using force upon the people without authority, and contrary to the trust put in him that does so, is a state of war with the people. ... In all states and conditions, the true remedy of force without authority, is to oppose force to it. The use of force without authority, always puts him that uses it into a state of war, as the aggressor, and renders him liable to be treated accordingly."[83] Simply said, when government exceeds its authority, it becomes the plunderer of property, the enslaver, or the life- taker. This places it in a state of war with the people it is supposed to protect.

Locke continued, "Tyranny is the exercise of power beyond right."[84] The people can only give the powers that they possess to their representative, the government. When government exceeds those limits, tyranny has begun. He explained that there are numerous ways that government exceeds its authority. When this occurs, the people have a right to dissolve the government and institute new means that will secure their rights.

> First, The [government] acts against the trust reposed in them, when they endeavour to invade the property of the subject, and to make themselves, or any part of the community, masters, or arbitrary disposers of the lives, liberties, or fortunes of the people. ... For since *it can never be supposed to be the will of the society, that the [government] should have a power to destroy that which everyone designs to secure,* by entering into society, and for which the people submitted themselves to [government] of their own making; whenever the [government] endeavor[s] to take away, and destroy the property of the people, or to reduce them to slavery under arbitrary power, they put themselves into a state of war with the people, who are thereupon absolved from any farther obedience, and are left to the common refuge, which God hath provided for all men, against force and violence. ... By this breach of trust they forfeit the power the people had put into their hands for quite contrary ends, and it devolves

to the people, who have a right to resume their original liberty, and, by the establishment of a new [government], (such as they shall think fit) provide for their own safety and security, which is the end for which they are in society.[85]

Whenever government invades the lives, liberty, or property of its citizens, demanding that they follow certain laws that one individual could not demand another individual to do, government places itself at war by using its arbitrary power that it has usurped.

Let's apply this understanding of government to our day. One individual cannot demand that another individual eat the proper foods, exercise, give charity to the poor, wear a seat belt, only use a bat to defend himself from thieves or others, or not destroy the wetland found on his property when he wants to turn it into a resort or farmland. Therefore, that individual who wishes to make such demands on another cannot bestow that power on government, his representative. In addition, why would the individual, who has demands made on him by another, give consent to a government that would make the same demands on him that the first individual demands? If the individual knew that government would make unwarranted and unauthorized demands, he or she would not enter into the compact. Individual citizens, together, form government and bestow authority upon that government. Government only possesses the authority bestowed; it can have no other authority.

A Change of Government

When government exceeds its limits, it is the right of the people to alter or abolish that government and form a new one that will best follow the principles of proper government and secure the rights of the people, which will provide for the safety and happiness of its citizens. However, the people may have consumed an enormous amount of time and effort to create their current government. To throw it off at the first sign of usurpation would be unfathomable. Making minor changes, adding stricter safeguards, strengthening the methods that government must use in order to prevent the abuses are more sensible methods than completely revamping the system. As Jefferson explained, "Prudence, indeed, will dictate that Governments long established should not be changed for light and transient causes." It is natural for those entrusted with government to make mistakes, which are typically light and transient causes. If remedied by various methods, including reparations of damages done directly to the citizen, then that government corrects its mistakes and returns itself to its correct principles and purpose. Locke argued that "Great mistakes in the ruling part, many wrong and inconvenient laws, and all the slips of human frailty will be borne by the people without mutiny or murmur."[86] The people recognize that human beings entrusted with government are like themselves—human beings with human tendencies to make mistakes.

What is not a mistake, however, is when those in government decide that they know better than citizens regarding their health, life, and so on, and then decide for citizens what they will allow them or forbid them to do. That is when government begins to trample the rights of its citizens. Jefferson, in his *Notes on Virginia*, warned: "Every government degenerates when trusted to the rulers of the people alone. The people themselves, therefore, are its only safe depositories."[87] Citizens should consider government mistakes excusable and temporary. But when government seeks to invade citizens' rights, citizens have the right to alter or abolish it in its present form. That is the power they have as sovereign over their government.

Despite this power, the sovereign is typically reluctant to change their form of government. Normally, they will suffer some "light and transient causes." History is replete with examples of the people suffering evils and oppression for a time before they revolt against their government to correct the wrongs done to them. For example, the Magna Carta is evidence of a revolt against an abusive monarch, King John, in which the people altered the affairs of their government. Then there was the brief period in England under a commonwealth protectorate, Oliver Cromwell, where the people had revolted and beheaded their king, Charles I, followed by yet another change, when the people restored the crown under William and Mary and devised yet another Bill of Rights in 1689. In the case of the Puritans under William Bradford, their revolt involved simply leaving the protection of the British government, trying another form of government in Holland, and then moving once again to America, where they formed their own government as best suited them. John Winthrop followed later. Numerous others, including William Penn, Roger Williams, and George Calvert also revolted by departing and forming their own colonies. All of these colonies later fell under the protection of England again. And these people and colonies soon suffered oppression in one form or another until they could no longer accept it and either violently revolted or peacefully revolted by moving on.

Locke explained in one section of his writing about the people's willingness to suffer "light and transient" abuses without attempting to make changes:

> People are not so easily got out of their old forms, as some are apt to suggest. They are hardly to be prevailed with to amend the acknowledged faults in the frame they have been accustomed to. And if there be any original defects, or adventitious ones introduced by time, or corruption; it is not an easy thing to get them changed, even when all the world sees there is an opportunity for it. This slowness and aversion in the people to quit their old constitutions, has, in the many revolutions which have been seen in this kingdom, in this and former ages, still kept us to, or, after some interval of fruitless attempts, still brought us back again to our old legislative of king, lords and commons: and whatever provocations have made the crown be taken from some of our princes heads, they never carried the people so far as to place it in another line.[88]

According to Locke, the people receive abuses to a point, revolt, and then alter their form of government. However, in his country of England, the people always seemed to restore the crown, which still managed to be abusive toward them and their rights.

In another section Locke wrote, "Till the mischief be grown general, and the ill designs of the rulers become visible, or their attempts sensible to the greater part, the people, who are more disposed to suffer than right themselves by resistance, are not apt to stir."[89] The people will suffer numerous abuses of trivial concern until the abuses become wanton and the citizens find the government "endeavoring" to abuse its citizens. Following Locke, Jefferson said in the Declaration, "Prudence, indeed, will dictate that Governments long established should not be changed for light and transient causes; and accordingly all experience hath shown that mankind are more disposed to suffer, while evils are sufferable, than to right themselves by abolishing the forms to which they are accustomed."

The next part of this paragraph of the Declaration begins laying out how the colonists concluded that there was a need to alter or abolish their form of government. It became "necessary for one People to dissolve the Political Bands which have connected them to another." As Jefferson states, "But when a long train of abuses and usurpations, pursuing invariably the same Object evinces a design to reduce them under absolute Despotism, it is their right, it is their duty, to throw off such Government, and to provide new Guards for their future security." Jefferson's point here is that the abuses of the crown against the colonies were not "light and transient causes." The abuses were a violation of the colonists' natural rights, which unalienable rights their Creator bestowed upon them; their earthly king did not grant them these rights. The government's abuses were numerous, the usurpations extensive, and the government's exercise of power was an "absolute despotism" and tyranny over the colonies. Jefferson used Locke in this statement in part. As Locke stated, "But if a long train of abuses, prevarications and artifices, all tending the same way, make the design visible to the people, and they cannot but feel what they lie under, and see whither they are going; it is not to be wondered, that they should then rouse themselves, and endeavour to put the rule into such hands which may secure to them the ends for which government was at first erected."[90] Once the people recognize that government has turned from the principles under which they founded it—the laws of nature—then the people will rise up and throw off the chains with which their government seeks to bind them. When government's design is to enslave its citizens by preventing them from deciding for themselves how they will live their lives, use their property and liberty, and prevent them from following their own will as long as it does not prevent others from acting similarly, then change must occur. It is the people's right and even duty to themselves, their friends and neighbors, and to their posterity to alter or abolish the system.

In this case, Jefferson summarizes that "Such has been the patient sufferance of these Colonies; and such is now the necessity which constrains them to alter their former Systems of Government." We have seen a little here and there of how the colonists arrived at this point of separation from the mother country. They and their ancestors had endured numerous abuses of the crown. They petitioned the crown many times for a redress of grievances, but all to no avail. Thus, of necessity they decided to change their government. And in the case of the American colonists, the change of government required the separation from England.

"The history of the present King of Great Britain is a history of repeated injuries and usurpations, all having in direct object the establishment of an absolute Tyranny over these States. To prove this, let Facts be submitted to a candid world." Speaking for the people, Jefferson claimed that the king had one purpose in his repeated actions: to establish an "absolute tyranny" over the colonies, usurping any authority of the colonists, and not granting them their rights as British subjects as well as refusing to recognize their God-given unalienable rights.

Locke, too, questioned how the people could *not* act when such events occur. "But if they universally have a persuasion, grounded upon manifest evidence, that designs are carrying on against their liberties, and the general course and tendency of things cannot but give them strong suspicions of the evil intention of their governors, who is to be blamed for it?"[91] That is, why would not the people act? Regardless of whether the people were negligent in watching the government in order to ensure that government not abuse their liberties, or whether the people did everything possible to prevent the need to rebel, once they understood the bad intentions of their government, they must act.

Jefferson clearly stated from whom the people derived their unalienable rights, and he articulated some of those rights. Furthermore, he showed the patience and perseverance of people in accepting limited abuse until the abuses became pervasive. Once that happened, Jefferson described why the people had a right to change their government. The people design government to protect their rights, not to abuse them.

In the next chapters, I will show how Jefferson provides ample evidence of the "long train of abuse(s) and usurpation(s)" that prove the design of the king to exercise an absolute tyranny over the colonists and therefore the need for a separation from that government. Put another way, the Declaration shows itself to be a justification for the American colonists' revolt from England's oppressive and abusive government.

The Charges: Abuses of Executive Power

He has refused his assent to laws, the most wholesome and necessary for the public good.

He has forbidden his governors to pass laws of immediate and pressing importance, unless suspended in their operation till his assent should be obtained; and when so suspended, he has utterly neglected to attend to them.

He has refused to pass other laws for the accommodation of large districts of people, unless those people would relinquish the right of representation in the legislature, a right inestimable to them and formidable to tyrants only.

He has called together legislative bodies at places unusual, uncomfortable, and distant from the depository of their public records, for the sole purpose of fatiguing them into compliance with his measures.

He has dissolved representative houses repeatedly, for opposing with manly firmness his invasions on the rights of the people.

He has refused for a long time, after such dissolutions, to cause others to be elected; whereby the legislative powers, incapable of annihilation, have returned to the people at large for their exercise; the state remaining in the meantime exposed to all the dangers of invasion from without, and convulsions within.

He has endeavored to prevent the population of these states; for that purpose obstructing the laws for naturalization of foreigners; refusing to pass others to encourage their migration hither, and raising the conditions of new appropriations of lands.

He has obstructed the administration of justice, by refusing his assent to laws for establishing judiciary powers.

He has made judges dependent on his will alone, for the tenure of their offices, and the amount and payment of their salaries.

He has erected a multitude of new offices, and sent hither swarms of officers to harass our people, and eat out their substance.

He has kept among us, in times of peace, standing armies without the consent of our legislature.

He has affected to render the military independent of and superior to civil power.

J efferson begins to list the facts that will prove the tyranny of the king of England and the reasons for the colonists' need for separation. In this chapter, I will discuss the usurpations and abuses of the king at the time of Jefferson. I will also cover the first twelve of twenty-eight evidences, which include one charge that the Founders removed by the amendment process.

I have divided Jefferson's list of charges into three parts for a couple of reasons. First, he provided a lengthy list of accusations against the crown. The discernable order of these charges comprises three different groups. Stephen E. Lucas of the University of Wisconsin, who wrote about the stylistic artistry of the Declaration of Independence, explained these groups:

Although one English critic assailed the Declaration for its "studied confusion in the arrangement" of the grievances against George III, they are not listed in random order but fall into four distinct groups. The first group, consisting of charges 1–12, refers to such abuses of the king's executive power as suspending colonial laws, dissolving colonial legislatures, obstructing the administration of justice, and maintaining a standing army during peacetime. The second group, consisting of charges 13–22, attacks the king for combining with "others" (Parliament) to subject America to a variety of unconstitutional measures, including taxing the colonists without consent, cutting off their trade with the rest of the world, curtailing their right to trial by jury, and altering their charters.

The third set of charges, numbers 23–27, assails the king's violence and cruelty in waging war against his American subjects.

The war grievances are followed by the final charge against the king—that the colonists' "repeated Petitions" for redress of their grievances have produced only "repeated injury."[92]

This chapter and the next two separate the charges against the king into each type of charge. First, this chapter examines the king's abuse of executive power. The next chapter focuses on the king's abuse of legislative powers to advance his tyrannical acts. The chapter after that explains the king's abuse of war powers against his subjects.

Finally, in this chapter, I will begin to compare the Declaration's concerns to today's political policies and rhetoric, showing what I believe to be America's current political condition. While I am not advocating for a revolution by violent means, I wonder if one through peaceful, political methods is called for. My central purpose is to show the dangerous scenario in which our government has placed itself. Moreover, I hope that my observations will serve as a warning to elected officials and other governmental employees to watch where they tread.

These charges against King George III are important in order to understand why the colonists deemed it necessary to separate themselves from their mother country and form a new government that would best provide for their safety and happiness. These charges are also important to understand because they reveal how government, including our current one, tends to follow the same path to tyranny that all governments designed with liberty tend to do. Understanding these charges will help citizens watch out for and hopefully prevent modern government from attempting to do what England did. If our government is already down that path, the Declaration of Independence lays out the rationale for citizens to exercise their duty and right to lead it back to the path of liberty or abolish it by reversing the actions of a tyrannical government.

Jefferson leveled charges against the king because the king was the one who had the ultimate responsibility for government actions. Still, Jefferson also found Parliament equally guilty of many of these charges. His approach exhibits the fact that charges may be leveled against governments as a whole, not just at the executive, legislative, or judicial branches individually. All branches of government may be found culpable, including the bureaucracies these branches create.

Charge 1: He has refused his assent to laws, the most wholesome and necessary for the public good.

Like Thomas Jefferson, writer Thomas Paine agreed with this first charge. In his pamphlet *Common Sense*, Paine wrote:

> The powers of governing still remaining in the hands of the king, he will have a negative over the whole legislation of this continent. And as he hath shown himself such an inveterate enemy to liberty, and discovered such a thirst for arbitrary power, is he, or is he not, a proper man to say to these colonies, "You shall make no laws but what I please?" And is there any inhabitant in America so ignorant, as not to know, that according to what is called the present constitution, that this continent can make no laws but what the king gives leave to? and is there any man so unwise, as not to see, that (considering what has happened) he will suffer no Law to be made here, but such as suit his purpose? We may be as effectually enslaved by the want of laws in America, as by submitting to laws made for us in England. After matters are made up (as it is called) can there be any doubt but the whole power of the crown will be

exerted, to keep this continent as low and humble as possible? Instead of going forward we shall go backward, or be perpetually quarrelling or ridiculously petitioning.[93]

Without the king giving his assent, the colonies could pass no laws. The colonies had no real voice in the actions of government. Furthermore, Parliament, as with the king, was unacquainted with the inhabitants of America and their circumstances, and yet it claimed to possess the responsibility to pass laws for colonists in a far distant land.

As I previously mentioned, Benjamin Franklin, in a letter to Dean Woodward in 1773, wrote about Pennsylvania's and Virginia's attempt at abolishing slavery from their colonies. And in this he observed that this attempt would likely be thwarted, not by fellow colonists, but by the governing authorities overseas. Franklin said:

A disposition to abolish slavery prevails in North America, that many of Pennsylvanians have set their slaves at liberty, and that even the Virginia Assembly have petitioned the King for permission to make a law for preventing the importation of more into that colony. This request, however, will probably not be granted as their former laws of that kind have always been repealed.[94]

Anti-slavery laws are laws that would have been wholesome and necessary for the public good. These laws would have been for the good of the colonies at that time. Furthermore, the continuation of these laws later led to severe bloodshed in America's Civil War. However, the king consistently vetoed any attempts to alter the pro-slavery laws imposed on the colonies.

Massachusetts also tried passing laws that banned the importation and sale of slaves. In May of 1766, Samuel Adams attended a Boston Town Meeting that instructed their representatives to try to pass the law.[95] But slavery continued by the design of the crown. Of course, according to the Mayflower Compact, the Puritans, when first founding the colony, formed themselves into "one body politic" for the purpose of forming government of the people and for their benefit. As I will later show, the king vested each of the colonies with power for enacting their laws without his consent. The king also vested these powers in the posterity of the colonists forever. That is, the king vested the colonies with all necessary powers unless, of course, the king changed his mind, as Bradford and the Pilgrims feared would happen.

Until 1764, the colonies issued their own paper bills of credit as legal tender for payment of money. However, England's Parliament issued the Currency Act in 1764, with the king's assent, which prohibited the colonies from issuing these bills of credit. In other words, the king failed to provide assent to the laws regarding bills of credit passed by the various colonies. This Act suspended the bills the colonies issued. The Act abolished any new currency except the reissue of currency previously in existence. With no hard currency, the colonies suffered economically at the hands of their mother country.

In the Declaratory Act of 1766, Parliament declared that it and the king alone possessed the authority to "make laws and statutes of sufficient force and validity to bind the colonies and people of America, subjects of the crown of Great Britain, in all cases whatsoever," and "all resolutions, votes, orders, and proceedings, in any of the said colonies or plantations, whereby the power and authority of the parliament of Great Britain, to make laws and statutes as aforesaid, is denied, or drawn into question, are and are hereby declared to be, utterly null and void to all in purposes whatsoever."[96] In short, the king "refused his assent to laws, the most wholesome and necessary for the public good." In fact, he even nullified the colonists' laws and prohibited their passage of new laws.

The federal government of today is guilty of a similar charge to that of King George. One major example of this is the landmark decision of the US Supreme Court in *Roe v. Wade*. This decision basically nullified all anti-abortion laws allowing for abortion on demand. It also ended any possible dissent to abortion in all the states. Until that judgment, forty-four of the fifty states had "outlawed abortion in nearly all situations that did not threaten the life or health of the mother."[97] Nearly 90 percent of the states believed these laws were wholesome and necessary for the public good. But in one decision rendered by a tyranny of nine judges, the US Supreme Court abolished these state laws—laws that the majority of the peoples' representatives had passed in nearly every state with the assent provided by their state executives and local courts.

Furthermore, the decision in *Roe v. Wade* violates the jurisdiction of the Supreme Court as defined in the US Constitution in Article III. Nowhere will one find that the Constitution grants the Supreme Court—or any federal court for that matter—any jurisdiction between a citizen of one state and the state in which that citizen resides. The Constitution grants the federal courts jurisdiction in cases between states, between citizens of two different states, between foreign governments or aliens against a state or against United States citizens, and nearly anything else to do with international affairs. However, the Constitution grants no jurisdiction between a state and its citizens. Put another way, the US Constitution grants the Texas Supreme Court jurisdiction in a Texas case. So in any case between the state of Texas and its citizens, the highest court is the Texas Supreme Court, not the US Supreme Court. The same applies to all other states. In *Roe v. Wade*, however, the US Supreme Court overstepped its constitutional boundaries: it accepted to hear a case that only concerned the state of Texas and an American citizen residing in it.

We must remember that the purpose of government is to protect life, liberty, and property, which are the natural rights of citizens. The Founders understood the concept of protecting these natural rights, including the rights of the unborn. James Wilson of Pennsylvania, a signer of the Declaration of Independence and the Constitution, spoke about the natural rights of all, including that the law protected all life. To support this, Wilson provided a history of other civilizations, including Rome, Germany, China, Sparta, and Athens. He described how these civilizations violated this right to life when they allowed and even promoted the purposeful taking of the lives of children. In Sparta, for example, if the examiner judged a child to be unhealthy or ill-formed, the examiner would have the child thrown into a pit. In contrast to this, Wilson argued that there was a natural right to life that all civilizations should acknowledge, respect, and follow. And this right was one of those rights the Founders built on in their establishment of the United States of America:

> With consistency, beautiful and undeviating, human life, from its commencement to its close, is protected by the common law. In the contemplation of law, life begins when the infant is first able to stir in the womb. By the law, life is protected not only from immediate destruction, but from every degree of actual violence, and, in some cases, from every degree of danger.[98]

Of course, the definition of "stir in the womb" was different in 1790 compared with today. When or at what point science recognizes what Wilson meant by the "stirring in the womb," now compared to then, will obviously be different. But even contemporary scientists have acknowledged that their research shows that human life begins at conception, when no stirring of life can even be felt in the womb—a fact that the decision in *Roe v. Wade* does not accommodate.[99] Even in spite of this, the *Roe v. Wade* ruling violates the powers of the states and natural law, and it is inconsistent with the concepts and beliefs of the Founders. These violations succinctly fall under the charge against the English crown and apply to our modern federal government.

In a similar manner, numerous other laws passed by legislatures or initiatives passed by a majority of the people have been struck down by the Court, many of these laws having been passed and assent provided by a president at the national level. For instance, Arizona, having a serious illegal immigration problem and believing that the federal government either was negligent in securing the US/Mexico border or was unable to enforce immigration law, enacted its own law, which it believed was wholesome and necessary for the public good. This law used similar wording and sited federal law for its basis in constitutional law.[100] In spite of this, the US Supreme Court failed to provide assent to Arizona's law as did the executive branch, which "sued to block"[101] the constitutionally passed law of Arizona. Moreover, the Supreme Court considered the Arizona law unconstitutional despite the fact that the law almost perfectly mirrored federal law.

Numerous other laws passed by the various states and initiatives passed by the majority of electors of states have been overturned, or not given assent, by the federal government, even when they mirror federal legislation. The federal government is over-reaching its constitutional bounds, imposing its will over that of the states and their residents, supplanting their liberties and laws for its own interests and views. King George III and his Parliament would have been proud.

Charge 2: He has forbidden his governors to pass laws of immediate and pressing importance, unless suspended in their operation till his assent should be obtained; and when so suspended, he has utterly neglected to attend to them.

In many respects, the king left the colonies to their own designs when it came to governing themselves, taxing themselves, and doing whatever they needed for their own good. They were generally independent of England. Historian David Ramsay confirms this:

> The inhabitants of the colonies from the beginning, especially in New-England, enjoyed a government, which was but little short of being independent. They had not only the image, but the substance of the English constitution. They chose most of their magistrates, and paid them all. They had in effect the sole direction of their internal government. The chief mark of their subordination consisted in their making no laws repugnant to the laws of their Mother Country—their submitting such laws as they made to be repealed by the King, and their obeying such restrictions, as were laid on their trade, by parliament. The latter were often evaded, and with impunity. The other small checks were scarcely felt, and for a long time were in no respects injurious to their interests.[102]

The king was uninvolved in the affairs of the colonies, except as needed and when it was in the interest of the king. However, as time passed and kings changed, more intrusion into the affairs of the colonists began to emerge. This is how the troubles between the colonies and the king began.

The aforementioned Currency Act provides one example of the king suspending the operation of laws until he gave his assent, if he provided that assent. The Act stated:

> If any governor or commander in chief for the time being, in all or any of the said colonies or plantations, shall ... give his assent to any act or order of assembly contrary to the true intent and meaning of this act, every such governor or commander in chief shall, for every such offence, forfeit and pay the sum of one thousand pounds, and shall be immediately dismissed from his government, and for ever after rendered incapable of any public office or place of trust.[103]

Through this Act, the king provided a punishment for governors who assented to laws of the colonies involving currency that violated the Act, regardless of the colonies' need for paper bills.

Two years before the Declaration of Independence, Jefferson wrote in *Summary View of the Rights of British America*, "With equal inattention to the necessities of his people here has his majesty permitted our laws to lie neglected in England for years, neither confirming them by his assent, nor annulling them by his negative."[104] Even if the king had annulled the laws, it would have been better than neglecting the confirmation or the annulment of the laws, which left the colonists wondering whether they were in violation of their own laws or being obedient to them. Without certainty regarding how to act, the colonists took no action whatsoever.

According to the Charter of Massachusetts, the Council, as the colony called it, maintained all authority to govern the colony. It possessed authority to pass laws for the public good, to tax as needed, and act on behalf of the colonists.[105] Samuel Adams explained:

> By the Royal Charter granted to our ancestors, the power of making laws for our internal government, and of levying taxes, is vested in the General Assembly. ... The most essential rights of British Subjects

are those of being represented in the same body which exercises the power of levying taxes upon them. … There are certain inherent rights belonging to the people, which the Parliament itself cannot divest them of, consistent with their own constitution.[106]

Simply stated, the king had granted Massachusetts the authority to act. This was to be perpetual, and neither the king nor Parliament possessed power to repeal the charter.

The Stamp Act, which Adams opposed, was a tax instituted by Parliament, not by the colonies, and it only benefited the mother country. This act taxed every bill of lading, magazines, newspapers, playing cards, wills and other legal documents, and many other items too numerous to list. The taxes paid for the king's troops stationed in America, a presence the colonies did not need or want. The Stamp Act was a clear violation of the rights of the colonies and their individual charters. It would take a year for Parliament to repeal it, only to replace it with the Declaratory Act, which forbade the colonies to pass laws of their own and bound them to every law of Parliament.

A circular letter to the governors in America, dated April 21, 1768, furnishes another example of the king's failure to provide assent and his suspension of anything the colonies did. It stated:

It is his Majesty's pleasure that you should immediately upon the receipt hereof exert your utmost influence to defeat this flagitious attempt to disturb the public peace by prevailing upon the Assembly of your province to take no notice of it, *which will be treating it with the contempt it deserves*. … If there should appear in the Assembly of your province a disposition to receive or give any countenance to this seditious paper, it will be your duty to prevent any proceeding upon it by an immediate prorogation or dissolution.[107]

Prorogation means that the governors will not suspend the assembly or its action but will discontinue the assembly's meeting, at least for a time. The king forbade his governors to provide assent to anything that the governors believed to be contrary to the king's wishes regardless of whether the colonists needed the law.

This charge against the king is not one that can be directly applied to the current American federal government. However, similar to the previous charge, we can see that any federal nullification of laws has the same effect as the king forbidding governors to pass laws of immediate importance, such as with the Arizona immigration law. Many state governors and even state legislatures will weigh what they assume the Supreme Court will rule before passing a controversial law, despite how necessary the law might be. So the effect is the same—namely, the federal government's wishes or designs weigh more heavily than do those of the states and local municipalities. Some needed legislation, therefore, may never be written, much less become law.

Charge 3: He has refused to pass other laws for the accommodation of large districts of people, unless those people would relinquish the right of representation in the legislature, a right inestimable to them and formidable to tyrants only.

In order to accommodate large districts of people, land is required. After the French and Indian War (1754–1763), the king made a proclamation that forbade the colonies from expanding beyond the Appalachian Mountains. This provided only a very narrow strip of land upon which the colonists could expand. Ironically, during the war the colonists fought for the land west of the Appalachian range (among other areas) only to have it stripped from their use.[108] The passage of this law was particularly unaccommodating.

England's king not only refused to pass laws for the people "unless those people would relinquish the right of representation," but the tyrant passed laws forcing the relinquishment of their right to representation. Once again, the Declaratory Act applies to this charge. Parliament, in passing this act with the king's consent, made themselves the sole legislative body of the colonies, regardless of the perpetual nature of the charters of the several colonies and the authority granted to them to pass their own laws, tax themselves, and so forth.

Any laws, any tax, any resolution—in short, anything that the colonies would legislate, the king deemed null and void with the passage of the Declaratory Act. This compelled by force of law the relinquishment of the colonies' right of representation.

Furthermore, in 1774, Parliament passed the Massachusetts Government Act, which came with numerous offenses to the colonists of Massachusetts and carried with it an evil omen of the king's continuing tyranny for the rest of the colonies. The following are a few items of the king forcing the colonists to relinquish their right of representation:

> Whereas the said method of electing such counsellors or assistants, to be vested with the several powers, authorities, and privileges, therein mentioned, although conformable to the practice theretofore used in such of the colonies thereby united, in which the appointment of the respective governors had been vested in the general courts or assemblies of the said colonies, hath, by repeated experience, been found to be extremely ill adapted to the plan of government established in the province of the Massachusetts Bay ... *the said method of annually electing the counsellors or assistants of the said province should no longer be suffered to continue* but that the appointment of the said counsellors or assistants should henceforth be put upon the like footing as is established in such other of his Majesty's colonies or plantations in America, the governors whereof are appointed by his Majesty's commission. ... And the council, or court of assistants of the said province for the time being, shall be composed of such of the inhabitants or proprietors of lands within the same as shall be thereunto nominated and appointed by his Majesty.[109]

Simply stated, the king required the relinquishment of Massachusetts' right to elect their own people as their representatives. The king would now nominate and appoint whomever he chose to govern the colony, and who would be loyal to the king rather than representative of the people. The king's subjects in

England would not have tolerated such an action, but the king expected his subjects in America to comply. Additionally, by the Act's own admission, the king perpetrated this upon other colonies too.

This was not all. The Act prohibited the colonists from choosing their own sheriffs and juries. In that day, the sheriffs, unless a party to a court case, would appoint the juries. Naturally, the crown-appointed sheriff would appoint juries that were loyal to the king rather than appointing people for the purpose of fairness.

In addition to dissolving the colony's legislature, the Act provided that "no meeting shall be called by the select men, or at the request of any number of freeholders of any township, district, or precinct, without the leave of the governor." The crown forbade assembly of the government, whether colonial or local, unless the crown-appointed governor granted permission.[110] Thus, if the governor never gave his permission, the colonists' government body could never assemble.

In the case of Virginia, the king prevented the creation of new counties with new representatives, a new county seat and courts, and other necessary governing units unless the colonists relinquished their right to representation. The king acted without regard for the needs of Virginia's citizens. About this, Jefferson wrote:

> Shall we speak of a late instruction to his majesty's governor of the colony of Virginia, by which he is forbidden to assent to any law for the division of a county, unless the new county will consent to have no representative in assembly? That colony has as yet fixed no boundary to the westward. Their western counties, therefore, are of indefinite extent; some of them are actually seated many hundred miles from their eastern limits. Is it possible, then, that his majesty can have bestowed a single thought on the situation of those people, who, in order to obtain justice for injuries, however great or small, must, by the laws of that colony, attend their county court, at such a distance, with all their witnesses, monthly, till their litigation be determined? Or does his majesty seriously wish, and publish it to the world, that his subjects

should give up the glorious right of representation, with all the benefits derived from that, and submit themselves the absolute slaves of his sovereign will? Or is it rather meant to confine the legislative body to their present numbers, that they may be the cheaper bargain whenever they shall become worth a purchase?[111]

The king routinely dissolved legislatures and forbade them from passing laws or doing anything that the colonies deemed necessary for the benefit of their citizens. Gratefully, this has yet to occur since the founding of the government under the current US Constitution, at least in part.

The part where representation has been lost began with the Seventeenth Amendment to the Constitution. The Founders designed the Senate for a specific purpose. Senators were to be elected by state legislatures and designed to work by different methods than the House of Representatives. In order to understand why the Seventeenth Amendment is a failure, it is important to understand the Founders' design.

First, the Founders designed America's government to be a republic. Realizing this is vital to understanding one of the problems of the Seventeenth Amendment, as well as how the ratification of the amendment applies to this charge. Initially, Madison designed the federal legislative branch with two branches, with rights of suffrage that "ought to be proportioned to the Quotas of contribution, or to the number of free inhabitants" (Federalist No. 51). In other words, the people voted for each of the two branches and each branch received its numbers by a census of the people. This, however, failed to unite the smaller states to the idea. So the delegates compromised and created a Senate "composed of two Senators from each State, chosen by the legislature thereof." This design appeared to be less democratic than Madison's original Virginia Plan was. Still, the Founders intentionally created the Senate this way. You see, they disliked democracies. In Federalist No. 10, Madison wrote, "democracies have ever been spectacles of turbulence and contention; have ever been found incompatible with personal security or the rights of property." Thus, the Founders created a republic, not a democracy.

The Founders intentionally designed the two houses of the legislative branch differently for a reason. Madison described the reason in Federalist No. 51:

> In republican government, the legislative authority necessarily predominates. The remedy for this inconveniency is to divide the legislature into different branches; and to *render them, by different modes of election and different principles of action, as little connected with each other as the nature of their common functions and their common dependence on the society will admit.* (Emphasis added.)

The fear of centralization of power always concerned the Founders. Therefore, they divided the most powerful branch into two houses, gave each specific powers, provided each house with a different mode of election, and made the length of the terms of office different for each house.

The House of Representatives received power to originate spending bills and impeach government officials, among possessing other powers. The Senate received power to ratify treaties, give advice, and consent to the nomination of ambassadors, federal judges, and other officials, and to try all impeachments decided in the House. The people elect the members of the House and the state legislatures elect the members of the Senate—this was the original design.

The Founders planned the legislative branch this way for a couple of reasons. First, by giving the states the power to vote for Senators, the Constitution recognized "the portion of sovereignty remaining in the individual States" and created "an instrument for preserving that residuary sovereignty" (Federalist No. 62). Thus, the Founders created a powerful check by the States on the federal government. The States, being bound by the Constitution to uphold the "Constitution, and the laws of the United States ... and all treaties," needed this fundamental check on the federal government. Second, "No law or resolution can now be passed without the concurrence, first, of a majority of the people, and then, of a majority of the States." This served to double "the security of the people, by requiring the concurrence of two distinct bodies in schemes of usurpation or perfidy" (Federalist No. 62). This double security that Madison wrote about served as a buffer against corruption. The difficulty of corrupting individual state legislatures, the people's representatives in the House, and the President would be a massive undertaking, which would be nearly impossible to accomplish.

The states voiced their desires through their representatives, the Senators. This gave the states a voice in federal laws, treaties, ambassadors involved in treaty making, and the choice of federal officials, such as the cabinet, those involved in federal law enforcement, and federal judges. The Senators' constitutional duty, then, is to protect the sovereignty and power of the states against the demands of the federal government.

The Seventeenth Amendment, however, eliminated this vital check of the states on the powers of the federal government. The Seventeenth Amendment put the selection of Senators in the hands of the people of each state. State legislatures no longer have the authority to select senators. Now this power rests in the popular vote of the people. Republicanism gave way to democracy.

The goal of the Seventeenth Amendment was to make the federal government result from a democratic form of selection. The Founders would have vehemently opposed this approach. They designed a representative government, not a democracy. With the passage of the Seventeenth Amendment, the people lost representation when the representatives of their states lost representation from their state legislatures. The end result was that the states lost their direct voice in Congress. This effectively centralized more power in the federal government. This is not quite the same as the king demanding that the people give up their representation in order to expand into new counties or territories, but the loss of representation of the states does provide a link to this historical event. Those representatives are to protect against tyranny. The Seventeenth Amendment stopped representation that did just that.

Without proper representation, tyranny prevails. The king is answerable to no one, but representatives are answerable to those who choose them. Thus, it is vitally important that the people be on guard so as not to lose their representative forms of government. Furthermore, the people should work to restore any representation they lose.

Charge 4: He has called together legislative bodies at places unusual, uncomfortable, and distant from the depository of their public records, for the sole purpose of fatiguing them into compliance with his measures.

In 1769, for example, Massachusetts' representatives assembled and passed resolutions opposing the recent deployment of British troops to Boston. The assembly demanded that the governor have the troops removed. Naturally, the king-appointed governor refused to comply with that demand, stating that he had no authority to do so and would likely be unable to influence the crown in requesting the removal of the troops. As the representatives reassembled, British troops marched and paraded around the assembly hall, making it impossible to conduct a meeting, which forced the assembly to move to Cambridge, distant from the public records they needed to access. This move against the Massachusetts assembly was an attempt to force compliance with the wishes of the king.[112] This harassment was also designed to disrupt the assembly's proceedings in order to convince the representatives to desist.

Later, the colonialists in Boston, not wishing to have tea forced upon them by Governor Hutchinson who had ulterior economic motives wrapped up in the sale of the tea, destroyed the tea by non-violently tossing it overboard. By 1774, when the crown appointed General Gage governor of Massachusetts, Gage ordered the assembly of representatives to Salem.

> He (General Gage) was at this time appointed governor and commander in chief of the province of Massachusetts Bay; directed to repair immediately there, and on his arrival to remove the seat of government from Boston, and to convene the general assembly to meet at Salem, a smaller town, situated about twenty miles from the capital. The governor, the lieutenant-governor, the secretary, the board of commissioners, and all crown officers were ordered by special mandate to leave Boston, and make the town of Salem the place of their future residence.[113]

This act, among other acts of General Gage, helped stoke the fires of revolution in Massachusetts and violated the people's right to have their seat of government where they designated—a place that was comfortable and usual and where they kept the public records.

The Stamp Act, which kindled the wrath of the colonists against the mother country, helped start this problem. After Parliament repealed the Stamp Act, it replaced the Act with the Declaratory Act and the Townsend Act of 1767 (see charge 9 below). Massachusetts was one of the first to address these problems, demanding that the king recognize their rights as British subjects and that Parliament repeal the acts. Massachusetts sent a circular to the rest of the colonial legislatures in early 1768. Virginia applauded the actions of Massachusetts and drafted a set of resolutions of their own. "Expressing their exclusive right to tax their constituents, and their right to petition their sovereign for redress of grievances, and the lawfulness of procuring the concurrence of the other colonies in praying for the royal interposition, in favour of the violated rights of America."[114]

The result was that the governor of Virginia, an appointed governor of the crown, Lord Botetourt, sent for the House of Burgesses the following day, having heard of their resolutions. At that point, the governor dissolved the House. So "The principle members, under [Patrick] Henry's leadership, reassembled nearby in the long-room of the Raleigh Tavern, known as the 'Apollo.'"[115] The governor left them little choice but to move to a different meeting place. They also could not include the whole assembly there because of that inconvenience, making it much more difficult and uncomfortable to conduct business.

Later, Governor Dunmore would also dissolve the assembly when Henry and others resolved to stand with Massachusetts in protesting Parliament's stripping of representation in Massachusetts—the previously mentioned Massachusetts Government Act.

Parliament, not just the British king, was culpable in these actions against the American colonists. Parliament was an ocean away from the colonies. And through the Declaratory Act, it stripped the colonies of their legislatures' authority. Consequently, these legislatures were left legally powerless to conduct needed business while also being forced to meet far away from the depository of their public records. Add to that the fact that they had no representatives in the

Parliament, and you can see how frustrating and fatiguing their plight was made by their mother country.

So far, America's current federal government has not done anything that would link it to this colonists' charge against England's monarchy, but Americans should always be on guard against such a disregard for their rights.

Charge 5: He has dissolved representative houses repeatedly, for opposing with manly firmness his invasions on the rights of the people.

Massachusetts' representative house was dissolved when Parliament dissolved the representative system so the king could appoint the colony's representatives. However, this was not all that the Massachusetts Government Act disbanded. It allowed for the crown-appointed governor to remove and appoint judges at all levels—namely, "the attorney general, provosts, marshals, justices of the peace, and other officers to the council or courts of justice"—and to nominate and appoint sheriffs as well as remove sheriffs. In addition, the Act provided for juries to be filled with those individuals selected by the appointed sheriff.[116]

Massachusetts protested this power grab, as did Virginia. Virginia's action led to the crown-appointed governor dissolving the colony's representative house. North Carolina, too, followed Massachusetts and Virginia's lead and adopted resolutions of their own. The response of North Carolina's governor, William Tryon, was similar; he dissolved his colony's assembly.[117] This was the standard operating procedure of the king's governors throughout the colonies.

The New York Suspending Act of 1767 is a classic case of denying representation. The Quartering Act of 1765 demanded that colonists provide needed quarters and other supplies for the defense of the colonists. Until New York provided for the king's soldiers, the New York Suspending Act forbade the executive appointed by the crown to assent to anything passed by the legislature of the colony, whether bills, resolutions, orders, or anything else that required a vote.[118] While not technically a dissolution, a suspension of the legislature has the same effect. Jefferson agreed that the New York Suspending Act in effect dissolved the legislature.

In his *A Summary View of the Rights of British America*, Jefferson wrote about the danger of this kind of action. Specifically mentioning The New York Suspending Act, he said:

> Shall these governments be dissolved, their property annihilated, and their people reduced to a state of nature, at the imperious breath of a body of men, whom they never saw, in whom they never confided, and over whom they have no powers of punishment or removal, let their crimes against the American public be ever so great? Can any one reason be assigned why 160,000 electors in the island of Great Britain should give law to four millions in the states of America, every individual of whom is equal to every individual of them, in virtue, in understanding, and in bodily strength? Were this to be admitted, instead of being a free people, as we have hitherto supposed, and mean to continue ourselves, we should suddenly be found the slaves, not of one, but of 160,000 tyrants, distinguished too from all others by this singular circumstance, that they are removed from the reach of fear, the only restraining motive which may hold the hand of a tyrant.[119]

Jefferson viewed the crown as tyrannical. He also viewed Parliament and all the electors of Great Britain as tyrants. As he reasoned, the danger of the situation was that the dissolution of the various legislative bodies paved the way to slavery, or, in other words, a loss of liberty.

Massachusetts, New York, North Carolina, and Virginia were among the colonies whose legislatures were suspended. Only a tyrant would move to suspend authority of the people in their legislatures. The legislative branch is the supreme authority of any government. When any chief executive suspends or dissolves bodies of legislative authority, he or she is becoming tyrannical and leading the people into servitude.

Technically speaking, the issue the colonies faced is not one we face today. However, Americans are at least seeing the weakening of their legislative branch of government. Consider: when an American president creates new laws through executive orders or when courts legislate from the bench, they bypass Congress and usurp its authority. This has the same effect as dissolving representative houses. The legislative branch becomes unnecessary if the executive and judicial branches do the legislating. Two examples will suffice to show this.

Among one of the first of President Barak Obama's executive orders was number 13503, "Establishment of White House Office of Urban Affairs." First, constitutionally the creation of any office or department is the responsibility of the legislative branch, not the executive branch. Moreover, President Obama's order created an office that spends money, and the disbursement of funds is the responsibility of the legislative branch.[120] This executive order violated the Constitution by bypassing Congress. Consequently, it had the same effect as dissolving representative houses.

Citing many other such examples is relatively simple. President George W. Bush, along with numerous other presidents in both major political parties, signed unconstitutional executive orders. President Bush's order called the "President's Commission to Strengthen Social Security" created a sixteen-member team and naturally spent money.[121] But it is the responsibility of Congress to allocate funds and create offices, regardless of how temporary or permanent the office may be. The president's order had the same effect as dissolving the representatives' authority to legislate.

Of course, the judicial branch has also acted in such a way as to have the same effect as dissolving a legislature. One such action came through the US Supreme Court's decisions in the cases of *Miranda v. Arizona* and *Gideon v. Wainwright*. In the *Miranda* case, despite a lack of statute that requires law enforcement to inform suspects or an arrested individual of their rights to remain silent, have an attorney, and so forth, the Court mandated they be informed of these rights. This was purely a judicial decision. No law existed that required it. The court's role, including that of the Supreme Court, under the Constitution is judgment, or judging whether a *law* has been violated, including the Constitution. While this decision in *Miranda* may appear as if the Court is protecting civil liberties, its decision was not for it to make. The Court's decision was properly legislative, not judicial. It falls under the responsibility of the legislative branch to enact laws that fulfill this responsibility.

In the *Wainwright* case, the Court held that it is the responsibility of the state to provide an attorney to an individual who cannot afford one. If one remembers that a right is one that is inherent and needs no outside permission or even assistance to exercise it, then one can clearly see that a right does not guarantee that one can exercise it. Requiring the state to pay for it, or in other words, for other taxpayers to pay for the attorney, does not constitute a right. This would be similar to requiring taxpayers to pay to publish my book. That does not fall under a right even though I have a constitutional right to free speech. Furthermore, the legislative branch now must allocate funds to pay for attorneys—something that the Court required but falls under the responsibility of the legislative branch.

When our executive and judicial branches assume the role of the legislative branch, they effectively circumvent and undermine the representatives' authority to legislate. If carried far enough, the executive and judicial branches will render Congress ineffective and obsolete, thereby removing from the people and their states their ability to stand up and oppose the tyranny emanating from their own government.

Charge 6: He has refused for a long time, after such dissolutions, to cause others to be elected; whereby the legislative powers, incapable of annihilation, have returned to the people at large for their exercise; the state remaining in the meantime exposed to all the dangers of invasion from without, and convulsions within.

The New York Suspending Act not only suspended or dissolved the legislature but also prohibited any vote whatsoever until the legislature fulfilled its requirements for quartering troops. This would expose the colony to "dangers from without." In other words, without the ability to appropriate funds for peace officers or other law enforcement, to tax itself so that it would have funds to appropriate, and to pass laws that were "wholesome and necessary for the public good," New York citizens' lives, liberty, and property would be in danger. The colonists of New York and other colonies did not want or see the need of having troops among them. They viewed this demand as an attempt by the king to control them with the threat of force from the military, especially since the war with the French had already ended and peace had been restored.

This Act left New York's citizens without an effective government—a government designed to protect their lives, liberties, and property. Without a legislative body to allocate funds, to provide for laws necessary for the public good, and to oversee the judicial and executive branches, the king left the colonists unprotected; he jeopardized their vital unalienable rights.

Under the assumption that government is for the people and by the people, when the king or any other body of government dissolves the people's legislative branch, the powers of that branch should return to the people at large. After all, it was the people who granted legislative power. In fact, because the people grant political power to all branches of government—legislative, executive, and judicial—only the people have the right to suspend or dissolve those branches. Neither the executive nor the judicial branch can procure legislative power without usurping the authority of the people. Nor can any other branch usurp authority not given it by the people.

Once again, Jefferson used Locke to form his argument against the king's terrible abuse of power regarding his suspension and dissolution of the colonies' legislatures. Locke stated:

> This legislative is not only the supreme power of the commonwealth, but sacred and unalterable in the hands where the community have once placed it; nor can any edict of anybody else, in what form soever conceived, or by what power soever backed, have the force and obligation of a law, which has not its sanction from that legislative which the public has chosen and appointed: for without this the law could not have that, which is absolutely necessary to its being a law, the consent of the society, over whom nobody can have a power to make laws, but by their own consent.[122]

Only the people may decide upon whom they desire to bestow legislative power. And only the people may decide to dissolve the body of representatives. No law is a law without the "sanction from that legislative which the public has chosen and appointed."

In the case of Massachusetts, the king and Parliament dissolved the legislature and gave the king, not the people, the power to make future appointments to the legislature. The appointees would therefore serve at "the pleasure of the king" rather than that of the people. The king's actions violated the colonists' right to self-government and gave him the power of a despot.

After Parliament passed the Stamp Act, the colonies recognized the need for unity and determined that it was necessary to form the Continental Congress. One of the internal convulsions that threatened the colonies was the passage of the Stamp Act. Many colonists opposed it and refused to follow the tyrannical demands of the crown.

However, despite this desire to form a congress, many of the crown-appointed governors refused to call sessions of their colonies' assemblies so they could elect delegations to the Congress. And in some of those cases where legislatures had already assembled, governors refused to allow them to elect and send delegations to the Congress. These governors were acting to protect the king and his interests. But preventing properly elected officials from meeting and conducting business violated the rights of the people who voted for their representatives. Concerning these tyrannical acts by the crown-appointed governors, David Ramsay wrote:

> The assemblies of Virginia, North Carolina, and Georgia, were prevented, by their governors, from sending a deputation to this Congress. Twenty eight deputies from Massachusetts, Rhode Island, Connecticut, New York, New Jersey, Pennsylvania, Delaware, Maryland, and South Carolina met at New York; and after mature deliberation agreed on a declaration of their rights, and on a statement of their grievances. They asserted in strong terms, their exemption from all taxes, not imposed by their own representatives.[123]

Historian Edmund S. Morgan observed that "Delaware and New Jersey met the same obstruction (as Virginia, North Carolina and Georgia) but sent representatives anyhow, chosen when some of the assemblymen defiantly held an informal election of their own." In the case of New York, representatives simply nominated themselves to attend.[124]

Today, the federal government has not abused its power by formally dissolving any legislating bodies. However, when federal courts can overturn any act of a state, regardless of whether the court has any authority or enumerated power regarding the act, the effect is the same. In such cases state legislatures are as impotent as if the federal courts had dissolved them.

However, as both Locke and Jefferson discussed, without the consent of the legislative body, no action taken by the executive or the judiciary branches are legally valid. Thus, when the executive branch orders an action not granted by the Constitution or by the legislative branch, the order is null and void and does not constitute law. The same requirement holds to the judiciary branch. Gag orders, which forbid individuals to freely speak on any subject they like, or restraining orders that try to divine whether an individual will commit a crime and thus prevent the individual's free movement are just two examples of arbitrary, unlawful, and unconstitutional actions taken by the judiciary branch. They have the same effect as the dissolution of the people's representatives.

Charge 7: He has endeavored to prevent the population of these states; for that purpose obstructing the laws for naturalization of foreigners; refusing to pass others to encourage their migration hither, and raising the conditions of new appropriations of lands.

One of the first items of England's poor immigration laws was not actually a prevention of migration to the colonies. In fact, it was the opposite. The crown, though not King George, had been exporting convicted felons to the colonies as part of their punishment for their crimes.[125] This perturbed the colonists. After all, why would a "caring mother" endanger her children by sending them dangerous criminals? Whether the criminals were non-violent or violent did not matter. The king's action helped create more lawlessness which could tend to anarchy. In 1751, Benjamin Franklin wrote about this matter in the *Pennsylvania Gazette*:

Such a tender parental concern in our mother country for the welfare of her children calls aloud for the highest returns of gratitude and duty. In some of the uninhabited parts of these provinces, there are numbers of these venomous reptiles we call rattlesnakes, felons-convict from the beginning of the world ... and if a small bounty were allowed per head, some thousands might be collected annually and transported to Britain ... [and] carefully distributed in St. James's Park ... in the gardens of the nobility and gentry throughout the nation ... for to them we are most particularly obliged.[126]

While the point made by Franklin is a bit tongue in cheek, the fact is that a caring parent would not free criminals and send them to her children. The king was simply looking for an easy way to rid England of the burden of its criminals. After the United States achieved its independence with the surrender of General Cornwallis at Yorktown in 1781, England searched for another colony to offload criminals. The British founded Australia as a penal colony and sent the first fleet of criminals there in 1788.[127]

Another instance where we see bad immigration law is the Proclamation of 1763. This act prohibited the colonists from expanding beyond the Appalachian Mountains, regardless of the colonists' need or desire to expand. This limitation was just one way used to prevent population growth as much as possible. It established an inadequate supply of land for the expansion of farming or whatever purpose the colonists had for the land. The king claimed that this limitation was necessary so he could effectively protect his subjects from Indians. This was a false claim. The colonists, not the British regulars, had fought in the majority of the battles in the French and Indian War. Indeed, from the early seventeenth century, the colonists had been defending themselves without British military assistance. They did not need the king's help in protecting themselves.

Beginning in 1660, Parliament passed several laws known as Navigation Acts that prevented skilled tradesmen from migrating to America or other western colonies of England without serious penalties. Furthermore, any trade of goods with the colonies was only to occur via British ships with British citizens at the helm.

Be it enacted, that no alien or person not born within the allegiance of our sovereign lord the king, his heirs and successors, or naturalized, or made a free denizen, shall ... exercise the trade or occupation of a merchant or factor in any the said places (Asia, Africa or America); upon pain of the forfeiture and loss of all his goods and chattels, or which are in his possession; one third to his Majesty, his heirs and successors; one third to the governor of the plantation where such person shall so offend; and the other third to him or them that shall inform or sue for the same in any of his Majesty's courts in the plantation where such offence shall be committed; no goods or commodities whatsoever, of the growth, production or manufacture of Africa, Asia, or America, or of any part thereof, or which are described or laid down in the usual maps or cards of those places, be imported into England, Ireland, or Wales, islands of Guernsey and Jersey, or town of Berwick upon Tweed, in any other ship or ships, vessel or commodities vessels whatsoever, but in such as do truly and without fraud belong only to the people of England or Ireland, dominion of Wales, or town of Berwick upon Tweed, or of the lands, islands, plantations or territories in Asia, Africa, or America, to his Majesty belonging, as the proprietors and right owners thereof, and whereof the master, and three fourths at least of the mariners are English; under the penalty of the forfeiture of all such goods and commodities, and of the ship or vessel in which they were imported, with all her guns, tackle, furniture, ammunition, and apparel.[128]

In 1696, the king renewed the Navigation Acts with the stipulation that governors would be required to enforce it and would become liable if they did not. The king prevented any transaction, including the transportation of goods, in anything but British vessels. Allowing only his colonies to trade with England served the king only and prevented the prosperity of the colonies.

When it came to the king's continued prohibition of individuals going to the American colonies, he enacted yet another law restricting immigration. While serving as an ambassador to England, Benjamin Franklin commented on this in 1774:

God commands to increase and replenish the earth; the proposed law would forbid increasing, and confine Britons to their present number, keeping half that number too in wretchedness. The common people of Britain and of Ireland contributed by the taxes they paid, and by the blood they lost, to the success of that war which brought into our hands the vast unpeopled territories of North America. … Shall Britons and Irelanders … be forbidden to share of it, and instead of enjoying there the plenty of happiness that might reward their industry, be compelled to remain here in poverty and misery?[129]

The crown continued its self-preserving, self-aggrandizing, and self-enriching programs with little regard for the welfare of his subjects on the North American continent and in England.

While the circumstances regarding immigration are different now, there are nevertheless serious problems of the same nature. One of the enumerated powers of the federal government is to create a uniform set of laws regarding naturalization and immigration. While there may be examples of such laws being passed, their enforcement has been lacking at best. Sometimes enforcement has been nearly non-existent. For example, it is well known that there are approximately eleven million illegal immigrants in the US, according to the Pew Research Center.[130] Similar to what the king was doing with offloading his criminals onto the American people, California, to site one example, signed a law that banned state authorities from transferring illegal immigrants to the federal authorities if an immigrant had not committed serious crimes[131]—that is, other than the crime of violating US federal law, which, depending upon the method of entry, can be a felony. This is only one of many examples of cities, counties, and even states that have provided sanctuary to criminals in violation of federal law. These actions have undercut the federal government's constitutional responsibility to regulate immigration.

Another example is the more current situation of refugees coming to the United States from war-torn Middle Eastern areas. High-level officials, including FBI Director James Comey, doubt that the vetting process could provide assurance that any of the refugees are not terrorists or do not have a criminal record, which would normally disqualify someone from entering the country. Comey stated that, despite improvements since the Iraq War refugee era and improved screening processes, "If we don't know much about somebody, there won't be anything in our data. I can't sit here and offer anybody an absolute assurance that there's no risk."[132] This is a dangerous situation, particularly when recent attacks against France, Belgium, and Germany and other serious refugee issues have demonstrated the burden at least some refugees bring. Most importantly is that the first responsibility of government is to protect its citizens from danger, not engage in importing danger.

Charge 8: He has obstructed the administration of justice, by refusing his assent to laws for establishing judiciary powers.

In earlier charges, I covered numerous problems between the crown and the colonies concerning the formation and operation of local colonial government. Many of these issues can also be included in charge 8. One such example is the New York Suspending Act, which dissolved New York's government and forbade any lawmaking, resolution-making, or any other necessary passage of laws or their execution. This led to further problems of establishing judiciary powers and administering justice. This charge is also applicable to every other act of the crown or his representatives that dissolved colonial governments and prohibited the passage of laws.

Consider North Carolina. It had serious problems with its court system; it did not have one established by the colonists. Without a system in place, there can be no administration of justice. The king refused to grant North Carolina's need for its own judicial system. After North Carolina became a royal colony in 1729, all functions of government were subject to the crown.

In 1767, a more elaborate system was set forth by the Legislature and was intended to last five years. Due partly to the continuing disagreement between local and royal partisans, however, it was not renewed at the end of the five year period. Thus, there were no higher courts in North

Carolina from the expiration of the courts created in 1767 until after the Revolution. Lower county court officials, such as justices of the peace, were appointed by the Royal Governor, and continued to exist throughout this period of time.[133]

When North Carolina had a judiciary, it favored the crown. The "inferior court's jurisdiction," according to Herman Husband of North Carolina, a member of the legislature, had "narrow limits" that favored neither the rich nor poor but favored the lawyers. Husband recognized the need to make "these men [the lawyers] subject to the laws, or they will enslave the whole community."[134]

Moreover, without higher courts to which the colonists could appeal for a redress of grievances, lower court officials collected excessive fees and provided excessive punishments. Despite the law affixing taxes and fees, government officials, clerks of the court, lawyers, entry takers, and so on demanded double or triple the fixed fee or tax. This was their standard practice. Governor William Tryon did little to redress the grievances of the colonists.[135]

These kinds of problems, excess regulations and taxes, and the sense that the crown would do little to address these grievances led to the small Battle of Alamance. A group of farmers and protesters, who were known as the "Regulators," swore they would pay no more taxes, believing they were over-taxed already. Governor Tryon ordered a special court in Hillsborough, believing that the Regulators would protest, which they did. This led to the Battle of Alamance. Of course, under Governor Tryon's command, he either killed in battle or captured the Regulators. However, as was typical for governors of the crown, Governor Tryon, without holding a trial, hanged one man who he believed was crazy. He then tried twelve others, six of whom he also hanged.[136]

Jefferson brought up charge 8 and directed it against the king of England. The fact remains, however, that this charge and many of the others could have been applied to the government of England as a whole.

Looking at the US government today, I would contend that Congress, as the Declaration says, "has obstructed the administration of justice, by refusing [their] assent to laws for establishing judiciary powers." Under Article III of the US Constitution, Congress has the power to establish lower courts, including determining their geographical jurisdictions. In addition, Congress has the power to setup lower courts, which includes the authority to dissolve lower courts that our representatives believe are using excessive powers. Moreover, though Congress may not dissolve the US Supreme Court, it has rarely used its powers to remove justices, including Supreme Court justices, when those justices use excessive powers—powers not granted to the federal government or to the judicial branch of government. Thus, by Congress failing to do its duty in keeping the judicial branch in check, it has contributed to the obstruction of "the administration of justice." The president appoints and the Senate consents to the appointment of justices for life based on their "good behavior." This would include the justices' behavior toward the Constitution. In these ways, the federal government has failed to provide for a proper judiciary and for the proper administration of justice by limiting the over-zealous and unconstitutional actions of the courts.[137]

Charge 9: He has made judges dependent on his will alone, for the tenure of their offices, and the amount and payment of their salaries.

Under a previous charge, I brought up the Massachusetts Government Act. Through it the crown made the governor and all appointees—including court officials, attorney generals, sheriffs, and other officials—dependent on the crown. The law stated that "The officers of chief justice and judges of the superior court," appointed by the crown-appointed governor, "shall hold their commissions during the pleasure of his Majesty, his heirs, and successors."[138] Holding office "during the pleasure" of the king demonstrates the disrespect the king had for his subjects.

Of course, the New York Suspending Act and Governor William Tryon of North Carolina also prevented the judiciary from doing their job, except by the king's will. In the case of New York, the king suspended its government until the colony agreed to "the pleasure of his Majesty," regardless of what might have been good for the colony. I also covered how the king provided for North Carolina's judiciary for five years, after which the king failed to continue the judiciary. Other colonies suffered similar tyrannical effects at the king's pleasure.

The Townsend Act of 1767 provided for numerous excessive taxes and required colonists to pay the tax at the time of the purchase of goods. These funds were to be used to defer the costs of the courts and for the administration of all other offices.

> His Majesty and his successors shall be, and are hereby, impowered, from time to time, by any warrant or warrants under his or their royal sign manual or sign manuals, countersigned by the high treasurer, or any three or more of the commissioners of the treasury for the time being, to cause such monies (taxes and duties paid by the colonies on the goods listed in the act) to be applied, out of the produce of the duties granted by this act, as his Majesty, or his successors, shall think proper or necessary, *for defraying the charges of the administration of justice, and the support of the civil government, within all or any of the said colonies or plantations.*[139]

The Townsend Act provided funds to pay down the crown's debts, including those incurred fighting the French and Indian War. The Act was especially enacted to pay the judges that the crown's governors who only the crown possessed authority to remove. This provided the incentive to ensure the payment of more taxes, duties, and fines, which allowed more money to fill the king's pockets and those he appointed to serve him.

One of the problems here was that since the crown appointed, commissioned, and paid for the judges, their tenure in office would be determined by how well they pleased the king. Of much lesser importance, if even much of a consideration at all, was how well these judges arrived at the truth of a case and administered genuine justice.

In modern times, the judicial branch of our federal government is dependent on Congress for its salaries. However, unlike the king who could remove or appoint judges at his whim, the executive and legislative branches must work together to appoint or remove judges. Though not a complete remedy, the Founders have provided a reasonably effective resolution for the problem with which they dealt under the crown. Congress, however, has rarely applied the remedy. Since the founding of the Constitution, Congress has impeached and removed only fifteen federal justices, with Justice John Pickering as the first in 1803 and G. Thomas Porteous Jr. the most recent in 2010. And Congress has impeached only one Supreme Court justice in its history. This judge was Samuel Chase who the House impeached in 1804. However, the Senate acquitted him, and in 1811 he resumed his judicial duties.[140] Evidently, Congress has completely reversed itself from King George, going to the opposite extreme with the judiciary not being dependent enough on the will of Congress.

Charge 10: He has erected a multitude of new offices, and sent hither swarms of officers to harass our people, and eat out their substance.

This charge is as applicable today as it was in the colonial era. Its wording is worthy of note and appears to be biblical. As Lucas points out, Jefferson's word choice

> conjures up Old Testament images of "swarms" of flies and locusts covering the face of the earth, "so that the land was darkened," and devouring all they found until "there remained not any green thing in the trees, or in the herbs of the field" (Exodus 10:14–15). It also recalls the denunciation, in Psalms 53:4, of "the workers of iniquity ... who eat up my people as they eat bread," and the prophecy of Deuteronomy 28:51 that an enemy nation "shall eat the fruit of thy cattle, and the fruit of thy land until thou be destroyed: which also shall not leave thee either corn, wine, or oil, or the increase of thy kine, or flocks of thy sheep, until he have destroyed thee."[141]

By using similar verbiage from the Old Testament, Jefferson depicted the king and England itself as a plague on the colonies. Through it Jefferson also showed his knowledge of the Bible and his ability to use it in his defense of the colonies.

Looking into this charge, let's start with its historical verification, beginning with the Quartering Act of 1765. This Act required the citizens of all the colonies "to quarter and billet the officers and soldiers" when there was not enough room in the regular barracks. The meaning of billeting is to provide the soldiers' required nutrition. Specifically, the Act stated that "the officers and soldiers so quartered and billeted as aforesaid (except such as shall be quartered in the barracks, and hired uninhabited houses, or other buildings as aforesaid) *shall be received and furnished with diet, and small beer, cyder, or rum mixed with water, by the owners of the inns, livery stables, alehouses, victualling-houses, and other houses.*"[142] This Act's requirements for compelling colonists to provide numerous provisions to British soldiers gave the occasion for the king to literally "eat out [the colonists'] substance."

In 1774, Parliament passed another Quartering Act, which continued this horrible practice. Similar to the Quartering Act of 1765, the new law sought to clarify any doubt about whether the troops of the king could requisition quarters. The Act stated; "Whereas doubts have been entertained, whether troops can be quartered otherwise in barracks … it shall be lawful … and they are hereby respectively authorised, impowered, and directed, on the requisition … to cause any officers or soldiers in his Majesty's service to be quartered and billetted in such manner as is now directed by law, where no barracks are provided by the colonies."[143] This Act also allowed for the requisition of property for this purpose, whether the property consisted of houses, barns, or other buildings. If the colonies, rather than the king, failed to provide for enough barracks, the army would seize houses and other buildings for their purposes.

New York was one of the colonies that failed to comply with the Act. The king's response was to pass the New York Suspending Act of 1767. This Act completely dissolved the New York legislature and government until the colony complied with the Act's provisions.

Other acts had similar effects. For instance, the Sugar Act of 1764 taxed many items such as sugar, wine, coffee, silk, herbs, and dyes. It also required affidavits to be signed by producers, shippers, and others, sworn before a justice of the peace, "expressing, in words at length and not in figure, the quality of the goods so shipped, with the number and denomination of the packages, and describing the name or names of the plantation or plantations, and the name

of the colony where the same grew or were produced and manufactured."[144]
Compliance with this Act was time consuming. Furthermore, the Stamp Act that
Parliament passed a year or so later charged for these kinds of documentation on
top of the taxes the Sugar Act required. Colonists ended up paying taxes on top
of taxes—essentially paying taxes on goods taxed previously.

The Sugar Act's punishments were also excessive. If violations occurred,
such as the quality or quantity of the goods showing a difference from what was
recorded on the documentation, or if colonists smuggled in goods and avoided
paying taxes on them, the government seized the goods. Moreover, every person
involved in the fraud "forfeit[ed] treble (triple) the value of such goods ... and
all the boats, horses, cattle, and other carriages whatsoever, made use of in the
loading, landing, removing, carriage, or conveyance, of any of the aforesaid goods,
shall also be forfeited and lost, and shall and may be seized and prosecuted, by any
officer of his Majesty's customs."[145] That is an excessively severe punishment—
charging triple the value, seizing the property used to violate the Act, *and* seizing
the goods involved. Such over-the-top punishments are likely one reason the
current US Constitution in the Eighth Amendment provides that "Excessive bail
shall not be required, nor excessive fines imposed."

The customs officials and others with ties to the crown had an enticing
incentive to prosecute for fraud or other actions that would permit the seizure of
goods and other property and increase the already excessive fines on the colonists.
The informant, the customs collector, and the governor (or commander in chief)
of the colony would each receive one third of the net produce of any successful
prosecution.[146] This, of course, would be exceedingly tempting for anyone who
might financially benefit from the enforcement of such laws.

The Stamp Act of 1765 was another harassing law that resulted in eating out
the people's substance. This Act required a tax paid on documents of all varieties
that a government or other private entity might issue. These included government
documents, such as court papers, customs papers, affidavits, warrants, and
licenses. Taxes would also have to be paid on items such as diplomas, bills of
lading, military commissions, newspapers, certificates, apprenticeship articles,
cards, dice, pamphlets, calendars, and a host of other items.[147] Of course,
commissioners needed to appoint numerous officers to make sure that the

crown's subjects followed the law and paid the taxes. As if these aspects of the Stamp Act were not bad enough, it had a still more onerous and atrocious part: if a certificate was found forged, counterfeited, erased, or altered, "ever such person so offending shall be guilty of felony, and *shall suffer death* as in cases of felony without the benefit of clergy."[148] Denying a person his or her life and religious freedom over paying taxes on whatever the king so desired was about as heinous an act as could be contrived.

The Stamp Act of 1765 led to protests throughout the colonies. Among the protests were the anti-Stamp Act resolutions of Virginia penned by Patrick Henry. The debates that followed included Henry's statement, "Caesar had his Brutus; Charles the First, his Cromwell; and George the Third ...." At this point, the Speaker cut off Henry, yelling "treason," to which Henry responded, "And if this be treason, make the most of it."[149]

Then there was the previously discussed Townsend Act of 1767 that exacted taxes on many of the goods sold to the colonists in order to pay for the numerous officers used to collect the taxes, the judiciary officers to enforce the taxes, and other officers. This had the same effect as eating out the colonists' substance, along with the erection of numerous offices and the sending forth of officers to harass the people. In fact, Parliament created this Act specifically for ensuring the acquisition of taxes and enforcement of their numerous laws in violation of the rights of the colonists.

I could cite many other acts enacted by England's king and Parliament that provide evidence for Charge 10 in the Declaration of Independence, but the ones I have mentioned already are enough to show the charge's justification. These examples also lay the foundation for charges against today's federal government. All the offices and the numbers of officers of the federal government create an intolerable tax and law enforcement burden on America's citizens. I will cite just a few examples of this, though countless volumes of books could be filled with examples.

One of the most egregious cases of this charge is the case of John Pozsgai, a Hungarian immigrant of Morrisville, Pennsylvania. Ironically, Pennsylvania named Morrisville after one of the Founders, Robert Morris, who signed *both* the Declaration of Independence and the Constitution. Pozsgai's alleged violation was the pollution of wetlands under the EPA's ambiguous definition of "wetland." The land that he purchased next to his home was a junkyard, a landfill of sorts. He proceeded to begin cleaning up the land by removing thousands of old tires and automobiles. One would think that the EPA would have been ecstatic about a self-motivated cleaner of the environment. However, because he cleaned up property that he owned and proceeded to bring in topsoil to fill in ditches on the property, the EPA deemed that topsoil a pollutant because the drainage ditch it filled was connected to a wetland. The EPA believed that Pozsgai violated their rules despite his efforts in cleaning up his property and therefore the environment.

The federal government arrested Pozsgai, imprisoned him for over a year, placed him on probation for five years, and fined him over $200,000.[150] Not only were the fine and imprisonment excessive, but the punishments violated the Declaration's own stated purpose of government, which is to protect property. Pozsgai was preserving and protecting his property, working to be a good steward of his own property—an act the EPA should have supported. Instead, the EPA imprisoned him, fined him, and bankrupted his family.[151] This seems eerily similar to the Sugar Act and its excessive punishments and violation of private property rights. The EPA alone can be charged with many other human rights violations, too many to list here and many of which are similar to Jefferson's charge against the king. Thus, the federal government, similar to the eighteenth century British government, is guilty of this charge.

Another case that occurred before Pozsgai's is found in *Wickard v. Filburn*. Here the federal government applied the Agricultural Adjustment Act of 1938—a law Congress passed as part of a slew of laws enacted during the Great Depression and used to try to boost the country's poor economy. In this case, Congress designed the Act to control the supply of agricultural goods so that prices would remain higher. The Act allowed farmers to grow 11.1 acres of wheat to sell on the open market. Roscoe Filburn went beyond this stipulation and grew twenty-three acres of wheat, but he had no intention of selling wheat beyond the 11.1 acres. His plan was to use the excess grain to feed his family and animals. However, the federal government saw Filburn's action as a violation of the Agricultural Adjustment Act of 1938, which had been created under the guise of the "*inter*state commerce" clause. Under Article I, Section 8 of the US Constitution, the interstate commerce clause allows Congress to "regulate Commerce with foreign Nations, and among the several States." In other words, Congress may regulate *inter*state commerce but not *intra*state commerce. If the transaction occurs between one individual in one state and another individual in another state, Congress may regulate it. For example, if one person buys an item on EBay or Amazon or some other similar commercial site, and the buyer and seller are in two different states, Congress may regulate the transaction. However, if both the buyer and seller are in the same state, then the transaction occurred within the state and is outside of Congress' jurisdiction. The Constitution grants no power to the federal government to regulate-intrastate commerce, only interstate commerce.

Now Filburn intended on selling only the government allotted 11.1 acres of wheat. With the rest of his wheat, he intended to feed his family and animals in the most economical way possible—by growing his own food on his own land. Moreover, concerning the other 11.9 acres of wheat, for which the courts fined Filburn, the wheat never entered into commerce. Therefore, it was illegal for Congress to regulate the wheat under the Constitution as either interstate or intrastate commerce.[152] No Founder would have found fault with Filburn, and our federal government should not have either. Instead, the US government violated Filburn's right to property, how he desired to use his property, and his liberty to take care of his family by growing as much as he needed for his family and himself. Furthermore, the government limiting his liberty to grow more grain for his own gain through its sale violates the Declaration's stated purpose of government.

In order to get an idea of the possibilities of the federal government's ability to harass the people by erecting a multitude of new offices and sending out swarms of officers to harass its citizens, you simply need look at one small document on USA.gov. It is the index of US government departments and agencies. It lists around 450 to 500 departments and agencies.[153] All of these require a large portion of the nation's production to function, or the "eating out our substance." Also consider the volumes upon volumes of laws passed by Congress, all of which are followed by volumes of rules and regulations created by each agency and department. The number of laws, rules, and regulations is so vast as to be mind-numbing, not to mention impossible for any citizen to know fully, much less follow. Concerning voluminous laws, James Madison stated, "It will be of little avail to the people that the laws are made by men of their own choice if the laws be so voluminous that they cannot be read, or so incoherent that they cannot be understood."[154]

It has become impossible for American citizens to adhere to all the laws of the land. Because of this, it is increasingly likely to have federal officers harassing citizens and the federal government seizing our property and threatening our livelihood. According to the Library of Congress website, the Justice Department "compiled a list of approximately 3,000 criminal offenses" with about "23,000 pages of federal law."[155] With many federal laws, the several federal agencies must create rules that have the force of law for each of the laws they are required to administer. Thus, the number of rules can exponentially multiply the number of laws, with these rules having the force of law.

These numerous agencies and departments, along with their rules and regulations, violate both the Constitution and the ideas of the Founders. Jefferson drew upon Locke's ideas in his formation of the Declaration. Regarding the formation of many government departments and agencies, Locke stated about the legislative branch that "The legislative cannot transfer the power of making laws to any other hands, for it being but a delegated power from the people, they who have it, cannot pass it over to others. … The power of the legislative being derived from the people by a positive grant and institution, can be no other, than what that positive grant conveyed, which being only to make laws, and not to make *legislators*."[156] But the creation of so many laws ends up requiring legislators to enlist more legislators, or as we call them today, bureaucrats, to compile, explain, distribute, and enforce those laws. More legislators create more offices, and officers are sent out as the arms of the legislators. And officers end up harassing we, the people, and take from us what government should protect—our lives, liberties, and properties.

Here is just one more example of how today's federal government comes under the indictment of the Declaration's charge 10. The Internal Revenue

Service estimates that businesses and citizens "spend about 6.1 billion hours a year complying with tax-filing requirements."[157] That is an excessive amount of time trying to comply with the laws and rules for just one federal agency. At the current federal minimum wage of $7.25 per hour, the hours expended amount to a cost of more than $44 billion of the people's substance. However, with a typical accountant making between double and triple the minimum wage, we can see that cost to Americans is closer to $100 billion. Never mind what it will cost in time and money if you fail to pay on time or at all. This is a huge cost in time and money that one federal agency alone has "eaten out" of America's citizens.

Charges 11 and 12: He has kept among us, in times of peace, standing armies without the consent of our legislature. He has affected to render the military independent of and superior to civil power.

At the end of the French and Indian War in 1763 (or the Seven Years' War, as Europe called it), the English king decided not to withdraw his troops. And he required the colonies to provide room and board for his troops, issuing the Quartering Act of 1765 and then another Quartering Act in 1774. The colonists opposed these laws, and New York's opposition led the king to dissolve the colony's government until it yielded provisions for his troops.

In his *A Summary View of the Rights of British America*, Thomas Jefferson had this to say about armies in the colonies that came and stayed without the consent of the governed:

> In order to enforce the arbitrary measures ... his majesty has from time to time sent among us large bodies of armed forces, not made up of the people here, nor raised by the authority of our laws: *Did his majesty possess such a right as this, it might swallow up all our other rights whenever he should think proper.* ... But his majesty has no right to land a single armed man on our shores, and those whom he sends here are liable to our laws made for the suppression and punishment of riots, routs, and unlawful assemblies; or are hostile bodies, invading us in defiance of

law. … Such a measure would have given just alarm to his subjects in Great Britain, whose liberties would not be safe if armed men of another country, and of another spirit, might be brought into the realm at any time without the consent of their legislature. To render these proceedings still more criminal against our laws, instead of subjecting the military to the civil powers, his majesty has expressly made the civil subordinate to the military.[158]

Jefferson understood the problems with standing armies that are not made up of local citizens and are not subject to their civil authority. Such a military presence can eliminate rights very quickly when so moved to act, especially when the armies are not subject to the governing body that should be raising the armies only as needed. As Jefferson noted, the danger is the loss of liberty with the possibility of the loss of property and even the loss of life.

None of the colonies provided for British troops after the end of the French and Indian War. The colonies had provided for their own militias *during* the war and quickly disbanded them at the conflict's conclusion. The remaining armies were the British regulars, which the king refused to withdraw. The armies created by the several colonies were subject to the authorities of those colonies, while the British regulars were subject to the king alone. British soldiers answered to the crown, which meant the king could use them to take liberties and property away from the colonists, including taking their lives.

This charge may have little to do with our modern situation, unless one wants to apply the charge to the various federal agencies that are well armed and enforce arbitrary federal laws. I have in mind such agencies as the FBI, BATFE, and even the IRS. Although these agencies are subject to civil authorities, there is no adequate reason for nearly any federal agency to purchase large amounts of ammunition when there is no civil unrest or threat of civil unrest. Only the military should have large amounts of ammunition at all times.

Consider, for example, one of the most outlandish requests for the acquisitions of ammunition. It came from the Social Security Administration (SSA) in 2012. This agency asked for 174,000 rounds of .357 Sig ammunition for its officers.[159] How likely is it that the disabled and senior population that the SSA services can be that much of a threat?

Or take as an example the National Oceanic and Atmospheric Administration (NOAA). In 2012, NOAA requested 76,000 rounds of 40 S&W ammunition.[160] What would be the need for all that?

One more example is the Department of Homeland Security. DHS is not the military but a federal law enforcement agency. Yet it ordered 1.6 billion rounds of ammunition, according to multiple sources, including the *Denver Post*[161] and *Bloomberg*.[162]

With no evidence of a possible internal insurrection, there is no reason for the federal government to need so much ammunition for non-military purposes. The threat to the lives, liberty, and property of citizens is very similar to the threat of the military of the king during the era when the Founders drafted the Declaration of Independence.

As a final thought, I urge American citizens to look at the situation of the colonists during their time and compare it to what the US does in other countries. Do we have armies based in other countries? Without question, we do. Can our army quickly apply force to the citizens of those countries if our commander-in-chief wishes? Yes, they can. Our federal government seems to be acting like King George. Once our military restores peace in a country, the commander-in-chief should withdraw our troops. We have no legitimate reason to remain, even for the protection of allies. Each nation is a sovereign nation and should provide for its own defense rather than relying on the US to fund their defense. This situation seems to fit with the above charges against King George. In many cases, our government is extending its authority and military where they do not belong.

Chapter 4

The Charges: Abuses
of Legislative Power

He has combined with others to subject us to a jurisdiction foreign to our constitution, and unacknowledged by our laws; giving his Assent to their Acts of pretended Legislation:

    For Quartering large bodies of armed troops among us:

    For protecting them, by a mock Trial, from punishment for any Murders which they should commit on the Inhabitants of these States:

    For cutting off our Trade with all parts of the world:

    For imposing Taxes on us without our Consent:

    For depriving us in many cases, of the benefits of Trial by Jury:

    For transporting us beyond Seas to be tried for pretended offences

    For abolishing the free System of English Laws in a neighbouring Province, establishing therein an Arbitrary government, and enlarging its Boundaries so as to render it at once an example and fit instrument for introducing the same absolute rule into these Colonies:

For taking away our Charters, abolishing our most valuable Laws, and altering fundamentally the Forms of our Governments:

For suspending our own Legislatures, and declaring themselves invested with power to legislate for us in all cases whatsoever.

This set of charges in the Declaration of Independence concerns the abuse of legislative powers. As we move through them, you will discover how King George III prevented the colonies from governing themselves and placed Parliament in charge. You will find that in all of the cases of colonial formation, the charters granted no authority to Parliament, with the arguable exception of Maryland, which I address in this chapter. The king granted authority to *all* the colonies, regardless of the type of colony, to form their own governments. The king granted general charters, including the aforementioned charter of the Puritans to settle in New England. However, these general charters and the various colonial charters, though created at different times, received authority to self-government to legislate for the good of the respective colony.

In this section of the Declaration, Jefferson continues to mount evidence that the king conspired with Parliament to abuse the colonies' rights as his subjects.

Charge 13: He has combined with others to subject us to a jurisdiction foreign to our constitution, and unacknowledged by our laws; giving his Assent to their Acts of pretended Legislation

This charge, leveled at the king, concerns combining with others (Parliament) to violate the rights of his subjects in the American colonies. The charters granted the colonies the authority to govern themselves or to legislate, including imposing taxes and providing for all needful laws. Given this, when the king joined with Parliament to make it the legislative authority over the colonies, he and Parliament breached the contracts made with Britain's American subjects. Thus, the altered jurisdiction over the colonists was foreign to their constitution or charter and thereby undermined the real authority in the colonies—namely, the local charter governments. The king's assent does not abrogate the original authority of local self-governance granted by charter. Therefore the legislation coming from Parliament is pretended or fake, even when the king gives "his Assent" to it.

While the king granted general charters, the colonial charters came at different times. The first attempt at colonization was Virginia. In 1606, King James I granted Virginia's first charter, which provided for a council. This council by the king's grant proclaimed, "we do also ordain, establish, and agree, for Us, our Heirs, and Successors, that each of the said Colonies shall have a Council, which shall govern and order all Matters-and Causes, which shall arise, grow, or happen, to or within the same several Colonies, according to such Laws, Ordinances, and Instructions, as shall be, in that behalf, given and signed with Our Hand or Sign Manual."[163] Clearly, they had full authority to make and pass laws and even make coin for the colonies.

The king issued a second charter in 1609. This charter granted "privileges and liberties to each colony, for their quiet settling and good government therein." Furthermore, this charter granted that those individuals mentioned in the charter

> and their successors shall be from henceforth *forever* enabled ... to make, ordain and establish laws, directions, instructions, forms and ceremonies of Government and Magistracy, fit and necessary for and concerning the Government of the said Colony and Plantation; And the same (the colonists and their successors), at all Times hereafter, to *abrogate, revoke, or change*, not only within the Precincts of the said Colony, but also upon the Seas, in going and coming to and from the said Colony, as they in their good Discretion, shall think to be fittest for the Good of the Adventurers and inhabitants there.[164]

The third and final charter of Virginia in 1611 did nothing to "abrogate or revoke" the previous charter and the authority vested in the colony to provide for their own government.

New England, more particularly Massachusetts, was the next colony to have a charter, which, once again, established self-government for the colony and its inhabitants. In similar language to the charter of Virginia, the king granted to the colonists and to their heirs and successors

> full power and authority to the said council and their successors ... as for the government of the said colony and plantation, and also to make, ordain, and establish all manner of orders, laws, directions, instructions, forms, and ceremonies of government and magistracy fit and necessary for and concerning the government of the said colony and plantation ... and the same at all times hereafter to abrogate, revoke, or change, not only within the precincts of the said colony, but also upon the seas in going and coming to and from the said colony, *as they in their good discretions shall think to be fittest for the good of the adventurers and inhabitants there.*[165]

Once again, the crown granted self-government to a specific colony and only its inhabitants could abrogate or revoke the authority as they "think fit." Like Virginia, they never thought it fit to abrogate their self-governing authority.

In Connecticut, the New Haven Colony was first created in 1643 and provided a government with the power to make and repeal laws, vote for all government officers, settle levy rates, and provide judges to pass judgment in "all weighty and capital cases, whether civil or criminal."[166]

A few years later when Connecticut became a charter colony, the king granted a charter that formed a government with a general assembly, governor, deputy-governor, and others. In addition, the settlers and the people elected into their government were to have "perpetual succession"[167]—that is, their right to self-government and choice of government was theirs forever.

New Hampshire started out under the jurisdiction of Massachusetts. By 1680, the king granted the creation of a full separate royal colony with John Cutt becoming the first president of the colony. The king presented Cutt and the Council or legislators with "full power and authority, to hold plea in all causes from time to time ... as in matters relating to the conservation of the peace, and punishment of offenders, as in civil suits and actions between party and party; or between us and any of our subjects there."[168] The charter provides for other crimes or judgments over which the colony has jurisdiction, including taxing. No mention of Parliament is included.

Delaware's charter of 1701 provided for an assembly with the power to prepare bills in order to pass laws and regulate elections. The charter provided for various counties to choose their officers to represent them in the assembly, choose sheriffs, coroners, and others. The only way to change the colony's authority was made very specific in the charter. "No Act, Law or Ordinance whatsoever, shall at any Time hereafter be made or done, to alter, change or diminish the Form or Effect of this Charter, or of any Part or Clause therein, contrary to the true Intent and Meaning thereof, without the Consent of the Governor for the Time being, and Six Parts of Seven of the Assembly met."[169] Notice it requires six-sevenths of the Assembly members to agree to alter the charter in any way. This is a steep requirement to meet. The colonizers of Delaware obviously intended the charter to continue for quite some time, if not perpetually.

Georgia's charter of 1732, the final colony to receive such a charter, also named their trustees and stated that "They and their successors, shall and may have perpetual succession ... and that it shall and may be lawful for them and their successors, to change, break, alter and make new the said seal, from time to time, and at their pleasure, and as they shall think best ... give and grant ... full power and authority to constitute, ordain and make, such and so many by-laws, constitutions, orders and ordinances, as to them, or the greater part of them, at their general meeting for that purpose."[170] Nowhere will one find any mention or allusion to Parliament in Georgia's charter nor was any authority granted to anybody except the charter members and their successors. Georgia was the last colony to receive a charter, even though it originally was part of the Carolina charter, which included North and South Carolina and Georgia, which charter granted and specifically named the officers of the government and how government was to be set up.[171] This is similar to New Hampshire, which started out as part of Massachusetts.

Maryland, the only colony that started as a colony for Roman Catholics, had the only charter that was slightly different. The charter granted the colony, or the Baron of Baltimore, Caecilius Calvert and his heirs, "Free, *full and absolute Power to Ordain, Make, and Enact Laws, of what Kind soever, according to their sound Discretions* whether relating to the Public State of the said Province, or the private Utility of Individuals, of and with the Advice, Assent, and Approbation of the Free-Men of the same Province, or the greater Part of them, or of their Delegates or Deputies."[172] The only stipulation was that the laws "be not repugnant or contrary but agreeable to the Laws, Statutes, Customs and Rights of this Our Kingdom of England."[173] This stipulation is what sets apart Maryland's charter from that of the other American colonies. However, even Maryland's charter makes no mention of any authority given to Parliament, only that the laws of Maryland should not contradict the laws of England. Still, Maryland's colonists knew their rights as Englishmen. Their representation was in the government of Maryland and nowhere else, and their local government had the right to legislate levies, criminal laws, and so on for the colony. This right did not exist in Parliament. Furthermore, the English Bill of Rights and Magna Carta prohibited Parliament from violating the rights of Englishmen. So the Maryland colonists should have remained free of Parliament's control.

In short, Rhode Island, New York, New Jersey, and every other American colony provided for its own government, taxing themselves, providing for the necessary laws as they saw fit, providing a voice to the people, and guaranteeing the people's liberties, all without the mother country's interference and infringement upon those liberties. The colonies formed their own courts, could raise their own armies, and do whatever else was needed to order themselves into a civil society and protect their interests. Parliament was unnecessary.

Parliament, however, later sought with the king's consent to take over jurisdiction of the colonies. Parliament passed numerous laws to which the king assented, including the Townsend Act, the Sugar Act, and the Stamp Act—all of which were "foreign to our constitution" and "unacknowledged by our laws." Thus, these became pretended acts—acts passed by England's Parliament without the proper authority or jurisdiction.

Moreover, Parliament and the crown crossed any line of possible reconciliation with the colonies with the passage of the Declaratory Act of 1766 wherein Parliament claimed full authority "to bind the colonies and people of America … in all cases whatsoever." Through this Act, Parliament declared null and void all laws, statutes, votes, and resolutions that had been passed by the colonies. Here is the full legislation:

> An act for the better securing the dependency of his majesty's dominions in America upon the crown and parliament of Great Britain.
>
> Whereas several of the houses of representatives in *his Majesty's colonies and plantations in America, have of late against law, claimed to themselves, or to the general assemblies of the same, the sole and exclusive right of imposing duties and taxes upon his majesty's subjects in the said colonies and plantations; and have in pursuance of such claim, passed certain votes, resolutions, and orders derogatory to the legislative authority of parliament*, and inconsistent with the dependency Of the said colonies and plantations upon the crown of Great Britain: may it therefore please your most excellent Majesty, that it may be declared; and be it declared by the King's most excellent majesty, by and with the advice and consent of the lords spiritual and temporal, and commons, in this present parliament assembled, and by the authority of the same, That *the said colonies and plantations in America have been, are, and of right ought to be, subordinate unto, and dependent upon the imperial crown and parliament of Great Britain*; and that the King's majesty, by and with the advice and consent of the lords spiritual and temporal, and commons of Great Britain, in parliament assembled, had hath, and *of right ought to have, full power and authority to make laws and statutes of sufficient force and validity to bind the colonies and people of America, subjects of the crown of Great Britain, in all cases whatsoever*,
>
> II. And be it further declared and enacted by the authority aforesaid, That *all resolutions, votes, orders, and proceedings, in any of the said colonies or plantations, whereby the power and authority of the parliament of Great Britain, to make laws and statutes as aforesaid, is denied, or drawn into question, arc, and are hereby declared to be, utterly null and void to all in purposes whatsoever.*[174]

Parliament took authority to itself. It usurped the authority that belonged to the colonies, and the king consented to this violation of rights. Parliament nullified everything that the colonies had done. In so doing, it stripped the colonies of any representation or authority whatsoever.

Parliament's declaration that the colonies claimed authority that was not theirs is false. From the beginning, the king and the individual charters of the colonies granted the colonies authority despite the fact that, in reality, all government authority comes from the people. In this case, the colonists had chosen their representatives and passed laws that they thought fit for themselves. In Parliament, of course, the colonists were completely void of representation. Moreover, to nullify everything was quite insulting and detrimental to the colonists as it would have been to the subjects of the crown in England itself if Parliament ever committed such an action against them.

Moreover, the king, too, conspired with Parliament to declare that Parliament had full authority and that the colonies' charters had no authority. Once the Revolution began, King George III, in a speech before Parliament, declared, "They have raised troops, and are collecting a naval force; they have seized the public revenue, and assumed to themselves legislative, executive and judicial powers, which they already exercise in the most arbitrary manner, over the persons and property of their fellow-subjects."[175] The king's words assume that he had already discounted or nullified all colonial charters, which he could not do according to the charters' language. In his statement, the king recognized that the colonists' possessed certain powers. The ironic part of his speech is that he claimed that the powers are exercised "in the most arbitrary manner," an act which he apparently reserved to himself alone. For he, in concert with Parliament, had arbitrarily abrogated all the colonial charters and all the actions the colonists had taken under the authority of those charters. Parliament and the king had violated the crown's own contracts.

Moving to our day, I can cite numerous examples of the federal government "subject[ing] us to a jurisdiction foreign to our constitution, and unacknowledged by our laws." However, I will mention just a couple of examples, which are enough to prove that this charge can be leveled against the current government.

Whether or not one agrees with homosexuality is unimportant in proving that the federal government is using foreign jurisdictions or foreign acts that subject the citizens of the United States to authorities foreign to our Constitution and unacknowledged by our laws. Such is the case of *Lawrence v. Texas*. Here, Justice Kennedy wrote for the opinion of the Supreme Court and cited foreign cases for support. Under the European Court of Human Rights, the Court decided that homosexual conduct was normal and a human right. The Supreme Court cited the case of *Dudgeon v. United Kingdom*, adding to their argument for "legalizing" sodomy.[176] In this case, the Supreme Court cited a foreign case, thus acknowledging a foreign jurisdiction over US law. By doing so, it broke its oath to protect and defend the Constitution. The Court, in effect, submitted its authority to that of another, making the Constitution no longer "the supreme law of the land." This placed us back under England's authority, against which we fought for our independence *twice*—once in 1776 and next in 1812!

In *Roper v. Simmons*—a case about the constitutionality of the death penalty for minors—the Supreme Court cites to support its decision the supposed civility of Europe and the UN Convention on the Rights of the Child, which the Court admits the United States failed to ratify.[177] The Constitution forbids the Supreme Court from using unratified treaties as a valid part of the Constitution or its laws. The whole Section IV of the Court's decision is dedicated to international standards. The first paragraph states in part:

> Our determination that the death penalty is disproportionate punishment for offenders under 18 finds confirmation in the stark reality that the United States is the only country in the world that continues to give official sanction to the juvenile death penalty. This reality does not become controlling, for the task of interpreting the Eighth Amendment remains our responsibility. Yet at least from the time of the Court's decision in *Trop*, the Court has referred to the laws of other countries and to international authorities as instructive for its interpretation of the Eighth Amendment's prohibition of "cruel and unusual punishments."

Despite the Court's claim that international decisions, laws, and the like are not "controlling" for its interpretation of the US Constitution's Eighth Amendment, it still sites them to declare juvenile executions unconstitutional. Citing the United Nations, the African Charter on the Rights and Welfare of the Child, surveys of foreign countries, reports of committees of Parliament of the United Kingdom, laws of Parliament, and so on, the Supreme Court made their decision. Our American Court is doing the same thing as King George; it is combining "with others to subject us to a jurisdiction foreign to our constitution and unacknowledged by our laws; giving its Assent to their Acts of pretended Legislation."

Charge 14: For Quartering large bodies of armed troops among us

Charges 11 and 12 discussed in the preceding chapter first mentioned this type of charge to expose the abuse of executive power: the king had sent British troops to the colonies to help in the French and Indian War but then refused to bring them home following the end of the war. Charge 14, on the other hand, cites this charge to highlight the abuse of legislative power.

I have already explained the background to the charge of quartering troops in the colonies. I cited two parliamentary acts in particular. Both are "Quartering Acts," one passed in 1765 and the other in 1774. The 1774 Act, in effect, continued the 1765 Act, which quartered troops in citizens' dwellings, barns, or other buildings and required the colonists to supply troops with the financial support of food, bedding, and other items. Moreover, in the case of New York, the king suspended the government of the colony until the colony met the demand for supporting the king's troops. Parliament passed the two quartering acts and the New York Suspending Act with the king's approval. Of course, this was an abuse of the authority of Parliament—a usurpation of authority that it did not possess. Furthermore, regardless of whether Parliament possessed authority to act, requiring the colonists to provide room and board for the king's troops was a grievous act itself.

One deadly result of the king demanding that the colonies pay for quartering his troops was a famous conflict between his troops and his subjects in Boston, which Sam Adams quickly dubbed the Boston Massacre. This occurred in 1770, and it caused the death of five and wounded six others. The Boston Massacre could have been avoided if the king would have ordered his troops home once the war ended. Rather than learn from this, the king combined with Parliament to force the colonists to quarter troops—an action that abused legislative authority. The king further doubled-down against Boston with the Boston Port Act of 1774. Here he used troops to end commerce in Boston until the colonists paid for the tea that the Boston Tea Party destroyed—tea the Bostonians did not even want. He seemed to care little that commerce is necessary for sustaining life.

Today, even though we are not required to quarter American troops in our dwellings and troops are not used against us (partly because of *posse comitatus* laws and the Third Amendment to the Constitution), we citizens should still be vigilant to ensure that this does not happen.

Charge 15: For protecting them, by a mock Trial, from punishment for any Murders which they should commit on the Inhabitants of these States

In this case, "them" means the king's troops. In the case of Massachusetts, John Adams—ardent independence advocate, member of the committee to draft the Declaration of Independence and signer of it, and future ambassador and president—provided the legal defense of the king's troops involved in the Boston Massacre and successfully brought acquittal to six of the eight soldiers on trial. Two of the soldiers were convicted of manslaughter. They had their left thumbs branded as punishment—a mild punishment considering Massachusetts' Puritan principles. In one other trial of Captain Preston, Adams was successful in acquiring a not guilty verdict.[178]

Despite the fact that Massachusetts proved that the troops could get a fair trial and this in the colony where the desire for independence was fiercest, the king and Parliament combined their efforts to protect their troops at all costs. Thus, in the Administration of Justice Act of 1774, Parliament and the king provided the abuse of power of protecting his troops, providing for the "mock" trials of so-called murderers of the king's subjects in America.

The governor of Massachusetts, a crown appointee of course, had full discretion to decide whether a trial in the colony would be fair. If he determined it would not be, the king granted the governor the choice to move a trial to another province or even to England. When the fastest means of travel was by horse or a ship with sails, this would be a major inconvenience, if not a complete impossibility, for witnesses against the accused to provide the court testimony needed to possibly achieve a conviction. This made it much easier to protect British officers and troops. After all, how can a conviction be reached if the needed witnesses are lacking? Any trial held would then be a mock trial, particularly if the king or governor moved the trial to England. This Act also eased the way for accused colonists to be convicted. If their trials were moved to a place far away from where their crime was allegedly committed, few, if any, witnesses who could vindicate them would be able to travel the distance and afford all the costs. A conviction in such instances would be much easier to obtain.

In light of such abuses of justice, Thomas Jefferson explained one of the clauses in the Administration of Justice Act this way:

> This is, in other words, taxing them to the amount of their recognizance, and that amount may be whatever a governor pleases; for who does his majesty think can be prevailed on to cross the Atlantic for the sole purpose of bearing evidence to a fact? His expences are to be borne, indeed, as they shall be estimated by a governor; but who are to feed the wife and children whom he leaves behind, and who have had no other subsistence but his daily labour? Those epidemical disorders, too, so terrible in a foreign climate, is the cure of them to be estimated among the articles of expence, and their danger to be warded off by the almighty power of parliament? And the wretched criminal, if he happen to have offended on the American side, stripped of his privilege of trial by peers of his vicinage, removed from the place where alone full evidence could be obtained, without money, without counsel, without friends, without exculpatory proof, is tried before judges predetermined to condemn. The cowards who would suffer a countryman to be torn from the bowels

of their society, in order to be thus offered a sacrifice to parliamentary tyranny, would merit that everlasting infamy now fixed on the authors of the act![179]

No matter what the actual cost to the witness, the Act required witnesses to pay their own way. It did not matter if they were witnesses for the defense or for the prosecution. Moreover, the crown-appointed governor possessed full authority to determine what that expense would be.

As if all this were not grievous enough, if the governor or judge found an error in the indictment, the judge possessed authority to quash the trial and return the witnesses, evidence, and anything else pertaining to the trial to the colony in which the alleged criminal act originated. After that, the prosecutors could bring another indictment, but how likely would that be, especially if the trial went to England and especially if it was against the king's troops?

The king and Parliament provided the means to protect the troops and other officers of the British government from acts perpetrated on the colonists.[180]

Another example that supports charge 15 comes from The Massachusetts Government Act, which I covered earlier. This Act stated that "The officers of chief justice and judges of the superior court," appointed by the crown-appointed governor, "shall hold their commissions during the pleasure of his Majesty, his heirs and successors."[181] This worked to protect the king's troops since judges served at his pleasure. Without the desired verdict against the king's troops, the king could remove the judge. So judges naturally wished to maintain their station by pleasing the king, regardless of whether their action and decision in court were just.

Moreover, the previously discussed New York Suspending Act made it impossible for trials to be held in that colony. The courts in England or in one of the other colonies had to provide New York with a court, a very inconvenient situation.

While there may not be any blatant examples of this occurring today, there are certainly problems with our government protecting government employees. Consider *Cleveland Board of Education v. Loudermill.* In this case, the board had hired James Loudermill as a security guard. Later, however, the board discovered that Loudermill had provided false information on his application about his criminal record. He had been convicted of grand larceny. Of course, once the Cleveland Board of Education learned of the conviction and deception, it took the proper, common sense action and terminated Loudermill's employment.

When the Supreme Court heard the case, the justices determined that because Loudermill was "classified civil servant," he had obtained a property right to that employment. In addition, the Court found that the board failed to provide a due process hearing for him in order that he might answer the charges. In other words, the Court decided that the school board had violated Loudermill's "future property" rights of employment by not providing him a hearing before termination. This decision, in effect, not only protected Loudermill as a civil servant but all future government employees from termination.[182]

This decision is absurd. First of all, Loudermill clearly lied on his application of employment, which was the first offense. And his deception was discovered when the education system did its job: it followed through with its requirement to perform a criminal background check on an employee. Schools do this for the safety of the children in their care. The Supreme Court's decision trumped the rights of the employer in favor of creating rights for government employees. And the enforcement of these new rights actually undermine the purpose for which government is created—the protection of life, liberty, and property. In Cleveland's case, it put children at risk from a convicted criminal.

What about this new right to "future property" that the Court allegedly discovered? Can this come under the unalienable right to property? Not at all. I own a house and a car. These are my property; I actually possess them. But what about a future house and future car? Are they my property even though I do not possess them? Can I claim them as my own into the future even though I do not own them and may never own them? To affirm this makes no sense.

What courts ought to protect is the current property of taxpayers. Instead, courts protect public employees from immediate termination for poor performance, failure to show up for work, and any number of other absurdities. Instead of permitting their firing, the courts require that they must receive their hearing in order to ensure that government employers avoid taking their "property" from them without due process; never mind the fact that they have not received or earned the property yet. This is a good example of the government protecting bad employees who have no right to protection for the various offenses they commit.

Charge 16: For cutting off our Trade with all parts of the world

The Navigation Act discussed in the previous chapter played an important role in limiting the amount of trade conducted by the colonies. By restricting the way that colonies shipped goods, it cut off trade with other parts of the world. The Act allowed colonies to transport their goods only "in such ships or vessels as do truly and without fraud belong only to the people of England."[183] This restriction severely limited the colonists' ability to trade with other countries. For example, if England had no trade relationship with a specific country, neither then would the colonists. This Act of Parliament was an abuse of legislative power. It was also a "pretended act" like those mentioned in Charge 13.

The Boston Port Act of 1774 is another legislative Act that cut off the colonists' trade. It prohibited trade until the Bostonians paid the cost of the tea that the Boston Tea Party destroyed.[184] This Act accomplished two things. It cut off trade, and it undercut any ability to sustain Boston. Moreover, this legislative action demonstrates what a "mother" country should not do and thereby violated the moral law of nature. As defined by Jefferson, the king and Parliament violated the purpose of government, which is to protect the life, liberty, and property of those persons under its jurisdiction. This Act endangered the colonists' lives and liberty—abuses they started to overcome the following year in 1775 by their rebellion in arms.

One of England's most well known members of Parliament, Edmund Burke, wanted only Samuel Adams and John Hancock punished for the actions of the Boston Tea Party. However, Parliament decided to punish the entire town of Boston. Burke responded that the Act was "the most dangerous unjust" bill "that ever was."[185] He was right. Legislating punishment against all of Boston without trial, without proof against every individual, made the legislation dangerous and unjust. And it helped initiate the only solution the colonists saw left to them—

revolution against England, which began one year to the day after Burke's warning speech.

The Constitution prohibits Congress from passing such a bill, known as a bill of attainder. This kind of bill declares an individual or a group guilty of a crime and typically targets their rights to life, liberty, and/or property. Still, our federal government is guilty of this abuse of power. While I can easily cite many instances of the government prohibiting trade or banning certain products, I will provide one example of an exportation prohibition and another example of an importation prohibition. These are enough to establish my point.

During the energy and oil crisis of the 1970s, Congress passed laws that prohibited the *exportation* of crude oil to other countries. While that may seem like a good idea for preserving resources for internal use, it perfectly aligns with this charge against the crown by cutting off trade. The laws passed by Congress include the 1975 Energy Policy Conservation Act and the 1979 Export Administration Act. Both of these, though not a total prohibition, severely limit the exportation abilities of numerous American companies. However, despite the energy oil crisis ending more than four decades ago, the laws are still in place.[186]

Regardless of the "good intentions" of Congress, with the crisis over, Congress should have repealed these laws. However, the issue I am raising concerns neither the crisis nor the motives of Congress. My point is that these laws prohibit the desired disposition of property of some American citizens. Prohibition against exportation limits the rights of US citizens to use their property the way they please. Additionally, it is a good example of a legislative body "cutting off our trade with all parts of the world."

The *importation* prohibition example concerns prohibitions placed on certain firearms. The ATF, in trying to be compliant with the law, has created several guidelines that identify what is acceptable to import, which, by implication, indicates what may not be imported. Firearms may be imported

1) for the purpose of scientific testing or research or for competition training under the provisions of Title 10, Chapter 401; (2) as unserviceable firearms, other than a machine gun as defined in 26 U.S.C. § 5844, (not readily restorable to firing condition) if imported as a curio or museum

piece; (3) if the firearms or ammunition are of a type generally recognized as particularly suitable for or readily adaptable to "sporting purposes"; or (4) the firearms or ammunition were previously taken out of the United States by the person who is bringing in the firearms or ammunition. Surplus military firearms and other non-sporting firearms qualifying as "curios or relics" may be imported. 18 U.S.C. § 925 (e). Title 18 U.S.C. § 925(a)(1) provides that the prohibition on the importation of firearms, firearm frames or receivers, firearm barrels and ammunition does not apply to the importation of firearms or ammunition sold or shipped to, or issued for the use of the United States or any department or agency thereof, or any State or any department, agency, or political division thereof.

In order to import under these conditions, a citizen must have a Federal Firearms License (FFL) or other license or permit that the government demands. An unlicensed citizen generally must go through an FFL dealer in order to purchase a firearm.[187] If a firearm fails to fall under the ATF's pre-determined rules, the ATF will not permit the importation of the firearm, thus cutting off American trade with other parts of the world.

Of course, Congress outright bans certain items from importation. And just as Parliament forced the colonists to use only certain ships, today's citizens can only purchase their imported item through the government-approved trader, in this case a licensed firearms dealer. This too is a good example of cutting off trade with all parts of the world.

Charge 17: For imposing Taxes on us without our Consent

Here is the first and only instance of "taxation without representation." This one charge, though very important, is by far not the only reason the colonists declared their independence. Still, the fact that it is singled out this way indicates its significance.

In the previous chapter, I discussed a couple of the laws of Parliament that fit this charge. The Sugar Act of 1764 and the Stamp Act of 1765 were two examples of taxing the colonists without their consent. Adams, Locke, and others voiced their opinions about the forfeiture of property without the consent of the owners. That consent may come through their voice via their representatives. That's how republics work. But in the case of the colonists, those who represented them locally for so long were shut down by Parliament. The colonies had no voice because they had no representatives in that legislative body. Representatives who originally had power to tax the colonists were those individuals for which the colonists voted in each of the legislative bodies of the colonies. But these same colonists did not have any representatives in Parliament for whom they voted nor did they have anyone appointed by the individual colonies or as a collective to voice their opinions in Parliament. So anyone in Parliament who cast a yea or nay vote on issues that affected the colonies did so without the authorization of the colonists themselves. The colonists were simply cut off from Parliament. There they had no voice. But that did not stop Parliament from passing laws of taxation on the colonies.

The philosopher John Locke addressed the issue of taxing without the consent of the governed. In describing the legislative power or the supreme governing power, he wrote: "The supreme power cannot take from any man any part of his property without his own consent. For the preservation of property, being the end of government, and that for which men enter into society, it necessarily supposes and requires, that the people should have property ... that no body hath a right to take their substance, or any part of it from them, without their own consent."[188]

Naturally, with no representatives in Parliament, the colonies were powerless to voice their opinion and provide or withhold their consent. *Within* the colonies, through their individual assemblies, the representatives heard the voices and provided or withheld consent. But that right was not honored or supported in Parliament.

Samuel Adams wrote about similar ideas in *The Rights of the Colonists,* even quoting Locke on occasion. Adams argued that his colony of Massachusetts received a charter granting authority to form a government for the purpose of passing laws, which included the authority of taxation. He then argued that the colonists could not rightly possess liberty without property:

Now what liberty can there be where property is taken away without consent? Can it be said with any color of truth and justice, that this continent of three thousand miles in length, and of a breadth as yet unexplored, in which, however, it is supposed there are five millions of people, has the least voice, vote, or influence in the British Parliament? Have they all together any more weight or power to return a single member to that House of Commons who have not inadvertently, but deliberately, assumed a power to dispose of their lives, liberties, and properties, than to choose an Emperor of China? Had the Colonists a right to return members to the British Parliament, it would only be hurtful; as, from their local situation and circumstances, it is impossible they should ever be truly and properly represented there. The inhabitants of this country, in all probability, in a few years, will be more numerous than those of Great Britain and Ireland together; yet it is absurdly expected by the promoters of the present measures that these, with their posterity to all generations, should be easy, while their property shall be disposed of by a House of Commons at three thousand miles' distance from them, and who cannot be supposed to have the least care or concern for their real interest; who have not only no natural care for their interest, but must be in effect bribed against it, as every burden they lay on the Colonists is so much saved or gained to themselves.[189]

With the king's consent, Parliament usurped the authority of the colonies and imposed unfair taxes on them. Parliament's taxation was unfair because it imposed these taxes without the consent of the governed.

In our governing system today, we have representation at all levels: federal, state, and local. We may not always like what our representatives do on our behalf, but we can vote them out of office and take other actions short of armed revolt. However, it's good to recall that the Seventeenth Amendment to the Constitution changed the representation in Congress to the detriment of the states and the people. And this has led to excessive taxes and spending that threaten the well-being of our nation.

Charge 18: For depriving us in many cases, of the benefits of Trial by Jury

Once you understand the importance of a trial by jury, you can see the gravity of this charge. In a republican form of government, or for that matter, in any form of government authorized by the people, jury trials are vitally important. The people have various methods of doing their own checks and balances on government. Voting, petitioning government for a redress of grievances, and other actions help maintain a balance and provide checks on a government that is constantly testing the limits that have been set and seeking to expand its authority beyond those limits. Trial by a jury of one's peers is a critical way that the people have to check the powers of government.

Thomas Jefferson plainly explained the purpose, importance, and benefit of a trial by a jury of one's peers. He explained that one of the purposes of the jury is to check the judge of the court. Knowing that judges can be bribed, misled by a spirit of their political party, improperly influenced by relationships or favors, and the like, juries can prevent that bias from deciding the fate of an individual. In fact, Jefferson stated that it is better to leave a decision to a game of cross and pile, the modern version of which is "heads or tails," than to a biased judge. However, better still is to acquire the opinion of a jury. As Jefferson explained, "It is in the power, therefore, of the juries, if they think permanent judges are under any bias whatever in any cause, to take on themselves to judge the law as well as the fact. They never exercise this power but when they suspect partiality in judges; and by this power they have been the firmest bulwarks of … liberty."[190] This is known as jury nullification.

Succinctly stated, juries can and should decide whether the law itself is in violation of the unalienable and natural rights of individuals. Juries can judge the law and then judge the facts of the case. If the jury believes the law is just, then they judge the facts and decide whether their fellow citizen is indeed guilty of violating the just law. These peers can also decide the government's justification in the use of force in taking the life, liberty, or property of an individual that the jury found guilty of violating the law. We who serve on juries need to understand and appreciate this vital role juries play. Without it, a government can easily usurp authority from its citizens, trample their rights to life, liberty, and property, and terrorize those they are to serve.

In the case of the colonists, the crown-appointed judges stayed on the bench as long as the king saw fit. To retain their position, these judges needed to follow the wishes of the king, regardless of justice or the facts of a case. This is the bias that Jefferson described when he made the claim that juries were important to justice.

Here's just one case in point. The Sugar Act provided for a trial by officers of the government who had a vested interest in the seizure of property and the administration of fines and penalties. Once an individual committed a crime in violation of the Act, the law prescribed adjudication. The Act prescribed that "all the forfeitures and penalties inflicted by this or any other act or acts of parliament relating to the trade and revenues of the said British colonies or plantations where such offence shall be appointed over all America (*which court of admiralty or vice admiralty are hereby respectively authorized and required to proceed, hear, and determine the same*) at the election of the informer or prosecutor."[191] In other words, the Act barred a trial by a jury of one's peers. The crown and Parliament mandated a military court rather than a civilian court. This was a clear form of abuse on top of the abuses of the Sugar Act. The colonists had little chance of seeing justice of any kind in this type of court, or, for that matter, in any court of England. Be it in England or the colonies, the king and Parliament ensured that cases would turn in their favor by requiring that the judges who sat on the bench made decisions "at the pleasure of his Majesty."[192]

Thankfully, this problem of not having a trial by jury does not exist in the United States today, with rare exception. However, one problem of jury trials today is that few juries understand the vital importance of "jury nullification." It is typically not taught in any schools or colleges. In fact, it is extremely unlikely that a judge would ever provide instructions to a jury that they have this authority, as this would weaken his own authority.

Trial by a jury of one's peers may be one of the most important checks on government that citizens possess. It would behoove all citizens to understand the real purpose of having a jury of one's peers deciding one's fate. All citizens should also understand their powers of jury nullification through which they provide a check against the intrusions of government. Having the knowledge that we can nullify a law that a jury believes to be unjust or that violates the purpose for which citizens created government is vitally important for maintaining our liberties.

Charge 19: For transporting us beyond Seas to be tried for pretended offences

We have discussed the numerous ways and poor methods of trials that the king and Parliament authorized. These included the Sugar Act, which provided for a court of admiralty or vice-admiralty rather than a trial by jury. Admiralty courts and many of the other courts were set in England rather than in the colony where the alleged crime occurred.[193]

The Administration of Justice Act allowed the crown-appointed governor to decide where to hold a trial. While the governor could decide to move a trial to a different colony, he could as easily decide to send the case to England. Of course, this would be quite prohibitive for the colonists, their witnesses, and the transportation of any evidence, particularly when the Act required the colonists to pay their own way.[194] And although the king originally provided each colony with the authority to pass laws and establish courts for trials, Parliament, with the king's consent, permanently suspended these provisions without the consent of the governed, thereby violating the colonists' rights. This, of course, led to trials for pretended offences. That is, the laws passed by Parliament were all pretended acts because Parliament received no authority from the governed to pass them. Moreover, the king conspired with Parliament to make laws, despite the colonies' previous and settled charters and compacts. Therefore, the colonists considered any violations perpetrated by pretended acts to be pretended offences.

The First Continental Congress of 1774 passed a resolution that included language regarding this problem of transporting colonists beyond seas for pretended offences:

And it has lately been resolved in Parliament, that by force of a statute, made in the thirty-fifth year of the reign of King Henry the Eighth, colonists may be transported to England, and tried there upon accusations for treasons, and misprisions, or concealments of treasons committed in the colonies; and by a late statute, such trials have been directed in cases therein mentioned.

Resolved, N.C.D. 5. That the respective colonies are entitled to the common law of England, and more especially to the great and inestimable privilege of being tried by their peers of the vicinage, according to the course of that law.[195]

By a unanimous vote, this Congress made it clear where its members stood on the issue of a change of venue and trials without a jury of peers. This resolution included other items that the Declaration addressed, including the quartering of troops and taxing without consent. By such actions, the colonists expressed their justification for concluding that the king had little regard for the real administration of justice in the colonies. They saw the king conspiring with Parliament to pass laws for England's benefit rather than the benefit of the king's subjects in America.

Returning to our day, I certainly believe that the federal government is guilty of pretended offences against its citizens. As I have shown in the case of John Pozsgai, the EPA pressed charges against him for cleaning up his property in a way not approved by the EPA. Yet no legislative body can delegate its authority, including to the EPA. Thus, violating the EPA's pretended regulations is merely a pretended offence.[196]

Charge 20: For abolishing the free System of English Laws in a neighbouring Province, establishing therein an Arbitrary government, and enlarging its Boundaries so as to render it at once an example and fit instrument for introducing the same absolute rule into these Colonies

This charge has to do with the Quebec Act passed in 1774. Quebec was a neighboring province to the thirteen American colonies. The Quebec Act voided the province's laws and abolished its government, similar to what Parliament and the crown did to Massachusetts, New York, and other colonies. Then the Act proceeded to setup government the way Parliament and the crown wanted it—at the king's pleasure. The Act completely changed the system of English laws to suit a king acting as a tyrant. Of course, the Continental Congress referenced this dangerous and autocratic act.[197]

However, for the colonists, an arbitrary government of absolute rule and the abolishment of free government in Quebec were not their only concern. As stated in charges 3 and 7, the king prohibited the expansion of the colonies with the Royal Proclamation of 1763.[198] The Quebec Act then enlarged the boundaries of the Quebec province through parts of the western side of the Appalachian Mountains into which the king forbade the colonists to expand.[199] The colonists viewed this as rubbing salt into an already sore and open wound.[200] The king allowed one group of his subjects to expand into areas that he forbade another to expand into, which clearly demonstrated the work of a tyrant.

With nowhere to expand and English troops surrounding the colonies on all sides, the king left the colonies with no choice but to submit their liberties to the crown and to despotic English rule. This is why this charge was as dastardly as the other charges. Submission to tyranny was not an option for the Founders.

Thankfully, today, this charge does not apply to the federal government as clearly as it applied to the crown at that time. However, with the federal government's continued expansion and intrusion into spheres that are rightfully those of the states or local governments, the arbitrary federal rules and laws are definitely instruments our national government uses to introduce their absolute rule over the states, local government, and therefore the people.

For example, one of the responsibilities of the federal government, according to Article IV of the Constitution, is to dispose of land: "The Congress shall have Power to dispose of and make all needful Rules and Regulations respecting … Property belonging to the United States." Two things are important to note. First, this clause is in the "States" Article, Article IV. This Article describes some interaction between the States, the creation method of new States, the designation of each States' form of government, and so on.

Article I, Section 8 vests Congress with power over the government's district as well as over all other property of the United States. It states that Congress shall have power "To exercise exclusive Legislation in all Cases whatsoever, over such District (the District of Columbia) ... and to exercise like Authority over all Places purchased by the Consent of the Legislature of the State in which the Same shall be." The question, then, is why insert a seemingly redundant power over US property in Article IV and more particularly in Section 3 regarding the addition of new states and territories? The purpose of this separate and distinct power is to facilitate the addition of new states. Furthermore, it requires Congress to relinquish or dispose of its property to the newly formed states, except those properties needed for the federal government to accomplish its responsibilities, such as military bases. In other words, once Congress forms a new state, Congress *must* dispose of its property to that state.

Hamilton showed the use of the word "dispose" concerning property in how he used the word in Federalist 83. The term did not mean to throw away property or trash it. It meant that the federal government had no more use for the property and was to sell it or give it away to either private ownership or state ownership. Hamilton wrote of how a person disposes of property in Federalist 83:

> Let us suppose that by the laws of this State a married woman was incapable of *conveying her estate*, and that the legislature, considering this as an evil, should enact that she might *dispose of her property* by deed executed in the presence of a magistrate. In such a case there can be no doubt but the specification would amount to an exclusion of any other *mode of conveyance*, because the woman having no previous power to *alienate her property*, the specification determines the particular mode which she is, for that purpose, to avail herself of. (Emphasis added.)

Hamilton used three different terms to describe the sale of or getting rid of property: "convey," "disposed," and "alienate." These terms all mean to transfer, deliver, or disassociate oneself from the property in question.

In the Constitution, placing this clause here with the section respecting the formation of new states, with the appearance of being redundant in making rules regarding property, makes it clear that the federal government, upon the formation of a state, should be "disposing," "conveying," or "alienating" the property it possesses. Only the property needed for military or other enumerated purposes should remain under the control of the federal government, and even that with the state legislature's permission.

To put this differently, the Department of Interior should exist only as long as the federal government is still processing the property for disposal. The Bureau of Land Management, the US Forest Service, and other land management agencies need to exist only until Congress creates a state and then transfers the requisite land to either the state or to private control and ownership. With about 64 percent of Idaho land, for instance, still controlled by the federal government and the state having entered the Union in 1890, Congress is clearly failing to follow the Constitution. This land should have been fully given over to Idaho more than 125 years ago.[201]

Furthermore, much of the federally controlled land is either completely off limits to the public or access severely limited. For example, the Frank Church River of No Return Wilderness, which covers over 2.3 million acres of land in Idaho, is more or less off limits to people. The restrictions are quite severe. A group of up to twenty may stay for a maximum of fourteen days in the wilderness and must follow the stated "Leave No Trace" rules. These rules include packing out your own feces if traveling by boat up the Salmon River, not being able to use dish soap or bathing soap within two hundred feet of water, only using trails, and camping at least two hundred feet away from water and trails (which you are supposed to stay on).[202]

This is only one example of many applicable to the federal government. Particularly in the western States, one can find many monuments, national parks, and open land—all severely restricted from any use or limited use.

In most cases, the federal government forbids settling on the land. In this and other cases, the federal government controls and restricts far more land than England's king ever hoped to control. Our government controls nearly a hundred million square miles, which only considers the land regulated by the BLM, the US Forest Service, the US Fish and Wildlife Service, and the National Parks Service. This figure does not include any land controlled by the military, other federal law enforcement controlled lands, or any other federal agency.[203] And there are between four hundred fifty and five hundred federal agencies that require offices and other facilities, including land, in order to operate. This situation bears an eerie similarity to the king's Royal Proclamation of 1763. And it is in clear violation of the US Constitution and the intent of the Founders. Charge 20 definitely applies to today's US federal government.

Charge 21: For taking away our Charters, abolishing our most valuable Laws, and altering fundamentally the Forms of our Governments

In previous chapters, I provided evidence for this charge against the king. However, this charge is applicable to Parliament as well. The king provided each colony with their own charter, which granted them their forms of representative government with power to tax, pass laws, form courts, and anything else the colony needed to secure the rights of its citizens. The charters also allowed abolishment—pardons of crimes committed—but only by the voice of the people or their representatives. For Parliament to pass their own laws over the colonies, they needed to abolish the charters in order to usurp authority, which is what Parliament did. For instance, the New York Suspending Act abolished the colony's government entirely. The Massachusetts Government Act took away the charter of the colony and altered its form of government. It stated that "all and every clause, matter, and thing, therein contained, which relates to the time and manner of electing the assistants or counsellors for the said province, be revoked, and is hereby revoked and made void and of none effect."[204] In short, Parliament and the king voided the colony's charter and fundamentally altered their form of government. Finally, Parliament, in the Declaratory Act of

1766, tactlessly abolished the colonies' laws, resolutions, and so forth. It stated, "That *all resolutions, votes, orders, and proceedings*, in any of the said colonies or plantations ... *are hereby declared to be, utterly null and void to all in purposes whatsoever.*"[205]

Clearly, Parliament was interested in becoming the sole legislative authority over the colonies, despite the charters granted by the king and despite whether its acts were good for the colonies or whether the acts were self-serving. Neither Parliament nor the king possessed the authority to take these actions—actions which left the colonists to the whim of a tyrant.

Is today's federal government guilty of this? Well, there are no more charters, so to speak. However, the individual states and their approved constitutions are similar to the charters of the colonies. One good example is that of the state of Idaho. In 2006, Idaho passed an amendment to its constitution concerning marriage. It states in Article III, Section 28 of Idaho's constitution: "Marriage. A marriage between a man and a woman is the only domestic legal union that shall be valid or recognized in this state."[206] Passed by the legislature, it went to the voice of the people for approval, which is according to the amending method of Idaho's constitution. The result was 63 percent to 37 percent in favor of the amendment.[207] Thus, under Idaho's constitution (think charter here), marriage is only between a man and a woman. Regardless of how one views the definition of marriage, this is the law passed by an overwhelming majority within the state and accomplished with the proper authority. Similar to every other state that enters the Union, the federal government approved and ratified the Idaho Constitution in 1890 when it became a state.

However, Chief Magistrate Judge Candy Wagahoff Dale of Idaho's federal district court ruled that Idaho's constitution violated the US Constitution under the Due Process and Equal Protection clauses of the fourteenth Amendment.[208] One federal judge abolished Idaho law and fundamentally altered its form of government. First, she struck down Idaho's amendment to its constitution, not a simple statute. By doing this, one federal judge essentially revoked the congressionally approved amendment process of Idaho.

A single federal judge can now void anything in a state's constitution. Thus, the form of government, which is a representative government and the voice of the people, is meaningless. Similar to what Parliament did to the colonies, federal courts can do to states. There is no point to having an amendment process or voting for representatives or voting for an item by the public at large or voting for the people's representatives to be our voice if a federal judge can render our exercise null and void. Federal judges who have such power have usurped authority from the people and their states, and they have rendered to themselves the ability to fundamentally alter the republican form of government on which our nation is built.

In this particular case, no violation of the amendment had occurred. Every individual had the same right and ability to marry whom each chose under the amendment—heterosexuals and homosexuals alike. Every individual was equal under the amendment to marry someone of the opposite sex, though they may want to marry someone of the same sex. The purpose of "Equal Protection" is to ensure that all are treated equally. The amendment did this. The law did not prohibit anyone from marriage. And no violation of due process existed.

The main point is that the US Constitution provided Idaho with a republican form of government, which constitution Congress approved, including its amendment process. The federal government, however, used its judicial power to nullify and abolish one of Idaho's most fundamental laws—one that had been properly and legally added to its constitution. The further effect of this decision was to alter Idaho's form of government, making the amendment process and the passage of laws a waste of time because one federal judge can nullify them all.

Recall as well the example I provided for Charge 1 concerning abortion. Before 1973, forty-four of fifty states had very restrictive laws on abortion. With the tyranny of the majority of Supreme Court judges, every state that passed a law prohibiting abortion had their charters revoked and their form of government fundamentally altered. Every state had representatives properly elected by the people. These representatives and state citizens voted for their state laws. In addition, governors elected by the people either signed the bills into law or vetoed them and the respective legislature overrode their vetoes to make the laws. Furthermore, the judges in each state, at the very least, failed to declare the laws unconstitutional. In counter to all of this, the Supreme Court alienated millions of people with their decision in *Roe v. Wade*. The state laws violated no civil liberty. Every law was constitutional and every law followed the purpose for which people created government, to protect human life. But the Supreme Court legislated from the bench and usurped the authority of the states and thereby violated the rights of American citizens and our nation's Constitution.

There can be no doubt that the federal government has altered the several forms of government of the states, abolished our most valuable laws, and taken away the charters of the states.

Charge 22: For suspending our own Legislatures, and declaring themselves invested with power to legislate for us in all cases whatsoever.

The Suspending Act of New York is a perfect example of Parliament and the crown suspending a legislature. The name of the law itself describes the intent and action taken by Parliament and the crown. The Massachusetts Government Act is another example of the suspension of legislatures, making Parliament the sole legislative body of the colony, abusing the legislative authority it did not possess.

The Declaratory Act of 1766 is the law from which Jefferson takes the wording of part of the charge. The Act declared that Parliament "of right ought to have, full power and authority to make laws and statutes of sufficient force and validity to bind the colonies and people of America, subjects of the crown of Great Britain, in all cases whatsoever."[209] Parliament, along with the crown, declared themselves tyrants with this legislation. It is an abuse of legislative authority when an entity legislates for the people when there is no representation of the people.

While there are no cases of suspending legislatures by the federal government today, in many ways the government still declares itself vested with power to legislate in all cases whatsoever. Citing numerous examples of how the federal government delves into areas that are the responsibility of states or local governments is relatively simple. Interstate commerce laws that Congress has passed have nothing to do with interstate commerce, such as the case with the previously mentioned *Wickard v. Filburn*. This was purely an *intra*state commerce case that Congress declared to be *inter*state. However, despite this obvious fact, Congress declared that the Constitution vested it with the authority dealt with in this case. Any power not enumerated in the Constitution and that Congress usurps for itself is unlawfully procured. In such cases our Congress does what Parliament did during the colonial period.

Section 8 of Article I of the Constitution provides a short summary of the powers granted to Congress. The powers are taxing by duties, imposts and excises, borrowing money, regulation of international and interstate commerce (not *intra*state commerce), naturalization and bankruptcy rules, coining and protecting money and providing standards of money, weights and measures, post offices, copyrights and patents, punishing international crimes, acts of war and providing a military and militia, making rules about federal lands, and forming federal courts below the Supreme Court. Legislating in all cases whatsoever where no authority was granted nor could be granted by the people would include licensing of firearms dealers, anything to do with education, labor, social security, healthcare, housing and urban development, agriculture, transportation, energy, the interior, protection of marriage, and too many other examples to list here. Where the Constitution fails to grant power, none exists, except by usurpation of authority.

This chapter has provided ample evidence of the abuse of power of the legislative branch of the English government against the colonies. The abuses by Parliament and the crown are many. Furthermore, a great deal of evidence exists of similar abuses perpetuated by the current federal government. There may be a few differences from the charges enumerated in the Declaration. Nevertheless, there is more than enough similarity for citizens to sit up and take note and begin considering how they can counter these abuses of power and their God-given rights. We must be on guard to push back against these abuses and prevent further ones by the federal government. If we fail, we will continue to lose more of our rights and authority.

The Charges: Abuses of War Power

···

He has abdicated Government here, by declaring us out of his Protection and waging War against us.

He has plundered our seas, ravaged our Coasts, burnt our towns, and destroyed the lives of our people.

He is at this time transporting large Armies of foreign Mercenaries to compleat the works of death, desolation and tyranny, already begun with circumstances of Cruelty & perfidy scarcely paralleled in the most barbarous ages, and totally unworthy of the Head of a civilized nation.

He has constrained our fellow Citizens taken Captive on the high Seas to bear Arms against their Country, to become the executioners of their friends and Brethren, or to fall themselves by their Hands.

He has excited domestic insurrections amongst us, and has endeavoured to bring on the inhabitants of our frontiers, the merciless Indian Savages, whose known rule of warfare, is an undistinguished destruction of all ages, sexes and conditions.

T hese charges have to do with the colonists' grievances against the king for his acts of war against his own subjects. These abuses were considered tyrannical. England's king should have protected and defended his people rather than trying to injure or destroy them. Tyrants, however, are not interested in their people's welfare. Despite this, the colonists still attempted reconciliation for a time.

Charge 23: He has abdicated Government here, by declaring us out of his Protection and waging War against us.

On April 19, 1775, the war for independence began even though it would be more than one year later when the Continental Congress formally declared independence from England. In the summer of 1775, Congress sent the king the Olive Branch Petition, which sought for reconciliation with him and England. However, two days after he received it, King George rejected it without even looking at it. He then proclaimed the colonies to be in open rebellion. For the mother country not to listen to the petitions of her children but begin punishing immediately, even by death, is extraordinary. But this is precisely what the king proclaimed on August 23, 1775:

> Whereas many of our subjects in divers parts of our Colonies and Plantations in North America, misled by dangerous and ill designing men, and *forgetting the allegiance which they owe to the power that has protected and supported them*; after various disorderly acts committed in disturbance of the publick peace, to the obstruction of lawful commerce, and to the oppression of our loyal subjects carrying on the same; have at length proceeded to open and avowed rebellion, by arraying themselves in a hostile manner, to withstand the execution of the law, and traitorously preparing, ordering and levying war against us ... *we do accordingly strictly charge and command all our Officers, as well civil as military, and all others our obedient and loyal subjects, to use their utmost endeavours to withstand and suppress such rebellion*, and to disclose and make known all treasons and traitorous

conspiracies which they shall know to be against us, our crown and dignity.[210]

The king moved from protecting his subjects to waging war against them. He conveniently forgot that the colonists risked life and limb alongside his troops in the French and Indian War only a few years before. They even taxed themselves to cover the costs for their own protection and army.

In addition, there is plenty of evidence to support the fact that the laws of the king undermined commerce for the colonists. I discussed some of these laws in previous chapters—laws such as the Navigation Acts. Finally, in violation of the rights of the colonists, the beginning of the war came because the king decided that disarming his subjects was the best way to force their submission to his will. The purpose of the army on that fateful day in 1775 was to seize arms and munitions the colonists had stored. The king sought to take their arms or property without cause and without trial, all in violation of their rights as British citizens.

Furthermore, later that year, the king provided more evidence to support the charge that he was waging war against his subjects. In October before Parliament, he gave a speech concerning the rebellion of the colonies: "The resolutions of Parliament breathed a spirit of moderation and forbearance; conciliatory propositions accompanied the measures taken to enforce authority." Regarding himself, he stated, "I have acted with the same temper; anxious to prevent, if it had been possible, the effusion of the blood of my subjects."[211] Despite his claims, he completely ignored the Olive Branch Petition, the colonists' offer of reconciliation. Even though he stated that he and Parliament had acted in a conciliatory manner, the evidence shows the contrary. The king tended to become more iron fisted when the colonies refused to cooperate as he desired. When the colonists sought for reconciliation with the Stamp Act, the king doubled-down and gave them the Declaratory Act. This was the king's typical pattern of "forbearance, moderation and desire to prevent bloodshed." However, it could be stated that he was conciliatory, but only after the manner of a tyrant who could have sent all his forces to utterly annihilate the colonies yet did not.

The tension escalated further with the royal proclamation titled "Appointing The Distribution Of Prizes Taken During The Continuance Or The Rebellion Now Subsisting In Divers Parts Of The Continent Of North America." This authorized the complete theft of any ships seized by the crown's ships for the use of the crown. The proclamation allowed for no trial, court, or any other legal action in order to seize the colonists' goods, including their ships.[212] This is just one of many reasons for the colonists to conclude that the king's actions resulted in the abdication of any form of rightful government.

In the case of America's current federal government, it certainly seems to have declared citizens out of their protection, which would allude to an abdication of rightful government. A perfect example is America's national border, particularly the border with Mexico, which the federal government refused to protect for so long. With about twelve million illegal immigrants living in the US, according to the Migration Policy Institute[213] (a non-partisan think-tank that uses numerous sources of data, including official government sources), and with multitudes continuing to cross the border, it is obvious that the protection of US citizens does not exist.

Charge 7 considered another instance of the failure of the federal government to protect the people. While the government admitted that the vetting process of Syrian refugees was somewhat lacking, officials continued to allow the refugees to come into the United States. Not knowing the kind of people they are— whether they are criminals, terrorists, or true refugees—creates a danger to the people already here.

In addition, the federal government allows states such as California to setup sanctuary cities for illegal immigrants. This practice has led to serious consequences for citizens, including theft, injury, death, and even murder. Citizens have even been compelled to pay for the subsistence of immigrants who receive financial assistance from the government in violation of federal laws.

These are just a few examples of many more I could cite. The federal government's failure to act is one way to abdicate government, with the other way being acting improperly in ways it has no authority to do.

Charge 24: He has plundered our seas, ravaged our Coasts, burnt our towns, and destroyed the lives of our people.

As shown in the last charge, the king declared his intentions of plundering the seas. The proclamation also included the ports where the crown considered traitorous actions to have taken place or actions that would take place, especially easy targets for plunder along the coasts.

One such event happened immediately following the battles of Lexington and Concord at the beginning of the war in 1775. Leading up to the Battle of Bunker Hill, Mercy Otis Warren noted: "The town of Charlestown was reduced to ashes by the fire of the shipping, while the land forces were storming the hills. Thus, in concert, was this flourishing and compact town destroyed, in the most wanton display of power. There were about four hundred dwelling-houses in the center of Charlestown, which, with the out-houses adjacent, and many buildings in the suburbs, were also sunk in the conflagration."[214] On top of the king plundering the seas, his soldiers began what was typical of the times: they destroyed everything they could and with no regard to the life or property of those whom they sought to bring back to obedience to the crown.

During this time, General Howe took over as the British commander-in-chief of the armies in the colonies. This changed how all parties fought the war. In the beginning, while Washington placed Boston under siege throughout most of 1775 and into 1776, Howe "published a proclamation, condemning to military execution any of the remaining inhabitants of Boston, who should attempt to leave the town; he compelled them to form themselves into bodies under officers he should appoint, and to take arms in case of attack, against their brethren in the country."[215] A complete and irresponsible tyrant would gladly force his subjects to fight against their own kin, their own neighbors, and their own town. He would also forbid the townspeople to leave, regardless of their condition, to sustain their own lives. These actions were reprehensible.

Another horrible proclamation was made after this one by General Howe as part of his overall strategy in the war. And another town was destroyed—

Falmouth, in eastern Massachusetts, which Mercy Warren described as having been built well and flourishing.[216]

Mercy Warren noted that the colonists were alarmed all along the coastline, stating that "their shipping were seized, their islands plundered, their harbors infested by the landing of marauding parties, and many places threatened with immediate conflagration." A town of Bristol, which was near Rhode Island, was burned to the ground by Captain Mowatt who stated, "He had orders to set on fire all the sea-port towns from Boston to Halifax." Mowatt ordered the inhabitants of the various towns to become compliant with the crown, deliver up their arms and other provisions for military use, and send a few important persons for hostages. If they failed to comply, "he [Mowatt] should lay the town in ashes within three hours."[217] In the end, the towns refused to comply. In just one town Mowatt "destroyed 139 houses and 278 stores, and other buildings."[218] In the case of Bristol, many of the inhabitants had been battling diseases. The destruction of their town left them exposed to the elements, without food, clothing, and shelter. This was the worst kind of war: a war that was utterly destructive and in which vengeance and power were ends to achieve. The crown's culpability in these dreadful acts is without question.

While charge 24 may not seem like one that can be applied to the federal government today, the government may certainly be charged with allowing others to wreck havoc in American cities and towns. One way this has occurred is through riots, such as the Watts riots[219] and the riots that more recently occurred in Ferguson, Missouri, over the fatal shooting of Michael Brown. Such violent acts have resulted in some locales being laid to ashes, at least in part.

We could also look to Arizona where the BLM (Bureau of Land Management) has installed signs warning citizens to avoid an area about ninety miles *north* of the US-Mexican border.[220] The reason: Mexican drug lords have taken over the area.

In all these cases, it is the government's responsibility to protect life, liberty, and property, which includes protecting the nation's borders and those who live near there from destructive elements, such as foreign drug lords. Concerning this charge, the federal government is once again failing to fulfill its duty to its citizens.

Charge 25: He is at this time transporting large Armies of foreign Mercenaries to compleat the works of death, desolation and tyranny, already begun with circumstances of Cruelty & perfidy scarcely paralleled in the most barbarous ages, and totally unworthy of the Head of a civilized nation.

The crown abdicated the colonies' authority of self-rule by waging war against them and doing it in the cruelest manner possible. Without regard to the people the crown claimed to want to protect, he allowed his troops to ransack towns, harbors, and so on. He allowed for the complete plundering of goods on ships, including the seizure of ships, as well as "laying to ashes" various towns.

The previous charges distinctly demonstrate the crown's "cruelty and perfidy" that parallels "the most barbarous ages" of the past. England should have been far beyond that kind of barbarity. England had moved toward civility with the Magna Carta and then the English Bill of Rights of 1689. England was well on its way to leaving barbarism behind. However, as autocrats seem to prove with relatively few exceptions, barbarism will always exist as long as they exist. England's own Lord Acton stated, "Despotic power is always accompanied by corruption of morality."[221] Evidently, the despotism of King George III was intent on proving Lord Acton correct.

In order to complete his "works of death, desolation and tyranny," the crown employed the use of mercenaries. These were dreaded foes. As the British, alongside the German Hessian mercenaries, traveled through the Jersies after the battle of New York, they tended to push many indifferent or neutral colonists to the side of the patriots. The reason was due to "the indiscriminate ravages of the Hessian and British soldiers. ... The elegant houses of some of their own most devoted partisans were burnt; their wives and daughters pursued and ravished in the woods to which they had fled for shelter."[222] Once King George went the way of a despot, he and his army tossed aside morality as Lord Acton predicted.

The crown employed thirty thousand German Hessians to fight the colonists.[223] Indeed, the king used this large army to help complete the "works of death, desolation and tyranny." He wanted these mercenaries to force the colonists into submission. He had no regard for his subjects, only for his own lust for power and riches. The barbarity of the Hessians and the crown's own soldiers provided the colonists with all the proof they needed to demand separation from their abusive, despotic king.

While this charge is inapplicable to the federal government today, it is within the government's reach to use its military power in an abusive way. It is always possible for those who believe they have the power of government behind them and are dissatisfied with their level of authority and wealth to use legitimate soldiers to acquire more. We must always be on guard regarding individuals and groups who receive the power of the people. As England's own Lord Acton so aptly stated: "Power tends to corrupt and absolute power corrupts absolutely. Great men are almost always bad men, even when they exercise influence and not authority; still more when you superadd the tendency of the certainty of corruption by authority."[224] Entrusting power to another will tend to corrupt. When government declares itself able to legislate for the people in all cases whatsoever, the corruption will become absolute. It is up to us to prevent an ongoing accumulation of power to those who represent us. One of the most important duties of all citizens is the responsibility of scaling back whatever power government has usurped and centralized.

Charge 26: He has constrained our fellow Citizens taken Captive on the high Seas to bear Arms against their Country, to become the executioners of their friends and Brethren, or to fall themselves by their Hands.

This charge relates to the Royal Proclamation Relating to America by the Parliament that was passed on December 22, 1775. However, before we explore this charge, I want to remind you of the British General Howe and what we covered under charge 24. Howe had already enacted a similar proclamation against Boston earlier in 1775. He forbade Bostonians from leaving Boston and forced them into his army to protect the city from Washington's siege against the British. If an actual battle had occurred, Howe would have forced the Bostonians to fight against their own brethren. Thankfully, this never happened. The Americans laid siege against the British, eventually forcing them to leave Boston on March 17, 1776.

General Howe, the king, and Parliament set precedent by continuing the abuse of war powers in their proclamation at the end of 1775. Any ship or vessel captured, not just war ships but also cargo ships found trading with the colonies, suffered the fate set forth in this Act. It forced into service for the British those who were captured, including their ships. The British seized cargo and anything else they decided to confiscate.[225] Forcing one to fight against one's own family, friends, town, or nation is an exceptionally heinous and barbaric act. And it was brutally and successfully applied. In 1775 alone, by one researcher's findings, about ten thousand American colonists had been pressed into service as British seamen.[226]

So far, this charge does not apply to America's federal government. However, as always, our vigilance is required. The closest that our government has come to this was the Civil War of the 1860s. Brother fought against brother. Families fought against each other. However, the combatants fought one another voluntarily. And typically, enemy soldiers were prisoners of war rather than forced to fight against the side for which they originally fought.

Charge 27: He has excited domestic insurrections amongst us, and has endeavoured to bring on the inhabitants of our frontiers, the merciless Indian Savages, whose known rule of warfare, is an undistinguished destruction of all ages, sexes and conditions.

One of the first instances of the British trying to use Indians in their war against the colonies occurred shortly after the colonists took Fort Ticonderoga in May 1775 under the command of Ethan Allen in order to secure cannons and other armaments so that Washington could lay siege to the British in Boston. When the king's governor, Sir Guy Carleton, in Canada learned of the fall of the fort, "he endeavored to induce the Canadians and Indians to cooperate with him."[227] Colonel Johnston of the British army held numerous conferences with the Indians to try to influence them to fight the colonists, but he had little success. He went so far as to invite them "to feast on a Bostonian and drink his blood."[228]

After the opening volleys of the Revolutionary War, Governor Dunmore of Virginia planned to promise freedom to slaves if they would proclaim loyalty to the crown and fight for it. In addition, he sent letters to Indian chiefs in hopes of employing them to fight. Part of this was because there were virtually no British troops in Virginia to defend the colony from the patriots. Slave owners feared possible insurrections from their slaves and attacks from Indians. Despite his efforts, Governor Dunmore failed. The governors of North and South Carolina fared a little better in recruiting Indians and slaves to fight for the king.[229]

Thomas Jefferson wrote many years after the Revolutionary War ended about what the colonists had tried to do before the war and the results of Britain's attempt to involve Indians in the war: "We spared nothing to keep them at peace with one another, to teach them agriculture and the rudiments of the most necessary arts, and to encourage industry."[230] Of course, the colonists' efforts were unraveled because of the enticements of the British, who would stoop as low as possible to bring their wayward subjects back into submission.

In South Carolina in 1776, Captain Andrew Pickens, who would later become a member of the House of Representatives, sent Captain McCall after some Tories in Georgia. The Cherokee attacked his detachment and captured him and some others. The Indians took McCall to their place of torture to show the witness their horrific acts on settlers and other captured individuals.

> Their treatment of captives … had more in common with the Pre-Colombian rituals of the Aztec and Maya. Excruciating tortures were inflicted to test the captive's soul. … burning was a common element in torture. The victim was frequently made to walk barefoot over fires, as well as being slowly roasted in other ways. … Hot irons or splinters would be thrust through limbs. … The whole village—men, women and children—would usually participate.[231]

Jefferson's description does not include all Indians, of course. However, charge 27 makes it clear that the king knew fully that inciting the Indians would horrify the colonists and hoped that it would frighten them into submission.

America's federal government has never succumbed to any actions that would bring on the indictment of this charge.

The Deleted Charge

In his draft of the Declaration of Independence, Jefferson leveled this charge against King George III:

> He has waged cruel war against human nature itself, violating its most sacred rights of life and liberty in the persons of a distant people who never offended him, captivating and carrying them into slavery in another hemisphere, or to incur miserable death in their transportation thither. This piratical warfare, the opprobrium of infidel powers, is the warfare of the Christian king of Great Britain. Determined to keep open a market where MEN should be bought and sold, he has prostituted his negative for suppressing every legislative attempt to prohibit or to restrain this execrable commerce: and that this assemblage of horrors might want no fact of distinguished die, he is now exciting those very people to rise in arms among us, and to purchase that liberty of which he has deprived them, by murdering the people upon whom he also obtruded them; thus paying off former crimes committed against the liberties of one people, with crimes which he urges them to commit against the lives of another.

In this charge, Jefferson articulated what he saw as one of the British king's most egregious offenses against the natural moral law. The king had forced slavery upon the colonies, then, as I mentioned earlier, began trying to coax the slaves to rise up against the colonists. In short, he first enslaved men (meaning men, women, and children) from another continent, transported them under horrific conditions to the colonies, and then tried to get those whom he had enslaved to enslave others. Jefferson and many other colonists could not find anything more appalling and barbaric than this practice—a practice promoted by a country claiming to be civilized and a king claiming to be Christian.

If you read the final draft of the Declaration of Independence, you will not find this to be one of the enumerated charges. The Founders removed it from the Declaration because Congress wanted a united front. Congress needed all the colonies to join in the fight for independence. Of the southern colonies, only South Carolina and Georgia refused to sign the Declaration unless the remaining colonies agreed to remove this charge. The slave holding colonies of Maryland, North Carolina, and Virginia were willing to sign. Jefferson was part of the Virginia delegation. Though himself a slave owner, he did not believe slavery was appropriate or moral, and he did not want slavery to continue in the colonies.

As part of the Fairfax county Virginia delegation to the colony's assembly, George Washington played a role in the Fairfax County resolutions that called for a stop to the importation of slaves into the colonies (see chapter 2). Although Washington owned slaves, he refused to sell them like cattle. Nor would he trade them or give them away for fear of splitting up their families, which he vehemently opposed. Thus, his beloved Mount Vernon was not as profitable as it could have been. In the end, using Virginia's law, he freed his slaves in his will upon his death and provided for their subsistence upon manumission.

Many of the colonies tried to abolish slavery in their legislative bodies before the Revolutionary War. Benjamin Franklin attested to this in a letter to Reverend Dean Woodward in London in 1773. Franklin stated that even Virginia petitioned the king to prevent more importation of slaves into the colony but to no avail.[232]

Unlike Washington, Jefferson was never able to free his slaves. Virginia law only allowed manumission of slaves as long as the slaves could support themselves or their former owners provided the means for their support.[233] However, by 1823, three years before Jefferson's death, Virginia banned any manumission of slaves by any private citizen, leaving no chance for Jefferson to free his slaves.[234]

In 1769, Jefferson became a member of Virginia's legislature. There, Jefferson "made one effort in that body for the permission of the emancipation of slaves, which was rejected."[235] Later, as president of the United States, he signed in 1807 the "Act Prohibiting the Importation of Slaves into the United States," which took effect in 1808.[236] Jefferson's life history from 1769 in the Virginia legislature to the Declaration in 1776 to his signature as president in 1807 demonstrates that he despised slavery and tried to end it.

Here I will provide another example of the British king's support for slavery and the negative effect he had on colonial legislative attempts to ban the practice.

In Massachusetts, the slave Felix Holbrook, along with other slaves, presented a petition for freedom and grants of land to the colony's legislature in 1773. The legislature passed the abolition of slavery act in 1774. However, governors Hutchinson and Gage (governors appointed by the British crown) refused to sign the legislation, which could not take effect until it was signed.[237]

Jefferson's final though deleted charge demonstrated that the government of England was not interested in doing the job of government—to protect life, liberty, and property. Rather, it was doing the opposite. The king continued to enslave Africans and sought to do the same to the American colonists. He tried to strip the colonists, similar to the African slaves, of their liberty and their property. The colonists, seeing the need to revolt against such dastardly acts, found that the king was willing to sacrifice their lives too.

Although the Founders removed this charge from the Declaration, it shows the depths of the king's depravity. I included it to show the attitude of the Founders during the Revolutionary era concerning slavery and what they really believed about the rights of the whole human family.

These charges against the king and his abuse of war powers show his barbarity and why the need for separation was required. Jefferson clearly defined the abuse of legislative powers, executive powers, and war powers and provided proof of those abuses. Despite these many and varied abuses, the colonists were "disposed to suffer, while evils are sufferable, than to right themselves." Furthermore, in the Declaration's next two paragraphs, Jefferson laid out the colonists' attempts to reconcile with the king and with all his other subjects.

Chapter 6

Reconciliation Attempts

In every stage of these Oppressions We have Petitioned for Redress in the most humble terms: Our repeated Petitions have been answered only by repeated injury. A Prince whose character is thus marked by every act which may define a Tyrant, is unfit to be the ruler of a free people.

Nor have We been wanting in attentions to our British brethren. We have warned them from time to time of attempts by their legislature to extend an unwarrantable jurisdiction over us. We have reminded them of the circumstances of our emigration and settlement here. We have appealed to their native justice and magnanimity, and we have conjured them by the ties of our common kindred to disavow these usurpations, which, would inevitably interrupt our connections and correspondence. They too have been deaf to the voice of justice and of consanguinity. We must, therefore, acquiesce in the necessity, which denounces our Separation, and hold them, as we hold the rest of mankind, Enemies in War, in Peace Friends.

T he colonists attempted many times to reconcile their differences with the crown and Parliament. When they thought that a bill before Parliament was wrong, they petitioned Parliament to repeal it. Sometimes this worked. In reality, however, anything passed by Parliament was wrong, was "foreign to [the colonies'] constitutions." Parliament had received no authority to govern the colonies. From their beginning, the crown had authorized the colonies to govern themselves. This did not stop Parliament from exercising power over the colonies.

To return to an earlier example, Parliament passed the Stamp Act of 1765, requiring any of the colonists' paper transactions to be taxed, including licenses, playing cards, and bills of lading. This was a usurpation of authority, of course. And it was a tax passed without the colonists being properly represented. Moreover, the colonists found the tax unwarranted. So they petitioned the crown regarding the Stamp Act and Parliament repealed it. Unfortunately, Parliament then passed the Declaratory Act, which stated that it had full authority over the colonies over all things whatsoever.[238] This is just one of many examples of the colonies petitioning Parliament only to be answered with further injury.

Another example involved New York, which disliked the act requiring their forced quartering of British troops. When the colonists refused to comply and petitioned the crown, Parliament passed the New York Suspending Act, which dissolved the legislature until the payment for the crown's soldiers was paid. Thus, the British government added another injury on top of the previous one.

Even after the battles of Lexington and Concord, the colonists sought reconciliation, despite the fact that there can be no true reconciliation when it comes to the lives lost in the battles. The Continental Congress drafted the Olive Branch Petition on July 8, 1775 and sent it to the king. The king would not even read it.

On numerous occasions the colonists insisted on reconciling with England, showing great devotion to their mother country. Even in the Olive Branch Petition, they stated that everything good had come to them under the crown's magnanimous actions. And this even after the king's most recent actions to seize the colonists' arms and kill more of his subjects.[239] The colonists strove to remain part of the mother country.

Furthermore, Congress offered to reconcile by discussing the differences that caused the dissensions and the need to take up arms. Congress reminded the king of their continued willingness "to assert and maintain the rights and interests of your Majesty, and of our Mother country."[240] Congress even flattered the crown in the next paragraph with this reconciliatory statement:

> We, therefore, beseech your Majesty, that your royal authority and influence may be graciously interposed to procure us relief from our afflicting fears and jealousies, occasioned by the system before mentioned, and to settle peace through every part of your dominions, with all humility submitting to your Majesty's wise consideration whether it may not be expedient for facilitating those important purposes, that your Majesty be pleased to direct some mode, by which the united applications of your faithful colonists to the throne, in pursuance of their common councils, may be improved into a happy and permanent reconciliation; and that, in the meantime, measures may be taken for preventing the further destruction of the lives of your Majesty's subjects; and that such statutes as more immediately distress any of your Majesty's colonies may be repealed.[241]

They recognized that the freedoms they had as British subjects were superior to anything else available. However, the evidence kept mounting that the crown endeavored to trample these freedoms.

After receiving this Olive Branch Petition, the king rejected the petition without reading it and then categorically declared the colonies to be in open rebellion. He had no intention of working with his subjects to reconcile any differences. He acted as a tyrant. Tyrants are never fit to be rulers of free people or anyone else. Tyranny should be opposed whenever and wherever possible. The Founders understood this and thus began taking steps toward independence.

The colonies petitioned the crown for a redress of grievances, as well as Parliament and the people of England. The colonies hoped they could influence the electorate who would then influence their elected officials.

Immediately following the Seven Years' War (or the French and Indian War, as the colonies called it), England was in serious debt. Parliament devised a way to pay for it by increasing taxes everywhere, including in the colonies. This came in the form of the Stamp Act, which Benjamin Franklin, the ambassador to England at the time, readily opposed and petitioned Parliament not to enact. Until this time, only the colonies taxed the colonies. Now Parliament began usurping the colonies' authority. Franklin met with George Grenville, the British minister of finance, in order to prevent the enactment of the bill. Franklin also went before Parliament to plead the colonies' case. Those in Parliament thoroughly questioned Franklin. In the end, he emphatically declared that the colonies would not submit to the legislation.[242]

By the end of 1767 and after the passage of the Townsend Act, Franklin began growing weary of the British government failing to listen to anything sent by the colonies. In his petitioning of Parliament, Franklin started realizing there was a "'new kind of loyalty' now required by Parliament, whereas the colonists up to that time had considered themselves bound only to the king."[243]

Franklin then turned to the British newspapers, more so than normal, along with William Strahan, and wrote an article describing the colonists' views on the government's abuses. This article dealt with taxation, bad governors appointed by the crown to do the will of the crown, the regulations prohibiting certain manufacturing, and other abuses of liberty. However, the editor softened the language before publishing the article. Franklin then understood "there is a malice against us"[244] in all of England, from the crown to his subjects.

After nearly three years of petitioning Parliament over the Townsend Act, Parliament finally repealed most of it, leaving the tax on tea in place. That ultimately led to the Boston Tea Party. Concerning this tax, Franklin wrote, "It is bad surgery to leave splinters in a wound which must prevent its healing, or in time occasion it to open afresh."[245] He clearly understood that Parliament and the king continued to add abuse upon abuse on the colonies.

Not everyone in Parliament or in England was blind to what the government was doing. For example, British Colonel Isaac Barré, who fought with the colonists in the French and Indian War, responded to Charles Townsend in the discussion on the Stamp Act in Parliament when Townsend claimed that the hand of the British government planted the Americans in America. Barré argued: "They planted by your care? No! Your oppressions planted them in America. They fled your tyranny, and believe me, remember I this day told you so, that this same spirit of freedom which actuated that people at first will accompany them still."[246] Barré's prediction of the American's thirst for freedom was quite accurate.

Others, including the well-known Edmund Burke, also opposed Parliament's actions. One year before the start of the American Revolution, Burke spoke at length on American taxation. Here is one of the most notable things he said:

> Could anything be a subject of more just alarm to America, than to see you go out of the plain high road of finance, and give up your most certain revenues and your clearest interests, merely for the sake of insulting your Colonies? No man ever doubted that the commodity of Tea could bear an imposition of three-pence. *But no commodity will bear three-pence, or will bear a penny, when the general feelings of men are irritated, and two millions of people are resolved not to pay. The feelings of the Colonies were formerly the feelings of Great Britain.* Theirs were formerly the feelings of Mr. Hampden when called upon for the payment of twenty shillings. Would twenty shillings have ruined Mr. Hampden's fortune? No! but the payment of half twenty shillings, on the principle it was demanded, would have made him a slave. It is the weight of that preamble, of which you are so fond, and not the weight of the duty, that the Americans are unable and unwilling to bear.[247]

He further stated that if the colonies can tax themselves, Parliament should let them for the sake of peace. Burke's warnings about taxation did little to persuade Parliament against taxing the colonies. The result was that one year from the date of that speech, the colonies erupted in revolution.

While not everyone supported the crown and Parliament, the majority of British citizens did, despite the colonists' numerous petitions to Parliament, the crown, and the people of England. Though I have provided just a handful of examples, many more exist of the colonists' efforts to educate the people of

England, the crown, and Parliament about what was fair and legal, all to no avail. The colonies even tried to flatter the king into doing what was right. They finally came to the conclusion that nothing but a total separation from England would work. Thus, Jefferson inserted these two paragraphs in order to show that the colonies tried to reconcile before the war commenced with the first shots fired as well as afterward. The choices of the colonies dwindled down to only one—independence.

Chapter 7

Separation and the Appeal to Heaven

We, therefore, the Representatives of the united States of America, in General Congress, Assembled, appealing to the Supreme Judge of the world for the rectitude of our intentions, do, in the Name, and by Authority of the good People of these Colonies, solemnly publish and declare, That these United Colonies are, and of Right ought to be Free and Independent States; that they are Absolved from all Allegiance to the British Crown, and that all political connection between them and the State of Great Britain, is and ought to be totally dissolved; and that as Free and Independent States, they have full Power to levy War, conclude Peace, contract Alliances, establish Commerce, and to do all other Acts and Things which Independent States may of right do. And for the support of this Declaration, with a firm reliance on the protection of divine Providence, we mutually pledge to each other our Lives, our Fortunes and our sacred Honor.

The Declaration was a history-changing act of declaring and justifying independence from a tyrannical form of government. In this announcement to Britain and the world, Jefferson laid out the history of what brought the colonies to the point of separation, declared what the proper role of government entailed, leveled charges exposing the despotic abuses of the executive and legislative branches, including their acts of aggression, and showed that the colonies tried to avoid a separation through reconciliation with the crown, Parliament, and the subjects of the crown. Now all that was left to do for the colonists to gain freedom from their abusers was to move toward independence.

The Case for Independence

The case laid out for independence in the Declaration is comprehensive and revealing. In its Introduction, Jefferson described why and how the physical separation became necessary. From the beginning, with the Magna Carta, there were certain rights enumerated for British subjects, many of which show similarities in the US Constitution. A major cause for separation was the inability to worship as one saw fit. Moreover, the king freely trampled other rights by seizing private property, failing to provide for proper trials, and detaining and imprisoning citizens without cause, to name but a few egregious actions.

Furthermore, Parliament inserted additional rights in the English Bill of Rights in 1689. This strengthened the rights in the Magna Carta. The purpose of these rights was to secure the liberty, lives, and property of British subjects wherever they might live. England failed to safeguard these rights as well. The history of the abuses and failures by the British government, as Jefferson would later describe, was such that the need for a political separation became necessary.

Jefferson also defined the purpose of government, which is to protect life, liberty, and property, among other natural and unalienable moral rights. He described the willingness of the people to suffer abuses for a time. He also stated when it becomes appropriate to alter or abolish the present form of government—namely, when the government fails to do its duty to protect the people or when it abusively exceeds its proper role.

Next, Jefferson provided for the indictment of the crown and the British government. The charges include the king's many abuses of his executive authority, which included dissolving legislatures, making government officers serve at the crown's pleasure, and adding a copious number of bureaucratic offices and officers to harass the crown's subjects and eat out their substance. Jefferson also addressed the king's abuse of legislative authority by conspiring with Parliament to pass oppressive laws, tax the people, and secure "absolute authority" to make all laws for the colonies, thereby abolishing colonial self-rule. Parliament never had authority over the colonies in any case whatsoever. Moreover, each colony had received a charter from the crown giving each one the power to regulate and tax itself and provide for their own representation regarding all their needs and desires.

In the final set of indictments, Jefferson directed attention to the crown's abuse of war powers. The king provided his troops with the ability to legally plunder the colonies' ships and houses and destroy anything the troops saw fit to destroy in the name of war. Moreover, he enslaved his subjects, while in the midst of war, by making them fight against fellow colonists. Furthermore, the king enslaved Africans for his own purposes, despite the protests of the colonies and their banishment of slavery in their own legislatures. In short, the crown declared war against humanity itself, which are typical acts of a tyrant.

The result of all of these abuses and infringements on the rights of the colonists was that the crown had setup himself to be a tyrant, to dictate his will at his whim. John Locke had defined tyranny before Jefferson's time:

> Tyranny is the exercise of power beyond right, which nobody can have a right to. And this is making use of the power any one has in his hands, not for the good of those who are under it, but for his own private separate advantage. When the governor, however entitled, makes not the law, but his will, the rule; and his commands and actions are not directed to the preservation of the properties of his people, but the

satisfaction of his own ambition, revenge, covetousness, or any other irregular passion.[248]

This description fit King George III perfectly. Jefferson's charges described how the crown had become tyrannical. In every case, in the legislative, executive, and war powers, the king had chosen his own advantage and ambition rather than the preservation of the liberties of his subjects.

Finally, Jefferson described the colonies' attempt to reconcile with the crown, despite the king's innumerable abuses. Occasionally the colonies' efforts met with success, but most often they failed. The colonies tried reconciliation before the shooting began, and even afterward they sent the Olive Branch Petition, which the king refused to look at or acknowledge. They also tried to reconcile through Parliament, publishing their issues in papers read by their fellow British subjects in England. But their attempts to describe their plight and find relief availed them little to nothing. All the efforts of the colonies to reconcile and petition the crown for a redress of grievances, the many abuses, the failure of government to fulfill its proper role, and the willingness of the crown to do whatever was necessary to use force through his own arbitrary laws and use of deadly force through the power of the military left the colonies no choice but to declare their separation and independence from England.

The Final Appeal

The colonies then made their final appeal to heaven and "the Supreme Judge of the world." Jefferson's reasoning here comes from Locke. Locke described the method for receiving restitution for abuses. First, the appeal should be made to the law. However, when government ignores the law, as well as the rights of the people to the extent that there is no justice or rectification, only one appeal remains—an appeal to heaven.

If the prince, or whoever they be in administration, decline that way of determination; the appeal then lies nowhere but to Heaven. Force between either persons, who have no known superior on earth, or which permits no appeal to a judge on earth, being properly a state of war, wherein the appeal lies only to Heaven; and in that state the injured party must judge for himself; when he will think fit to make use of that appeal, and put himself upon it.[249]

This is exactly what Jefferson and the Founders did. They had no other superior to which they might appeal, so they appealed to the God who had given humankind their rights in the first place, and then they judged for themselves when and how to enforce that judgment.

In order to properly abolish and change their government, the Founders declared that the colonies were free and independent states, absolved themselves from the crown, ended any political connection with Britain, and finally declared that they could act as all other nations could act. These acts included forming their own government, beginning and ending wars, forming alliances, trading their goods with whomever they chose, and other necessary acts of government. In short, the colonies declared themselves free to form a government that would do as described by Jefferson in the Preamble of the Declaration. They would work to form a government that they designed to protect life, liberty, and property.

In all of this, the Founders placed their trust in divine Providence. It would only be, as Jefferson wrote, "with a firm reliance on the protection of divine Providence," "appealing to the Supreme Judge of the world," that the colonies would be successful in enforcing the ideas of the Declaration. Their reliance on the protection of divine Providence called for numerous days of "humiliation and prayer." These colonists humbled themselves before the "Supreme Judge," with mayors, governors, and Congress all called for numerous days of prayer. By humbling themselves, calling for the protection of God and seeking only for that which were their unalienable rights and a government that would safeguard those rights, they believed that the blessings of liberty would come to them. In order to prove their dedication, they pledged everything they had in order to support the Declaration of Independence. All they had was their property, their lives, and their sacred honor.

The Cost of Liberty

Many people mistakenly thought that the Founders committed treason. However, the law and the enumerated rights in both the Magna Carta and the English Bill of Rights of 1689 proved quite the opposite. But human and civil rights mean nothing to a tyrant. The Founders recognized this. They also understood that if they were caught, the king would execute them, alleging they were traitors though they were really opponents of the king's abuses of power. Franklin said it best when he signed the Declaration: "We must indeed all hang together, or most assuredly we shall all hang separately!"[250]

So the Founders stayed united. But at what cost? Just looking at several of the signers of the Declaration of Independence will show that the cost they paid was high indeed.

Francis Lewis of New York forfeited all property that he owned on Long Island when the British invaded New York and took over Long Island near the opening of the Revolutionary War.[251] Furthermore, the British "had the brutality to confine his wife in a close prison for several months, without a bed or a change of raiment, whereby her constitution was ruined, and she died two years afterward."[252]

After signing the Declaration and serving honorably in Congress until the end of 1778, George Walton of Georgia received a commission as a colonel in the army that worked to defend Savannah from the invading British military. In that defense, Walton received a severe gunshot wound to his thigh, and the British took him prisoner. Soon after, he returned to Georgia after a prisoner exchange, worked as a governor, and then as the chief justice of the state until his death.[253]

John Hart of New Jersey had his property looted during the war. His wife died just months after he signed the Declaration, and in 1778 he invited the Continental army to encamp on his farm, which happened to be during growing season—a bad time for his fields to be trampled on.[254] In 1776 when Washington fled New York and New Jersey with the British chasing him, Hart learned of the coming of the British and Hessian armies. He and his family fled. As a result, the armies ravaged his farm, destroyed his timber, and used his livestock to feed the armies that Hart opposed. "He did not live to see the sunlight of Peace and Independence gladden the face of his country. He died in the year 1780 (the gloomiest period of the War of Independence)."[255]

Robert Morris of Pennsylvania helped in numerous ways, including loaning the government $10,000 of his own money, which was a substantial sum in 1776.[256] In 1781, near the conclusion of the war, Congress could obtain no loans for continuing the war. However, "Robert Morris effected loans upon his own credit of tens of thousands. … There is no doubt that these patriotic services of Robert Morris present the chief reason why the Continental army was not at that time disbanded by its own act."[257]

Carter Braxton of Virginia, along with Robert Morris and others, invested heavily in shipping in order to assist the army by transporting cotton, food supplies, and other needed goods. Braxton and his associates took damaging losses. "Beginning in 1777, when the British blockade was first tightened around Chesapeake Bay, Braxton and his associates incurred heavy losses to enemy cruisers until at least half of the vessels they had outfitted were swept from the seas."[258] One ship alone, The Bird, was lost totaling "no less than £40,000—and this in a single disaster."[259] In today's dollars, this would roughly estimate to a loss of close to $1 million. This was only one of the many ships that Braxton and his associates utilized and lost.

In spite of his worldly interests, Lewis Morris of New York signed the Declaration. As a result his house was ruined, his farm and a thousand acres of forest on his land destroyed or despoiled, his cattle and other animals stolen, and "his family driven into exile by the invading foe. … When peace was restored, he returned to his scathed and almost ruined estate."[260]

Thomas Heyward Jr. of South Carolina was a bold patriot. After signing the Declaration and serving in Congress until 1778, he returned to South Carolina and became a judge. Despite having the means to live a comfortable retirement, he chose to act as a judge. Even though the enemy was in the vicinity of his judging, it had no effect on him. "He tried, and caused to be executed, virtually within sight of the British lines, several persons who were found guilty of treason."[261] Heyward also held a military commission, and in one skirmish received a wound that scarred him for life. In addition, the British took him prisoner, and while prisoner, "soldiers were sent to his plantation and carried off all his slaves," most of which he never recovered. Though today it is a horrible thought to price human beings, his loss of his slaves cost him over fifty thousand dollars, which is equal to hundreds of thousands of dollars today. He also lost his wife during this time.[262]

The British accused Georgian Lyman Hall of high treason and then burned his property in Savannah. He fled to Charleston and then to Connecticut where he stayed with family.[263] He would later return to Georgia but would not live long enough to see the greatest fruit of Independence, the US Constitution. He died in 1784.

After signing the Declaration, Joseph Hewes of North Carolina placed all his ships in the service of the armed forces.[264] He was the first of the signers to die while serving in Congress. He passed away before the end of the War for Independence.[265]

New Yorker Philip Livingston was yet another Founder dedicated to the cause of independence. After signing the Declaration and despite suffering from dropsy (also known as edema), "he obeyed the calls of duty, and took his seat in Congress" for a second time. Within nine months of his election in 1777, "his disease then suddenly terminated his life."[266] He heeded the call to duty and it cost him his life.

Richard Stockton of New Jersey was captured by the British because of the treachery of a friend's neighbor. Stockton had been staying with a friend to avoid capture by the British. Due to Stockton's "position as one of the signers of the Declaration of Independence, [he] was treated with great severity." The hardships he endured physically, as well as the vandalism and destruction of his estate, left him in a "despondency from which he never recovered." He died about eight months before the surrender of British General Cornwallis at Yorktown.[267]

One of South Carolina's signers, Edward Rutledge, worked tirelessly to defend his colony from invasion. Eventually, Rutledge took up arms as the head of a corps of artillery. In 1780, while trying to insert troops into the besieged city of Charleston, the British took him prisoner and sent him to St. Augustine, Florida. The British held him for nearly a year before his release in a prisoner exchange. Thus, in the midst of fighting for the liberties of his countrymen, he lost his own liberty for a time.[268]

The British seized the estate of signer William Floyd of New York and used it as a rendezvous point for their cavalry. They also confiscated Floyd's sheep and cattle to provide themselves provisions. Floyd was never paid for the many years of the use of his estate or for his animals. Still, "he abated not a jot in his zeal for the cause." After the war ended and Floyd returned to his estate, from which the British had exiled him for many years, he found it terribly dilapidated.[269]

One of the most remarkable instances of pledging life, fortune, and sacred honor was that of Thomas Nelson Jr. of Virginia. After signing and returning home to Virginia to recover from illness, Virginia called on him to lead the militia to defend against the fleet of Lord Howe. Rather than landing in Virginia, British commander Howe landed in Philadelphia, which created a need for defense there in 1777. Congress called upon all men for aid in recruiting an army. Nelson used his influence and money to raise a volunteer army. He knew of the tough financial situations of those who volunteered and used all in his means to support them, including giving money to ameliorate the condition of their families and sending his own numerous servants to help in their fields. In 1780, Congress felt that the soon-to-be-arriving French needed provisions supplied to them, yet Congress was powerless to borrow money and collect taxes. Nelson immediately sought to raise money from many wealthy persons who refused to lend Congress money but would contribute on the basis of Nelson granting them his personal security. Later in 1781, even after becoming governor of Virginia, he raised and led an army to help stop Cornwallis, which led to the eventual capture of Cornwallis at Yorktown. With Washington laying siege on Yorktown, Nelson found the American army sparing his own mansion out of respect, to which "he begged them not to make any difference on that account, and at once a well-directed fire was opened upon it."[270] All of Nelson's time, money, and property he freely and gladly gave to the cause of independence. His example shows the deep level of commitment the signers had in the cause for independence.

Of course, many others signed the Declaration of Independence. And far more fought, bled, and died, giving along with the signers their fortune, sacred honor, and very lives.

Forward with Freedom

The principles of the Declaration of Independence stand the test of time. Human nature does not change. Humankind naturally possesses an inherent desire for freedom, a desire to do as one sees fit, a desire to act without interference from others.

The purpose for entering into society is for the mutual protection of the natural, unalienable rights of man. All of us—male and female—have the right to live and to live according to the dictates of our conscience as long as we do not infringe on the rights of others.

We also have the natural right to liberty. Liberty allows each of us to pursue our own dreams and ideas and to make plans for the future or squander our time. No other person has the right to infringe on another's liberty, and this includes by slavery, unjust confinement, and the excessive regulation of what one may or may not do.

Finally, we human beings have the natural, unalienable right to property. After all, what is an individual if he or she has no property? Property is what we possess when we apply our labor to an item. This may involve picking a peach off a tree owned in common—in other words, a tree no one has purchased or has laid claim to or put forth any labor to take care of. This may also involve our working for money and then using our funds to purchase an item from a store. Our labor makes the peach we pick, the money we earn, or the items we buy our property. Property is essential to life and to liberty. Life, liberty, and property are all essential to our existence. Human beings are nothing without any one of these three. If a person is not at liberty to acquire property to sustain life, such as shelter, clothing, and food, and if that person cannot own these items needed to sustain life, this individual will soon lose his or her life. Therefore, *both* liberty and property are essential to life. Thus, the proper role of government is to protect man's unalienable rights to life, liberty, and property.

Of course, the Declaration of Independence is a declaration of separation from England. But it is also a declaration for the unalienable rights of all human beings—rights given to us by our Creator. Only the Creator may revoke these rights. And no human authority or government has the right to trump these God-given human rights. Jefferson's words are not for Americans alone. They are for all humankind, declaring to all human governments and all human authorities that the supreme Authority has endowed humankind with certain unalienable rights that must be upheld lest severe consequences may follow.

On July 4, 1826, fifty years after the signing of the Declaration of Independence, both the author of the Declaration, Thomas Jefferson, and one of the greatest advocates for independence, John Adams, died. Later, Daniel Webster eulogized John Adams in Boston's Faneuil Hall. While Adams never gave the speech, Webster captured the essence of Adams' feelings about the Declaration and the independence that followed. His eulogy provides a fitting conclusion to this book, and I present it here in its entirety:

Sink or swim, live or die, survive or perish, I give my hand and my heart to this vote. It is true, indeed, that in the beginning we aimed not at independence. But there's a Divinity which shapes our ends. The injustice of England has driven us to arms; and, blinded to her own interest for our good, she has obstinately persisted, till independence is now within our grasp. We have but to reach forth to it, and it is ours. Why, then, should we defer the Declaration? Is any man so weak as now to hope for a reconciliation with England, which shall leave either safety to the country and its liberties, or safety to his own life and his own honor? Are not you, sir, who sit in that chair, is not he, our venerable colleague, near you, are you not both already the proscribed and predestined objects of punishment and of vengeance? Cut off from all hope of royal clemency, what are you, what can you be, while the power of England remains, but outlaws? If we postpone independence, do we mean to carry on, or to give up, the war? Do we mean to submit to the measures of Parliament,

Boston Port Bill and all? Do we mean to submit, and consent that we ourselves shall be ground to powder, and our country and its rights trodden down in the dust? I know we do not mean to submit. We never shall submit. Do we intend to violate that most solemn obligation ever entered into by men, that plighting, before God, of our sacred honor to Washington, when, putting him forth to incur the dangers of war, as well as the political hazards of the times, we promised to adhere to him, in every extremity, with our fortunes and our lives? I know there is not a man here, who would not rather see a general conflagration sweep over the land, or an earthquake sink it, than one jot or tittle of that plighted faith fall to the ground. For myself, having, twelve months ago, in this place, moved you, that George Washington be appointed commander of the forces raised, or to be raised, for defence of American liberty, may my right hand forget her cunning, and my tongue cleave to the roof of my mouth, if I hesitate or waver in the support I give him.

The war, then, must go on. We must fight it through. And if the war must go on, why put off longer the Declaration of Independence? That measure will strengthen us. It will give us character abroad. The nations will then treat with us, which they never can do while we acknowledge ourselves subjects, in arms against our sovereign. Nay, I maintain that England herself will sooner treat for peace with us on the footing of independence, than consent, by repealing her acts, to acknowledge that her whole conduct towards us has been a course of injustice and oppression. Her pride will be less wounded by submitting to that course of things which now predestinates our independence, than by yielding the points in controversy to her rebellious subjects. The former she would regard as the result of fortune; the latter she would feel as her own deep disgrace. Why, then, why then, sir, do we not as soon as possible change this from a civil to a national war? And since we must fight it through, why not put ourselves in a state to enjoy all the benefits of victory, if we gain the victory?

If we fail, it can be no worse for us. But we shall not fail. The cause will raise up armies; the cause will create navies. The people, the people, if we are true to them, will carry us, and will carry themselves, gloriously, through this struggle. I care not how fickle other people have been found. I know the people of these Colonies, and I know that resistance to British aggression is deep and settled in their hearts and cannot be eradicated. Every Colony, indeed, has expressed its willingness to follow, if we but take the lead. Sir, the Declaration will inspire the people with increased courage. Instead of a long and bloody war for the restoration of privileges, for redress of grievances, for chartered immunities, held under a British king, set before them the glorious object of entire independence, and it will breathe into them anew the breath of life. Read this Declaration at the head of the army; every sword will be drawn from its scabbard, and the solemn vow uttered, to maintain it, or to perish on the bed of honor. Publish it from the pulpit; religion will approve it, and the love of religious liberty will cling round it, resolved to stand with it, or fall with it. Send it to the public halls; proclaim it there; let them hear it who heard the first roar of the enemy's cannon; let them see it who saw their brothers and their sons fall on the field of Bunker Hill, and in the streets of Lexington and Concord, and the very walls will cry out in its support.

Sir, I know the uncertainty of human affairs, but I see, I see clearly, through this day's business. You and I, indeed, may rue it. We may not live to the time when this Declaration shall be made good. We may die; die colonists; die slaves; die, it may be, ignominiously and on the scaffold. Be it so. Be it so. If it be the pleasure of Heaven that my country shall require the poor offering of my life, the victim shall be ready, at the appointed hour of sacrifice, come when that hour may. But while I do live, let me have a country, or at least the hope of a country, and that a free country.

But whatever may be our fate, be assured, be assured that this Declaration will stand. It may cost treasure, and it may cost blood; but it will stand, and it will richly compensate for both. Through the thick gloom of the present, I see the brightness of the future, as the sun in heaven. We shall make this a glorious, an immortal day. When we are in our graves, our children will honor it. They will celebrate it with thanksgiving, with festivity, with bonfires, and illuminations. On its annual return they will shed tears, copious, gushing tears, not of subjection and slavery, not of agony and distress, but of exultation, of gratitude, and of joy. Sir, before God, I believe the hour is come. My judgment approves this measure, and my whole heart is in it. All that I have, and all that I am, and all that I hope, in this life, I am now ready here to stake upon it; and I leave off as I begun, that live or die, survive or perish, I am for the Declaration. It is my living sentiment, and by the blessing of God it shall be my dying sentiment, Independence, now, and Independence forever![271]

May we all mutually pledge, as did the Founders, to support this Declaration "with a firm reliance on the protection of divine Providence … [dedicating] our Lives, our Fortunes and our sacred Honor." With Abraham Lincoln, I urge "you to come back. … [C]ome back to the truths that are in the Declaration of Independence."

APPENDICES

The Magna Carta

Preamble: John, by the grace of God, king of England, lord of Ireland, duke of Normandy and Aquitaine, and count of Anjou, to the archbishop, bishops, abbots, earls, barons, justiciaries, foresters, sheriffs, stewards, servants, and to all his bailiffs and liege subjects, greetings. Know that, having regard to God and for the salvation of our soul, and those of all our ancestors and heirs, and unto the honor of God and the advancement of his holy Church and for the rectifying of our realm, we have granted as underwritten by advice of our venerable fathers, Stephen, archbishop of Canterbury, primate of all England and cardinal of the holy Roman Church, Henry, archbishop of Dublin, William of London, Peter of Winchester, Jocelyn of Bath and Glastonbury, Hugh of Lincoln, Walter of Worcester, William of Coventry, Benedict of Rochester, bishops; of Master Pandulf, subdeacon and member of the household of our lord the Pope, of brother Aymeric (master of the Knights of the Temple in England), and of the illustrious men William Marshal, earl of Pembroke, William, earl of Salisbury, William, earl of Warenne, William, earl of Arundel, Alan of Galloway (constable of Scotland), Waren Fitz Gerold, Peter Fitz Herbert, Hubert De Burgh (seneschal of Poitou), Hugh de Neville, Matthew Fitz Herbert, Thomas Basset, Alan Basset, Philip d'Aubigny, Robert of Roppesley, John Marshal, John Fitz Hugh, and others, our liegemen.

1. In the first place we have granted to God, and by this our present charter confirmed for us and our heirs forever that the English Church shall be free, and shall have her rights entire, and her liberties inviolate; and we will that it be thus observed; which is apparent from this that the freedom of elections, which is reckoned most important and very essential to the English Church, we, of our pure and unconstrained will, did grant, and did by our charter confirm and did obtain the ratification of the same from our lord, Pope Innocent III, before the quarrel arose between us and our barons: and this we will observe, and our will is that it be observed in good faith by our heirs forever. We have also granted to all freemen of our kingdom, for us and our heirs forever, all the underwritten liberties, to be had and held by them and their heirs, of us and our heirs forever.

2. If any of our earls or barons, or others holding of us in chief by military service shall have died, and at the time of his death his heir shall be full of age and owe "relief," he shall have his inheritance by the old relief, to wit, the heir or heirs of an earl, for the whole barony of an earl by £100; the heir or heirs of a baron, £100 for a whole barony; the heir or heirs of a knight, 100s, at most, and whoever owes less let him give less, according to the ancient custom of fees.

3. If, however, the heir of any one of the aforesaid has been under age and in wardship, let him have his inheritance without relief and without fine when he comes of age.

4. The guardian of the land of an heir who is thus under age, shall take from the land of the heir nothing but reasonable produce, reasonable customs, and reasonable services, and that without destruction or waste of men or goods; and if we have committed the wardship of the lands of any such minor to the sheriff, or to any other who is responsible to us for its issues, and he has made destruction or waster of what he holds in wardship, we will take of him amends, and the land shall be committed to two lawful and discreet men of that fee, who shall be responsible for the issues to us or to him to whom we shall assign them; and if we have given or sold the wardship of any such land to anyone and he has therein made destruction or waste, he shall lose that wardship, and it shall be transferred to two lawful and discreet men of that fief, who shall be responsible to us in like manner as aforesaid.

5. The guardian, moreover, so long as he has the wardship of the land, shall keep up the houses, parks, fishponds, stanks, mills, and other things pertaining to the land, out of the issues of the same land; and he shall restore to the heir, when he has come to full age, all his land, stocked with ploughs and wainage, according as the season of husbandry shall require, and the issues of the land can reasonable bear.

6. Heirs shall be married without disparagement, yet so that before the marriage takes place the nearest in blood to that heir shall have notice.

7. A widow, after the death of her husband, shall forthwith and without difficulty have her marriage portion and inheritance; nor shall she give anything for her dower, or for her marriage portion, or for the inheritance which her husband and she held on the day of the death of that husband; and she may remain in the house of her husband for forty days after his death, within which time her dower shall be assigned to her.

8. No widow shall be compelled to marry, so long as she prefers to live without a husband; provided always that she gives security not to marry without our consent, if she holds of us, or without the consent of the lord of whom she holds, if she holds of another.

9. Neither we nor our bailiffs will seize any land or rent for any debt, as long as the chattels of the debtor are sufficient to repay the debt; nor shall the sureties of the debtor be distrained so long as the principal debtor is able to satisfy the debt; and if the principal debtor shall fail to pay the debt, having nothing wherewith to pay it, then the sureties shall answer for the debt; and let them have the lands and rents of the debtor, if they desire them, until they are indemnified for the debt which they have paid for him, unless the principal debtor can show proof that he is discharged thereof as against the said sureties.

10. If one who has borrowed from the Jews any sum, great or small, die before that loan be repaid, the debt shall not bear interest while the heir is under age, of whomsoever he may hold; and if the debt fall into our hands, we will not take anything except the principal sum contained in the bond.

11. And if anyone die indebted to the Jews, his wife shall have her dower and pay nothing of that debt; and if any children of the deceased are left under age, necessaries shall be provided for them in keeping with the holding of the

deceased; and out of the residue the debt shall be paid, reserving, however, service due to feudal lords; in like manner let it be done touching debts due to others than Jews.

12. No scutage not aid shall be imposed on our kingdom, unless by common counsel of our kingdom, except for ransoming our person, for making our eldest son a knight, and for once marrying our eldest daughter; and for these there shall not be levied more than a reasonable aid. In like manner, it shall be done concerning aids from the city of London.

13. And the city of London shall have all it ancient liberties and free customs, as well by land as by water; furthermore, we decree and grant that all other cities, boroughs, towns, and ports shall have all their liberties and free customs.

14. And for obtaining the common counsel of the kingdom anent the assessing of an aid (except in the three cases aforesaid) or of a scutage, we will cause to be summoned the archbishops, bishops, abbots, earls, and greater barons, severally by our letters; and we will moreover cause to be summoned generally, through our sheriffs and bailiffs, and others who hold of us in chief, for a fixed date, namely, after the expiry of at least forty days, and at a fixed place; and in all letters of such summons we will specify the reason of the summons. And when the summons has thus been made, the business shall proceed on the day appointed, according to the counsel of such as are present, although not all who were summoned have come.

15. We will not for the future grant to anyone license to take an aid from his own free tenants, except to ransom his person, to make his eldest son a knight, and once to marry his eldest daughter; and on each of these occasions there shall be levied only a reasonable aid.

16. No one shall be distrained for performance of greater service for a knight's fee, or for any other free tenement, than is due therefrom.

17. Common pleas shall not follow our court, but shall be held in some fixed place.

18. Inquests of novel disseisin, of mort d'ancestor, and of darrein presentment shall not be held elsewhere than in their own county courts, and that in manner following; We, or, if we should be out of the realm, our chief justiciar, will send two justiciaries through every county four times a year, who shall alone with four

knights of the county chosen by the county, hold the said assizes in the county court, on the day and in the place of meeting of that court.

19. And if any of the said assizes cannot be taken on the day of the county court, let there remain of the knights and freeholders, who were present at the county court on that day, as many as may be required for the efficient making of judgments, according as the business be more or less.

20. A freeman shall not be amerced for a slight offense, except in accordance with the degree of the offense; and for a grave offense he shall be amerced in accordance with the gravity of the offense, yet saving always his "contentment"; and a merchant in the same way, saving his "merchandise"; and a villein shall be amerced in the same way, saving his "wainage" if they have fallen into our mercy: and none of the aforesaid amercements shall be imposed except by the oath of honest men of the neighborhood.

21. Earls and barons shall not be amerced except through their peers, and only in accordance with the degree of the offense.

22. A clerk shall not be amerced in respect of his lay holding except after the manner of the others aforesaid; further, he shall not be amerced in accordance with the extent of his ecclesiastical benefice.

23. No village or individual shall be compelled to make bridges at river banks, except those who from of old were legally bound to do so.

24. No sheriff, constable, coroners, or others of our bailiffs, shall hold pleas of our Crown.

25. All counties, hundred, wapentakes, and trithings (except our demesne manors) shall remain at the old rents, and without any additional payment.

26. If anyone holding of us a lay fief shall die, and our sheriff or bailiff shall exhibit our letters patent of summons for a debt which the deceased owed us, it shall be lawful for our sheriff or bailiff to attach and enroll the chattels of the deceased, found upon the lay fief, to the value of that debt, at the sight of law worthy men, provided always that nothing whatever be thence removed until the debt which is evident shall be fully paid to us; and the residue shall be left to the executors to fulfill the will of the deceased; and if there be nothing due from him to us, all the chattels shall go to the deceased, saving to his wife and children their reasonable shares.

27. If any freeman shall die intestate, his chattels shall be distributed by the hands of his nearest kinsfolk and friends, under supervision of the Church, saving to every one the debts which the deceased owed to him.

28. No constable or other bailiff of ours shall take corn or other provisions from anyone without immediately tendering money therefor, unless he can have postponement thereof by permission of the seller.

29. No constable shall compel any knight to give money in lieu of castle-guard, when he is willing to perform it in his own person, or (if he himself cannot do it from any reasonable cause) then by another responsible man. Further, if we have led or sent him upon military service, he shall be relieved from guard in proportion to the time during which he has been on service because of us.

30. No sheriff or bailiff of ours, or other person, shall take the horses or carts of any freeman for transport duty, against the will of the said freeman.

31. Neither we nor our bailiffs shall take, for our castles or for any other work of ours, wood which is not ours, against the will of the owner of that wood.

32. We will not retain beyond one year and one day, the lands those who have been convicted of felony, and the lands shall thereafter be handed over to the lords of the fiefs.

33. All kydells for the future shall be removed altogether from Thames and Medway, and throughout all England, except upon the seashore.

34. The writ which is called praecipe shall not for the future be issued to anyone, regarding any tenement whereby a freeman may lose his court.

35. Let there be one measure of wine throughout our whole realm; and one measure of ale; and one measure of corn, to wit, "the London quarter"; and one width of cloth (whether dyed, or russet, or "halberget"), to wit, two ells within the selvedges; of weights also let it be as of measures.

36. Nothing in future shall be given or taken for a writ of inquisition of life or limbs, but freely it shall be granted, and never denied.

37. If anyone holds of us by fee-farm, either by socage or by burage, or of any other land by knight's service, we will not (by reason of that feefarm, socage, or burgage), have the wardship of the heir, or of such land of his as if of the fief of that other; nor shall we have wardship of that feefarm, socage, or burgage, unless such fee-farm owes knight's service. We will not by reason of any small serjeancy

which anyone may hold of us by the service of rendering to us knives, arrows, or the like, have wardship of his heir or of the land which he holds of another lord by knight's service.

38. No bailiff for the future shall, upon his own unsupported complaint, put anyone to his "law," without credible witnesses brought for this purposes.

39. No freemen shall be taken or imprisoned or disseised or exiled or in any way destroyed, nor will we go upon him nor send upon him, except by the lawful judgment of his peers or by the law of the land.

40. To no one will we sell, to no one will we refuse or delay, right or justice.

41. All merchants shall have safe and secure exit from England, and entry to England, with the right to tarry there and to move about as well by land as by water, for buying and selling by the ancient and right customs, quit from all evil tolls, except (in time of war) such merchants as are of the land at war with us. And if such are found in our land at the beginning of the war, they shall be detained, without injury to their bodies or goods, until information be received by us, or by our chief justiciar, how the merchants of our land found in the land at war with us are treated; and if our men are safe there, the others shall be safe in our land.

42. It shall be lawful in future for anyone (excepting always those imprisoned or outlawed in accordance with the law of the kingdom, and natives of any country at war with us, and merchants, who shall be treated as if above provided) to leave our kingdom and to return, safe and secure by land and water, except for a short period in time of war, on grounds of public policy reserving always the allegiance due to us.

43. If anyone holding of some escheat (such as the honor of Wallingford, Nottingham, Boulogne, Lancaster, or of other escheats which are in our hands and are baronies) shall die, his heir shall give no other relief, and perform no other service to us than he would have done to the baron if that barony had been in the baron's hand; and we shall hold it in the same manner in which the baron held it.

44. Men who dwell without the forest need not henceforth come before our justiciaries of the forest upon a general summons, unless they are in plea, or sureties of one or more, who are attached for the forest.

45. We will appoint as justices, constables, sheriffs, or bailiffs only such as know the law of the realm and mean to observe it well.

46. All barons who have founded abbeys, concerning which they hold charters from the kings of England, or of which they have long continued possession, shall have the wardship of them, when vacant, as they ought to have.

47. All forests that have been made such in our time shall forthwith be disafforsted; and a similar course shall be followed with regard to river banks that have been placed "in defense" by us in our time.

48. All evil customs connected with forests and warrens, foresters and warreners, sheriffs and their officers, river banks and their wardens, shall immediately by inquired into in each county by twelve sworn knights of the same county chosen by the honest men of the same county, and shall, within forty days of the said inquest, be utterly abolished, so as never to be restored, provided always that we previously have intimation thereof, or our justiciar, if we should not be in England.

49. We will immediately restore all hostages and charters delivered to us by Englishmen, as sureties of the peace of faithful service.

50. We will entirely remove from their bailiwicks, the relations of Gerard of Athee (so that in future they shall have no bailiwick in England); namely, Engelard of Cigogne, Peter, Guy, and Andrew of Chanceaux, Guy of Cigogne, Geoffrey of Martigny with his brothers, Philip Mark with his brothers and his nephew Geoffrey, and the whole brood of the same.

51. As soon as peace is restored, we will banish from the kingdom all foreign born knights, crossbowmen, serjeants, and mercenary soldiers who have come with horses and arms to the kingdom's hurt.

52. If anyone has been dispossessed or removed by us, without the legal judgment of his peers, from his lands, castles, franchises, or from his right, we will immediately restore them to him; and if a dispute arise over this, then let it be decided by the five and twenty barons of whom mention is made below in the clause for securing the peace. Moreover, for all those possessions, from which anyone has, without the lawful judgment of his peers, been disseised or removed, by our father, King Henry, or by our brother, King Richard, and which we retain in our hand (or which as possessed by others, to whom we are bound to warrant

them) we shall have respite until the usual term of crusaders; excepting those things about which a plea has been raised, or an inquest made by our order, before our taking of the cross; but as soon as we return from the expedition, we will immediately grant full justice therein.

53. We shall have, moreover, the same respite and in the same manner in rendering justice concerning the disafforestation or retention of those forests which Henry our father and Richard our brother afforested, and concerning the wardship of lands which are of the fief of another (namely, such wardships as we have hitherto had by reason of a fief which anyone held of us by knight's service), and concerning abbeys founded on other fiefs than our own, in which the lord of the fee claims to have right; and when we have returned, or if we desist from our expedition, we will immediately grant full justice to all who complain of such things.

54. No one shall be arrested or imprisoned upon the appeal of a woman, for the death of any other than her husband.

55. All fines made with us unjustly and against the law of the land, and all amercements, imposed unjustly and against the law of the land, shall be entirely remitted, or else it shall be done concerning them according to the decision of the five and twenty barons whom mention is made below in the clause for securing the pease, or according to the judgment of the majority of the same, along with the aforesaid Stephen, archbishop of Canterbury, if he can be present, and such others as he may wish to bring with him for this purpose, and if he cannot be present the business shall nevertheless proceed without him, provided always that if any one or more of the aforesaid five and twenty barons are in a similar suit, they shall be removed as far as concerns this particular judgment, others being substituted in their places after having been selected by the rest of the same five and twenty for this purpose only, and after having been sworn.

56. If we have disseised or removed Welshmen from lands or liberties, or other things, without the legal judgment of their peers in England or in Wales, they shall be immediately restored to them; and if a dispute arise over this, then let it be decided in the marches by the judgment of their peers; for the tenements in England according to the law of England, for tenements in Wales according

to the law of Wales, and for tenements in the marches according to the law of the marches. Welshmen shall do the same to us and ours.

57. Further, for all those possessions from which any Welshman has, without the lawful judgment of his peers, been disseised or removed by King Henry our father, or King Richard our brother, and which we retain in our hand (or which are possessed by others, and which we ought to warrant), we will have respite until the usual term of crusaders; excepting those things about which a plea has been raised or an inquest made by our order before we took the cross; but as soon as we return (or if perchance we desist from our expedition), we will immediately grant full justice in accordance with the laws of the Welsh and in relation to the foresaid regions.

58. We will immediately give up the son of Llywelyn and all the hostages of Wales, and the charters delivered to us as security for the peace.

59. We will do towards Alexander, king of Scots, concerning the return of his sisters and his hostages, and concerning his franchises, and his right, in the same manner as we shall do towards our other barons of England, unless it ought to be otherwise according to the charters which we hold from William his father, formerly king of Scots; and this shall be according to the judgment of his peers in our court.

60. Moreover, all these aforesaid customs and liberties, the observances of which we have granted in our kingdom as far as pertains to us towards our men, shall be observed by all of our kingdom, as well clergy as laymen, as far as pertains to them towards their men.

61. Since, moreover, for God and the amendment of our kingdom and for the better allaying of the quarrel that has arisen between us and our barons, we have granted all these concessions, desirous that they should enjoy them in complete and firm endurance forever, we give and grant to them the underwritten security, namely, that the barons choose five and twenty barons of the kingdom, whomsoever they will, who shall be bound with all their might, to observe and hold, and cause to be observed, the peace and liberties we have granted and confirmed to them by this our present Charter, so that if we, or our justiciar, or our bailiffs or any one of our officers, shall in anything be at fault towards anyone, or shall have broken any one of the articles of this peace or of this security, and

the offense be notified to four barons of the foresaid five and twenty, the said four barons shall repair to us (or our justiciar, if we are out of the realm) and, laying the transgression before us, petition to have that transgression redressed without delay. And if we shall not have corrected the transgression (or, in the event of our being out of the realm, if our justiciar shall not have corrected it) within forty days, reckoning from the time it has been intimated to us (or to our justiciar, if we should be out of the realm), the four barons aforesaid shall refer that matter to the rest of the five and twenty barons, and those five and twenty barons shall, together with the community of the whole realm, distrain and distress us in all possible ways, namely, by seizing our castles, lands, possessions, and in any other way they can, until redress has been obtained as they deem fit, saving harmless our own person, and the persons of our queen and children; and when redress has been obtained, they shall resume their old relations towards us. And let whoever in the country desires it, swear to obey the orders of the said five and twenty barons for the execution of all the aforesaid matters, and along with them, to molest us to the utmost of his power; and we publicly and freely grant leave to everyone who wishes to swear, and we shall never forbid anyone to swear. All those, moreover, in the land who of themselves and of their own accord are unwilling to swear to the twenty five to help them in constraining and molesting us, we shall by our command compel the same to swear to the effect foresaid. And if any one of the five and twenty barons shall have died or departed from the land, or be incapacitated in any other manner which would prevent the foresaid provisions being carried out, those of the said twenty five barons who are left shall choose another in his place according to their own judgment, and he shall be sworn in the same way as the others. Further, in all matters, the execution of which is entrusted, to these twenty five barons, if perchance these twenty five are present and disagree about anything, or if some of them, after being summoned, are unwilling or unable to be present, that which the majority of those present ordain or command shall be held as fixed and established, exactly as if the whole twenty five had concurred in this; and the said twenty five shall swear that they will faithfully observe all that is aforesaid, and cause it to be observed with all their might. And we shall procure nothing from anyone, directly or indirectly, whereby any part of these concessions and liberties might be revoked or diminished; and if any such things has been procured, let it be void and null, and we shall never use it personally or by another.

62. And all the will, hatreds, and bitterness that have arisen between us and our men, clergy and lay, from the date of the quarrel, we have completely remitted and pardoned to everyone. Moreover, all trespasses occasioned by the said quarrel, from Easter in the sixteenth year of our reign till the restoration of peace, we have fully remitted to all, both clergy and laymen, and completely forgiven, as far as pertains to us. And on this head, we have caused to be made for them letters testimonial patent of the lord Stephen, archbishop of Canterbury, of the lord Henry, archbishop of Dublin, of the bishops aforesaid, and of Master Pandulf as touching this security and the concessions aforesaid.

63. Wherefore we will and firmly order that the English Church be free, and that the men in our kingdom have and hold all the aforesaid liberties, rights, and concessions, well and peaceably, freely and quietly, fully and wholly, for themselves and their heirs, of us and our heirs, in all respects and in all places forever, as is aforesaid. An oath, moreover, has been taken, as well on our part as on the art of the barons, that all these conditions aforesaid shall be kept in good faith and without evil intent. Given under our hand—the above named and many others being witnesses—in the meadow which is called Runnymede, between Windsor and Staines, on the fifteenth day of June, in the seventeenth year of our reign.

The English Bill of Rights of 1689

An Act Declaring the Rights and Liberties of the Subject and Settling the Succession of the Crown.

Whereas the Lords Spiritual and Temporal and Commons assembled at Westminster, lawfully, fully and freely representing all the estates of the people of this realm, did upon the thirteenth day of February in the year of our Lord one thousand six hundred eighty-eight [old style date] present unto their Majesties, then called and known by the names and style of William and Mary, prince and princess of Orange, being present in their proper persons, a certain declaration in writing made by the said Lords and Commons in the words following, viz.:

Whereas the late King James the Second, by the assistance of divers evil counsellors, judges and ministers employed by him, did endeavour to subvert and extirpate the Protestant religion and the laws and liberties of this kingdom;

By assuming and exercising a power of dispensing with and suspending of laws and the execution of laws without consent of Parliament;

By committing and prosecuting divers worthy prelates for humbly petitioning to be excused from concurring to the said assumed power;

By issuing and causing to be executed a commission under the great seal for erecting a court called the Court of Commissioners for Ecclesiastical Causes;

By levying money for and to the use of the Crown by pretence of prerogative for other time and in other manner than the same was granted by Parliament;

By raising and keeping a standing army within this kingdom in time of peace without consent of Parliament, and quartering soldiers contrary to law;

By causing several good subjects being Protestants to be disarmed at the same time when papists were both armed and employed contrary to law;

By violating the freedom of election of members to serve in Parliament;

By prosecutions in the Court of King's Bench for matters and causes cognizable only in Parliament, and by divers other arbitrary and illegal courses;

And whereas of late years partial corrupt and unqualified persons have been returned and served on juries in trials, and particularly divers jurors in trials for high treason which were not freeholders;

And excessive bail hath been required of persons committed in criminal cases to elude the benefit of the laws made for the liberty of the subjects;

And excessive fines have been imposed;

And illegal and cruel punishments inflicted;

And several grants and promises made of fines and forfeitures before any conviction or judgment against the persons upon whom the same were to be levied;

All which are utterly and directly contrary to the known laws and statutes and freedom of this realm;

And whereas the said late King James the Second having abdicated the government and the throne being thereby vacant, his Highness the prince of Orange (whom it hath pleased Almighty God to make the glorious instrument of delivering this kingdom from popery and arbitrary power) did (by the advice of the Lords Spiritual and Temporal and divers principal persons of the Commons) cause letters to be written to the Lords Spiritual and Temporal being Protestants, and other letters to the several counties, cities, universities, boroughs and cinque ports, for the choosing of such persons to represent them as were of right to be sent to Parliament, to meet and sit at Westminster upon the two and twentieth day of January in this year one thousand six hundred eighty and eight [old style date], in order to such an establishment as that their religion, laws and liberties might not again be in danger of being subverted, upon which letters elections having been accordingly made;

And thereupon the said Lords Spiritual and Temporal and Commons, pursuant to their respective letters and elections, being now assembled in a full and free representative of this nation, taking into their most serious consideration the best means for attaining the ends aforesaid, do in the first place (as their ancestors in like case have usually done) for the vindicating and asserting their ancient rights and liberties declare

That the pretended power of suspending the laws or the execution of laws by regal authority without consent of Parliament is illegal;

That the pretended power of dispensing with laws or the execution of laws by regal authority, as it hath been assumed and exercised of late, is illegal;

That the commission for erecting the late Court of Commissioners for Ecclesiastical Causes, and all other commissions and courts of like nature, are illegal and pernicious;

That levying money for or to the use of the Crown by pretence of prerogative, without grant of Parliament, for longer time, or in other manner than the same is or shall be granted, is illegal;

That it is the right of the subjects to petition the king, and all commitments and prosecutions for such petitioning are illegal;

That the raising or keeping a standing army within the kingdom in time of peace, unless it be with consent of Parliament, is against law;

That the subjects which are Protestants may have arms for their defence suitable to their conditions and as allowed by law;

That election of members of Parliament ought to be free;

That the freedom of speech and debates or proceedings in Parliament ought not to be impeached or questioned in any court or place out of Parliament;

That excessive bail ought not to be required, nor excessive fines imposed, nor cruel and unusual punishments inflicted;

That jurors ought to be duly impanelled and returned, and jurors which pass upon men in trials for high treason ought to be freeholders;

That all grants and promises of fines and forfeitures of particular persons before conviction are illegal and void;

And that for redress of all grievances, and for the amending, strengthening and preserving of the laws, Parliaments ought to be held frequently.

And they do claim, demand and insist upon all and singular the premises as their undoubted rights and liberties, and that no declarations, judgments, doings or proceedings to the prejudice of the people in any of the said premises ought in any wise to be drawn hereafter into consequence or example; to which demand of their rights they are particularly encouraged by the declaration of his Highness the prince of Orange as being the only means for obtaining a full redress and remedy therein. Having therefore an entire confidence that his said Highness the prince of Orange will perfect the deliverance so far advanced by him, and will still preserve them from the violation of their rights which they have here asserted, and from all other attempts upon their religion, rights and liberties, the said Lords Spiritual and Temporal and Commons assembled at Westminster do resolve that William and Mary, prince and princess of Orange, be and be declared king and queen of England, France and Ireland and the dominions thereunto belonging, to hold the crown and royal dignity of the said kingdoms and dominions to them, the said prince and princess, during their lives and the life of the survivor to them, and that the sole and full exercise of the regal power be only in and executed by the said prince of Orange in the names of the said prince and princess during their joint lives, and after their deceases the said crown and royal dignity of the same kingdoms and dominions to be to the heirs of the body of the said princess, and for default of such issue to the Princess Anne of Denmark and the heirs of her body, and for default of such issue to the heirs of the body of the said prince of Orange. And the Lords Spiritual and Temporal and Commons do pray the said prince and princess to accept the same accordingly.

And that the oaths hereafter mentioned be taken by all persons of whom the oaths have allegiance and supremacy might be required by law, instead of them; and that the said oaths of allegiance and supremacy be abrogated.

I, A.B., do sincerely promise and swear that I will be faithful and bear true allegiance to their Majesties King William and Queen Mary. So help me God.

I, A.B., do swear that I do from my heart abhor, detest and abjure as impious and heretical this damnable doctrine and position, that princes excommunicated or deprived by the Pope or any authority of the see of Rome may be deposed or murdered by their subjects or any other whatsoever. And I do declare that no foreign prince, person, prelate, state or potentate hath or ought to have any jurisdiction, power, superiority, pre-eminence or authority, ecclesiastical or spiritual, within this realm. So help me God.

Upon which their said Majesties did accept the crown and royal dignity of the kingdoms of England, France and Ireland, and the dominions thereunto belonging, according to the resolution and desire of the said Lords and Commons contained in the said declaration. And thereupon their Majesties were pleased that the said Lords Spiritual and Temporal and Commons, being the two Houses of Parliament, should continue to sit, and with their Majesties' royal concurrence make effectual provision for the settlement of the religion, laws and liberties of this kingdom, so that the same for the future might not be in danger again of being subverted, to which the said Lords Spiritual and Temporal and Commons did agree, and proceed to act accordingly. Now in pursuance of the premises the said Lords Spiritual and Temporal and Commons in Parliament assembled, for the ratifying, confirming and establishing the said declaration and the articles, clauses, matters and things therein contained by the force of law made in due form by authority of Parliament, do pray that it may be declared and enacted that all and singular the rights and liberties asserted and claimed in the said declaration are the true, ancient and indubitable rights and liberties of the people of this kingdom, and so shall be esteemed, allowed, adjudged, deemed and taken to be; and that all and every the particulars aforesaid shall be firmly and strictly holden and observed as they are expressed in the said declaration, and all officers and ministers whatsoever shall serve their Majesties and their successors according to the same in all time to come. And the said Lords Spiritual and Temporal and Commons, seriously considering how it hath pleased Almighty God in his marvellous providence and merciful goodness to this nation to provide and preserve their said Majesties' royal persons most happily to reign over us upon the throne of their ancestors, for which they render unto him from the bottom of their hearts their humblest thanks and praises, do truly, firmly, assuredly and in the sincerity of their hearts think, and do hereby recognize, acknowledge and declare, that King James the Second having abdicated the government, and their Majesties having accepted the crown and royal dignity as aforesaid, their said Majesties did become, were, are and of right ought to be by the laws of this realm our sovereign liege lord and lady, king and queen of England, France and Ireland and the dominions thereunto belonging, in and to whose princely persons the royal state, crown and dignity of the said realms with all honours, styles, titles, regalities, prerogatives, powers, jurisdictions and authorities to the same belonging and appertaining are most fully, rightfully and entirely invested and incorporated, united and annexed. And for preventing all questions and divisions in this realm by reason of any pretended titles to the crown, and for preserving a certainty in the succession thereof, in and upon which the unity, peace, tranquility and safety of this nation doth under God wholly consist and depend, the said Lords Spiritual and Temporal and Commons do beseech their Majesties that it may be enacted, established and declared, that the crown and regal government of the said kingdoms and dominions, with all and singular the premises thereunto belonging and appertaining, shall be and continue to their said Majesties and the survivor of them during their lives and the life of the survivor of them, and that the entire, perfect and full exercise of the regal power and government be only in and executed by his Majesty in the names of both their Majesties during their joint lives; and after their deceases the said crown and premises shall be and remain to the heirs of the body of her Majesty, and for default of such issue to her Royal Highness the Princess Anne of Denmark and the heirs of the body of his said Majesty; and thereunto the said Lords Spiritual and Temporal and Commons do in the name of all the people aforesaid most humbly and faithfully submit themselves, their heirs and posterities for ever, and do faithfully promise that they will stand to, maintain and defend their said Majesties, and also the limitation and succession of the crown herein specified and contained, to the utmost of their powers with their lives and estates against all persons whatsoever that shall attempt anything to the contrary. And whereas it hath been found by experience that it is inconsistent with the safety and welfare of this Protestant kingdom to be governed by a popish prince, or by any king or queen marrying a papist, the said Lords Spiritual and Temporal and Commons do further pray that it may be enacted, that all and every person and persons that is, are or shall be reconciled to or shall hold communion with the see or Church of Rome, or shall profess the popish religion, or shall marry a papist, shall be excluded and be for ever incapable to inherit, possess or enjoy the crown and government of this realm and Ireland and the dominions thereunto belonging or any part of the same, or to have, use or exercise any regal power, authority or jurisdiction within the same; and in all and every such case or cases the people of these realms shall be and are hereby absolved of their allegiance; and the said crown and government shall from time to time descend to and be enjoyed by such person or persons being Protestants as should have inherited and enjoyed the same in case the said person or persons so reconciled, holding communion or professing or marrying as aforesaid were naturally dead; and that every king and queen of this realm who at any time hereafter shall come to and succeed in the imperial crown of this kingdom shall on the first day of the meeting of the first Parliament next after his or her coming to the crown, sitting in his or her throne in the House of Peers in the presence of the Lords and Commons therein assembled, or at his or her coronation before such person or persons who shall administer the coronation oath to him or her at the time of his or her taking the said oath (which shall first happen), make, subscribe and audibly repeat the declaration mentioned in the statute made in the thirtieth year of the reign of King Charles the Second entitled, _An Act for the more effectual preserving the king's person and government by disabling papists from sitting in either House of Parliament._ But if it shall happen that such king or queen upon his or her succession to the crown of this realm shall be under the age of twelve years, then every such king or queen shall make, subscribe and audibly repeat the same declaration at his or her coronation or the first day of the meeting of the first Parliament as aforesaid which shall first happen after such king or queen shall have attained the said age of twelve years. All which their Majesties are contented and pleased shall be declared, enacted and established by authority of this present Parliament, and shall stand, remain and be the law of this realm for ever; and the same are by their said Majesties, by and with the advice and consent of the Lords Spiritual and Temporal and Commons in Parliament assembled and by the authority of the same, declared, enacted and established accordingly.

II. And be it further declared and enacted by the authority aforesaid, that from and after this present session of Parliament no dispensation by _non obstante_ of or to any statute or any part thereof shall be allowed, but that the same shall be held void and of no effect, except a dispensation be allowed of in such statute, and except in such cases as shall be specially provided for by one or more bill or bills to be passed during this present session of Parliament.

III. Provided that no charter or grant or pardon granted before the three and twentieth day of October in the year of our Lord one thousand six hundred eighty-nine shall be any ways impeached or invalidated by this Act, but that the same shall be and remain of the same force and effect in law and no other than as if this Act had never been made.

The Declaration of Independence

IN CONGRESS, July 4, 1776.

The unanimous Declaration of the thirteen united States of America,

When in the Course of human events, it becomes necessary for one people to dissolve the political bands which have connected them with another, and to assume among the powers of the earth, the separate and equal station to which the Laws of Nature and of Nature's God entitle them, a decent respect to the opinions of mankind requires that they should declare the causes which impel them to the separation.

We hold these truths to be self-evident, that all men are created equal, that they are endowed by their Creator with certain unalienable Rights, that among these are Life, Liberty and the pursuit of Happiness.—That to secure these rights, Governments are instituted among Men, deriving their just powers from the consent of the governed,—That whenever any Form of Government becomes destructive of these ends, it is the Right of the People to alter or to abolish it, and to institute new Government, laying its foundation on such principles and organizing its powers in such form, as to them shall seem most likely to effect their Safety and Happiness. Prudence, indeed, will dictate that Governments long established should not be changed for light and transient causes; and accordingly all experience hath shewn, that mankind are more disposed to suffer, while evils are sufferable, than to right themselves by abolishing the forms to which they are accustomed. But when a long train of abuses and usurpations, pursuing invariably the same Object evinces a design to reduce them under absolute Despotism, it is their right, it is their duty, to throw off such Government, and to provide new Guards for their future security.—Such has been the patient sufferance of these Colonies; and such is now the necessity which constrains them to alter their former Systems of Government. The history of the present King of Great Britain is a history of repeated injuries and usurpations, all having in direct object the establishment of an absolute Tyranny over these States. To prove this, let Facts be submitted to a candid world.

He has refused his Assent to Laws, the most wholesome and necessary for the public good.

He has forbidden his Governors to pass Laws of immediate and pressing importance, unless suspended in their operation till his Assent should be obtained; and when so suspended, he has utterly neglected to attend to them.

He has refused to pass other Laws for the accommodation of large districts of people, unless those people would relinquish the right of Representation in the Legislature, a right inestimable to them and formidable to tyrants only.

He has called together legislative bodies at places unusual, uncomfortable, and distant from the depository of their public Records, for the sole purpose of fatiguing them into compliance with his measures.

He has dissolved Representative Houses repeatedly, for opposing with manly firmness his invasions on the rights of the people.

He has refused for a long time, after such dissolutions, to cause others to be elected; whereby the Legislative powers, incapable of Annihilation, have returned to the People at large for their exercise; the State remaining in the mean time exposed to all the dangers of invasion from without, and convulsions within.

He has endeavoured to prevent the population of these States; for that purpose obstructing the Laws for Naturalization of Foreigners; refusing to pass others to encourage their migrations hither, and raising the conditions of new Appropriations of Lands.

He has obstructed the Administration of Justice, by refusing his Assent to Laws for establishing Judiciary powers.

He has made Judges dependent on his Will alone, for the tenure of their offices, and the amount and payment of their salaries.

He has erected a multitude of New Offices, and sent hither swarms of Officers to harrass our people, and eat out their substance.

He has kept among us, in times of peace, Standing Armies without the Consent of our legislatures.

He has affected to render the Military independent of and superior to the Civil power.

He has combined with others to subject us to a jurisdiction foreign to our constitution, and unacknowledged by our laws; giving his Assent to their Acts of pretended Legislation:

For Quartering large bodies of armed troops among us:

For protecting them, by a mock Trial, from punishment for any Murders which they should commit on the Inhabitants of these States:

For cutting off our Trade with all parts of the world:

For imposing Taxes on us without our Consent:

For depriving us in many cases, of the benefits of Trial by Jury:

For transporting us beyond Seas to be tried for pretended offences

For abolishing the free System of English Laws in a neighbouring Province, establishing therein an Arbitrary government, and enlarging its Boundaries so as to render it at once an example and fit instrument for introducing the same absolute rule into these Colonies:

For taking away our Charters, abolishing our most valuable Laws, and altering fundamentally the Forms of our Governments:

For suspending our own Legislatures, and declaring themselves invested with power to legislate for us in all cases whatsoever.

He has abdicated Government here, by declaring us out of his Protection and waging War against us.

He has plundered our seas, ravaged our Coasts, burnt our towns, and destroyed the lives of our people.

He is at this time transporting large Armies of foreign Mercenaries to compleat the works of death, desolation and tyranny, already begun with circumstances of Cruelty & perfidy scarcely paralleled in the most barbarous ages, and totally unworthy of the Head of a civilized nation.

He has constrained our fellow Citizens taken Captive on the high Seas to bear Arms against their Country, to become the executioners of their friends and Brethren, or to fall themselves by their Hands.

He has excited domestic insurrections amongst us, and has endeavoured to bring on the inhabitants of our frontiers, the merciless Indian Savages, whose known rule of warfare, is an undistinguished destruction of all ages, sexes and conditions.

In every stage of these Oppressions We have Petitioned for Redress in the most humble terms: Our repeated Petitions have been answered only by repeated injury. A Prince whose character is thus marked by every act which may define a Tyrant, is unfit to be the ruler of a free people.

Nor have We been wanting in attentions to our Brittish brethren. We have warned them from time to time of attempts by their legislature to extend an unwarrantable jurisdiction over us. We have reminded them of the circumstances of our emigration and settlement here. We have appealed to their native justice and magnanimity, and we have conjured them by the ties of our common kindred to disavow these usurpations, which, would inevitably interrupt our connections and correspondence. They too have been deaf to the voice of justice and of consanguinity. We must, therefore, acquiesce in the necessity, which denounces our Separation, and hold them, as we hold the rest of mankind, Enemies in War, in Peace Friends.

We, therefore, the Representatives of the united States of America, in General Congress, Assembled, appealing to the Supreme Judge of the world for the rectitude of our intentions, do, in the Name, and by Authority of the good People of these Colonies, solemnly publish and declare, That these United Colonies are, and of Right ought to be Free and Independent States; that they are Absolved from all Allegiance to the British Crown, and that all political connection between them and the State of Great Britain, is and ought to be totally dissolved; and that as Free and Independent States, they have full Power to levy War, conclude Peace, contract Alliances, establish Commerce, and to do all other Acts and Things which Independent States may of right do. And for the support of this Declaration, with a firm reliance on the protection of divine Providence, we mutually pledge to each other our Lives, our Fortunes and our sacred Honor.

Georgia:
Button Gwinnett
Lyman Hall
George Walton
North Carolina:
William Hooper
Joseph Hewes
John Penn

South Carolina:
Edward Rutledge
Thomas Heyward, Jr.
Thomas Lynch, Jr.
Arthur Middleton

Massachusetts:
John Hancock

Maryland:
Samuel Chase
William Paca
Thomas Stone
Charles Carroll of
Carrollton

Virginia:
George Wythe
Richard Henry Lee
Thomas Jefferson
Benjamin Harrison
Thomas Nelson, Jr.
Francis Lightfoot Lee
Carter Braxton

Pennsylvania:
Robert Morris
Benjamin Rush
Benjamin Franklin
John Morton
George Clymer
James Smith
George Taylor
James Wilson
George Ross

Delaware:
Caesar Rodney
George Read
Thomas McKean

New York:
William Floyd
Philip Livingston
Francis Lewis
Lewis Morris

New Jersey:
Richard Stockton
John Witherspoon
Francis Hopkinson
John Hart
Abraham Clark

New Hampshire:
Josiah Bartlett
William Whipple

Massachusetts:
Samuel Adams
John Adams
Robert Treat Paine
Elbridge Gerry

Rhode Island:
Stephen Hopkins

William Ellery

Connecticut:

Roger Sherman

Samuel Huntington

William Williams

Oliver Wolcott

New Hampshire:

Matthew Thornton

Bibliography

Acton, Lord John Emerich Edward Dalberg. n.d. "Lord Acton Quote Archive."
    Acton Institute for the Study of Religion and Liberty. Accessed October
    13, 2014. http://www.acton.org/research/lord-acton-quote-archive.

Adams, John. 1776. "From John Adams to James Sullivan." May 26. National
    Archives. Founders Online. https://founders.archives.gov/documents/
    Adams/06-04-02-0091.

———. 1856. *The Works of John Adams, Second President of the United States:
    With a Life of the Author, Notes and Illustrations, by His Grandson Charles
    Francis Adams.* 10 vols. Vol. 6, chap. 1. Boston: Little, Brown and
    Company.

———. 1954. *Political Writings of John Adams.* Edited by George A. Peek Jr.
    American Heritage Series. New York: Liberal Arts Press.

Adams, John Quincy. 1837. *An Oration Delivered before the Inhabitants of the
    Town of Newburyport at Their Request on the Sixty-first Anniversary of the
    Declaration of Independence.* July 4. Newburyport: Charles Whipple.

Adams, Samuel. 1772. *The Rights of the Colonists.* November 20. http://www.
    constitution.org/bcp/right_col.htm.

Allison, Andrew M. 1983. *The Real Thomas Jefferson.* Second edition. American
    Classic Series. Malta: National Center for Constitutional Studies.

Allison, Andrew M., W. Cleon Skousen, and M. Richard Maxfield. 2009. *The Real Benjamin Franklin*. American Classic Series. Malta: National Center for Constitutional Studies.

America's Founding Fathers—Delegates to the Constitutional Convention. n.d. Accessed September 22, 2011. https://www.archives.gov/founding-docs/founding-fathers-virginia#toc--john-blair-virginia.

Arizona State Legislature. 2010. House Bill 2162. http://www.azleg.gov//FormatDocument.asp?inDoc=/legtext/49leg/2r/bills/hb2162c.htm&Session_ID=93.

Associated Press. 2013. "Homeland Security Aims to Buy 1.6 Billion Rounds of Ammo." *Denver Post*, February 14. http://www.denverpost.com/nationworld/ci_22594279/homeland-security-aims-buy-1-6-billion-rounds.

Australian Government. n.d. "Convicts and the British Colonies in Australia." Accessed April 6, 2016. http://www.australia.gov.au/about-australia/australian-story/convicts-and-the-british-colonies.

Barton, David. 2008. "As a Reformer." In *Benjamin Rush: Signer of the Declaration of Independence*. First edition. Aledo: Wallbuilders Press.

Blackstone, William. 1803. *Commentaries on the Laws of England*. Edited by George Tucker. Philadelphia. http://www.constitution.org/tb/tb-1102.htm.

Blake, W. O. 1857. *The African Slave Trade and the Political History of Slavery in the United States*. http://books.google.com/books?id=UgwZAAAAYAAJ&printsec=frontcover&dq=w.o.+blake+the+history+of+slavery&hl=en&ei=WzB4TqWLE4XisQKx28HADQ&sa=X&oi=book_result&ct=result&resnum=1&ved=0CC0Q6AEwAA#v=onepage&q&f=false.

Boersma, Tim, and Charles K. Ebinger. 2014. "Lift the Ban on U.S. Oil Exports." Brookings Institute. January 23. http://www.brookings.edu/research/papers/2014/01/lift-ban-us-oil-exports-boersma-ebinger.

Bradford, William. 1856. *History of Plymouth Plantation*. Boston: Massachusetts Historical Society.

"British Royal Proclamations Relating to America, 1603–1783." n.d. Archive. org. Accessed September 18, 2014. http://www.archive.org/stream/ royalproclamations12brigrich/royalproclamations12brigrich_djvu.txt.

Bui, Quoctrung, and Margot Sanger-Katz. 2016. "Why the Government Owns so Much Land in the West." *New York Times*, January 5. http://www. nytimes.com/2016/01/06/upshot/why-the-government-owns-so-much-land-in-the-west.html?_r=0.

Burke, Edmund. 1999. *Select Works of Edmund Burke*. Payne Edition. Vol. 1. Indianapolis: Online Liberty Fund. http://oll.libertyfund.org/titles/ burke-select-works-of-edmund-burke-vol-1--5.

Bush, George W. 2001. Executive Order: President's Commission to Strengthen Social Security. White House. May 2. http://georgewbush-whitehouse.archives.gov/news/releases/2001/05/20010502-5.html.

Cali, Jeanine. 2013. "Frequent Reference Question: How Many Federal Laws Are There?" Library of Congress. March 12. https://blogs.loc.gov/ law/2013/03/frequent-reference-question-how-many-federal-laws-are-there/.

CBS News. 2010. "Feds Sue to Block Arizona Immigration Law." July 6. http:// www.cbsnews.com/stories/2010/07/06/politics/main6651468.shtml.

A Century of Lawmaking for a New Nation. n.d. Washington, D.C.: Library of Congress. Accessed April 2, 2015. http://memory.loc.gov/cgi-bin/ ampage.

Charles I. 1632. The Charter of Maryland. The Avalon Project, Yale Law School. http://avalon.law.yale.edu/17th_century/ma01.asp.

Charles II. 1662. Charter of Connecticut. The Avalon Project, Yale Law School. http://avalon.law.yale.edu/17th_century/ct03.asp.

———. 1663. Charter of Carolina. The Avalon Project, Yale Law School. March 24. http://avalon.law.yale.edu/17th_century/nc01.asp.

———. 1665. Charter of Carolina. The Avalon Project, Yale Law School. June 30. http://avalon.law.yale.edu/17th_century/nc04.asp.

Cicero, Marcus Tullius. 52. *De Republica*. Constitution Society. http:// constitution.org/rom/republica0.htm.

Circular Letter to the Governors in America. 1768. The Avalon Project, Yale Law School. April 21. http://avalon.law.yale.edu/18th_century/circ_let_gov_1768.asp.

Cleveland Board of Education v. Loudermill. 1985. 470 U.S. 532. Oyez, IIT Chicago-Kent College of Law. http://www.oyez.org/cases/1980-1989/1984/1984_83_1362.

Commission of John Cutt. 1680. The Avalon Project, Yale Law School. http://avalon.law.yale.edu/17th_century/nh08.asp.

Constitutional Convention of Idaho. 1890. Constitution of the State of Idaho. http://legislature.idaho.gov/idstat/IC/ArtIIISect28.htm.

Devin, Leonard. 2014. "Why Is the Post Office Buying Bullets?" *Bloomberg Businessweek*, April 21. http://www.bloomberg.com/news/articles/2014-04-21/why-is-the-post-office-buying-bullets.

Dill, Thomas Alonzo. 1983. *Carter Braxton, Virginia Signer: A Conservative in Revolt*. Lanham: University Press of America.

Elliot, Jonathan. 1836. *The Debates in the Several State Conventions on the Adoption of the Federal Constitution as Recommended by the General Convention at Philadelphia in 1787 Together with the Journal of the Federal Convention, Luther Martin's Letter, Yates's Minutes, Congressional Opinions, Virginia and Kentucky Resolutions of '98–99, and Other Illustrations of the Constitution*. 5 vols. Second edition. Liberty Fund. Digital eBook. files.libertyfund.org/files/1905/1314.01_Bk.pdf.

English Bill of Rights: An Act Declaring the Rights and Liberties of the Subject and Settling the Succession of the Crown. 1689. The Avalon Project, Yale Law School. http://avalon.law.yale.edu/17th_century/england.asp.

Fairfax County Resolves.1774. July 18. http://constitution.org/bcp/fairfax_res.htm.

Federal Judicial Center. n.d. History of the Federal Judiciary. Accessed April 8, 2016. http://www.fjc.gov/history/home.nsf/page/judges_impeachments.html.

Few, William. 1804. "Slavery in the Early Republic." Digital History. http://www.digitalhistory.uh.edu/disp_textbook.cfm?smtID=3&psid=234.

Finkelman, Paul. 1994. "Thomas Jefferson and Antislavery: The Myth Goes On." *The Virginia Magazine of History and Biography* 102, no. 2 (April): 193–228.

First Continental Congress. 1774. Declaration and Resolves on Colonial Rights of the First Continental Congress. Constitution Society. October 14. http://www.constitution.org/bcp/colright.htm.

Franklin, Benjamin. 1839. *The Works of Benjamin Franklin.* Vol. 8. Edited by Jared Sparks. Boston: Tappan, Whittemore, and Mason.

Fundamental Orders. 1639. The Avalon Project, Yale Law School. January 14. http://avalon.law.yale.edu/17th_century/order.asp.

George II. 1732. Charter of Georgia. The Avalon Project, Yale Law School. http://avalon.law.yale.edu/18th_century/ga01.asp.

George III. 1763. *The Royal Proclamation.* The Avalon Project, Yale Law School. October 7. http://avalon.law.yale.edu/18th_century/proc1763.asp.

———. 1775. *Royal Proclamation of Rebellion.* Digital History. August 23. http://www.digitalhistory.uh.edu/disp_textbook. cfm?smtID=3&psid=4105.

———. 1775. *King George III's Address to Parliament.* Library of Congress. October 27. http://www.loc.gov/teachers/classroommaterials/ presentationsandactivities/presentations/timeline/amrev/shots/address. html.

Government of New Haven Colony. 1643. The Avalon Project, Yale Law School. October 27/November 6. http://avalon.law.yale.edu/17th_ century/ct02.asp.

Hancock, John. 1865. *The Great Question for the People!: Essays on the Elective Franchise; or, Who Has the Right to Vote?* Philadelphia: Merrihew & Son.

Hawks, Francis L., David L. Swain, and William A. Graham. 1853. *Revolutionary History of North Carolina, in Three Lectures.* Compiled by William D. Cooke. Raleigh: William D. Cooke; New York: G. P. Putnam and Co.

Head, David. n.d. "Hessians." *The Digital Encyclopedia of George Washington.* Accessed October 10, 2014. http://www.mountvernon.org/research-collections/digital-encyclopedia/article/hessians/.

Hobbes, Thomas. 1651. *Leviathan*. Constitution Society. http://constitution. org/th/leviatha.htm.

Husband, Herman. n.d. *An Impartial Relation of the First Rise and Cause of the Recent Differences in Publick Affairs, in the Progress of the So Much Talked of Regulation in North Carolina*. Learn NC. Accessed June 13, 2014. http://www.learnnc.org/lp/editions/nchist-revolution/4939.

Idaho Secretary of State. n.d. "November 7, 2006 General Election Results." Accessed September 12, 2014. http://www.sos.idaho.gov/elect/ RESULTS/2006/general/tot_stwd.htm.

James I. 1606. The First Charter of Virginia. The Avalon Project, Yale Law School. April 10. http://avalon.law.yale.edu/17th_century/va01.asp.

———. 1609. The Second Charter of Virginia. The Avalon Project, Yale Law School. May 23. http://avalon.law.yale.edu/17th_century/va02.asp.

———. 1620. Charter of New England. The Avalon Project, Yale Law School. http://avalon.law.yale.edu/17th_century/mass01.asp.

Jefferson, Thomas. 1774. *A Summary View of the Rights of British America*. The Avalon Project, Yale Law School. http://avalon.law.yale.edu/18th_ century/jeffsumm.asp#back10.

———. 1811. "Jefferson to Benjamin Rush." Library of Congress. http:// memory.loc.gov/cgi-bin/ampage?collId=mtj1&fileName=mtj1page045. db&recNum=55.

Johnson, Edward A. 1890. *A School History of the Negro Race in America, from 1619 to 1890, with a Short Introduction as to the Origin of the Race; Also a Short Sketch of Liberia*. Raleigh: Edwards & Broughton. http://docsouth. unc.edu/church/johnson/johnson.html.

Journals of the Continental Congress. 1775. *Petition to the King*. The Avalon Project, Yale Law School. http://avalon.law.yale.edu/18th_century/ contcong_07-08-75.asp.

Kaminski, John P., ed. 1995. *A Necessary Evil? Slavery and the Debate over the Constitution*. Madison, WI: Madison House.

Kliff, Sarah. 2013. "Charts: How Roe v. Wade Changed Abortion Rights." *Washington Post*, January 22. http://www.washingtonpost.com/blogs/

wonkblog/wp/2013/01/22/charts-how-roe-v-wade-changed-abortion-rights/.

Krogstad, Jens Manuel, Jeffrey S. Passell, and D'Vera Cohn. 2016. "5 Facts about Illegal Immigration in the U.S." Pew Research Center. November 3. http://www.pewresearch.org/fact-tank/2015/11/19/5-facts-about-illegal-immigration-in-the-u-s/.

Latta et al v. Otter et al. 2014. No. 1:13-cv-00482. http://www.plainsite.org/dockets/uoehxt8w/idaho-district-court/latta-et-al-v-otter-et-al/.

Lawrence et al v. Texas. 2003. No. 02-102. FindLaw. http://caselaw.lp.findlaw.com/scripts/getcase.pl?court=US&vol=000&invol=02-102#opinion1.

Lee, Tony. 2013. "Jerry Brown Signs Bill Making CA Sanctuary State for Most Illegals." *Breitbart*, October 6. http://www.breitbart.com/big-government/2013/10/06/ca-gov-signs-bill-making-ca-sanctuary-state-for-most-illegals/.

Lincoln, Abraham. 1858. "Speech at Lewistown, Illinois." August 17. In the *Collected Works of Abraham Lincoln*, 1809–1865, edited by Roy P. Basler. Vol. 2. New Brunswick: Rutgers University Press, 1953.

Locke, John. 1690. *The Second Treatise of Civil Government*. Constitution Society. http://constitution.org/jl/2ndtreat.htm.

Lossing, B. J. 1866. *Biographical Sketches of the Signers of the Declaration of American Independence*. Philadelphia: Davis, Porter and Co.

Lucas, Stephen E. 1989. *The Stylistic Artistry of the Declaration of Independence*. National Archives. https://www.archives.gov/founding-docs/stylistic-artistry-of-the-declaration.

Madison, James. 1787. *The Debates in the Federal Convention of 1787*. Constitution Society. http://constitution.org/dfc/dfc_0915.htm.

———. 1788. "The Powers Conferred by the Constitution Further Considered." Federalist No. 42 in *Federalist Papers*. January 22. Constitution Society. http://constitution.org/fed/federa42.htm.

———. n.d. "Selected Quotes of James Madison." Constitution Society. Accessed May 22, 2015. http://www.constitution.org/jm/jm_quotes.htm.

The Magna Carta. 1215. Constitution Society. http://constitution.org/eng/magnacar.htm.

Malone, Dumas. 1981. *Jefferson and His Time: The Sage of Monticello*. Boston: Little Brown and Co.

Markon, Jerry. 2015. "Senior Obama Officials Have Warned of Challenges in Screening Refugees from Syria." *Washington Post*, November 17. https://www.washingtonpost.com/news/federal-eye/wp/2015/11/17/senior-obama-officials-have-warned-of-challenges-in-screening-refugees-from-syria/.

McCullough, David. 2001. *John Adams*. New York: Simon & Schuster.

Morgan, Edmund S. 1975. *American Freedom, American Slavery*. New York: W. W. Norton & Co.

Morgan, Edmund S., and Helen M. Morgan. 1995. *The Stamp Act Crisis: Prologue to Revolution*. Chapel Hill: University of North Carolina Press.

Nash, Francis. 1903. *Hillsboro: Colonial and Revolutionary*. Raleigh: Edwards & Broughton. http://books.google.com/books?id=YF0dAAAAMAAJ&pg=PA1&lpg=PA1&dq=francis+nash+hillsboro+colonial+and+revolutionary&source=bl&ots=9ef1wvLiYh&sig=s3INENFayYrS8XZLi74Ffo-Jj-8&hl=en&ei=K8t6Tqf0DMKIsQKfzs29Aw&sa=X&oi=book_result&ct=result&resnum=2&sqi=2&ved=0CCEQ6AEwAQ#v=onepage&q=william%20few&f=false.

National Oceanic and Atmospheric Administration. n.d. "13—Ammunition and Shooting Targets." Accessed April 14, 2016. https://www.fbo.gov/index?s=opportunity&mode=form&tab=core&id=4370194550dd10f4aae476069e17eb85&_cview=1.

Navigation Acts. n.d. Digital History. Accessed January 9, 2014. http://www.digitalhistory.uh.edu/disp_textbook.cfm?smtID=3&psid=4102.

"North Carolina Court History of Interest." n.d. Accessed June 13, 2014. http://www.nccourts.org/County/Orange/Interest.asp.

Obama, Barack Hussein. 2009. Executive Order 13503. White House. February 24. https://www.gpo.gov/fdsys/pkg/FR-2009-02-24/pdf/E9-4068.pdf.

O'Laughlin, Jay. 2011. "Fact Sheet #8: Federal Land as a Percentage of Total State Land Area." College of Natural Resources Policy Analysis Group, University of Idaho. http://www.idahoforests.org/img/pdf/ CQHSNFPAG-factsheet.pdf.

"Olive Branch Petition." 1775. Digital History. July 8. http://www. digitalhistory.uh.edu/disp_textbook.cfm?smtID=3&psid=3881.

Paine, Thomas. 1776. *Common Sense*. Philadelphia. http://constitution.org/tp/ comsense.htm.

Papenfuse, Edward C., Alan F. Day, David W. Jordan, and Gregory A. Stiverson, eds. 2002. *A Biographical Dictionary of the Maryland Legislature 1635–1789*. Archives of Maryland Online. http://msa. maryland.gov/megafile/msa/speccol/sc2900/sc2908/000001/000426/ html/am426--589.html

Parliament, Great Britain. 1764. The Currency Act. The Avalon Project, Yale Law School. April 19. http://avalon.law.yale.edu/18th_century/curency_ act_1764.asp.

———. 1764. The Sugar Act. The Avalon Project, Yale Law School. http:// avalon.law.yale.edu/18th_century/sugar_act_1764.asp.

———. 1765. The Stamp Act. The Avalon Project, Yale Law School. March 22. http://avalon.law.yale.edu/18th_century/stamp_act_1765.asp.

———. 1765. The Quartering Act. The Avalon Project, Yale Law School. May 15. http://avalon.law.yale.edu/18th_century/quartering_act_165.asp.

———. 1766. The Declaratory Act. The Avalon Project, Yale Law School. March 18. http://avalon.law.yale.edu/18th_century/declaratory_ act_1766.asp.

———. 1767. The New York Suspending Act. TeachingAmericanHistory. org. Ashbrook Center, Ashland University. July 20. http:// teachingamericanhistory.org/library/document/the-new-york- suspending-act/.

———. 1767. The Townsend Act. The Avalon Project, Yale Law School. November 20. http://avalon.law.yale.edu/18th_century/townsend_ act_1767.asp.

———. 1774. The Administration of Justice Act. The Avalon Project, Yale Law School. May 20. http://avalon.law.yale.edu/18th_century/admin_of_justice_act.asp.

———. 1774. The Massachusetts Government Act. The Avalon Project, Yale Law School. May 20. http://avalon.law.yale.edu/18th_century/mass_gov_act.asp.

———. 1774. The Boston Port Act. The Avalon Project, Yale Law School. May 31. http://avalon.law.yale.edu/18th_century/boston_port_act.asp.

———. 1774. The Quartering Act. The Avalon Project, Yale Law School. June 2. http://avalon.law.yale.edu/18th_century/quartering_act_1774.asp.

———. 1774. The Quebec Act: An Act for Making More Effectual Provision for the Government of the Province of Quebec in North America. The Avalon Project. October 7. http://avalon.law.yale.edu/18th_century/quebec_act_1774.asp.

Parry, Jay A., Andrew M. Allison, and W. Cleon Skousen. 2009. *The Real George Washington: The True Story of America's Most Indispensable Man.* Malta: National Center for Constitutional Studies.

Paul, Rand. 2011. "Paul: EPA Regulations Violate Constitutional Rights." *Washington Times*, August 31. http://www.washingtontimes.com/news/2011/aug/31/epa-regulations-violate-constitutional-rights/.

Penn, William. 1701. Charter of Delaware. The Avalon Project, Yale Law School. http://avalon.law.yale.edu/18th_century/de01.asp.

Pierson, Hamilton. 1971. *Jefferson at Monticello:; The Private Life of Thomas Jefferson.* Freeport, N.Y: Books for Libraries Press.

Proper, Emberson Edward. 1900. *Colonial Immigration Laws: A Study of the Regulation of Immigration by the English Colonies in America.* Studies in History, Economics and Public Law. New York: The Columbia University Press.

The Quebec Act: An Act for Making More Effectual Provision for the Government of the Province of Quebec in North America. 1774 .The Avalon Project, Yale Law School. October 7. http://avalon.law.yale.edu/18th_century/quebec_act_1774.asp.

Ramsay, David. 1789. *The History of the American Revolution*. 2 vols. Edited by Lester H. Cohen. Indianapolis: Liberty Fund, 1990. http://oll. libertyfund.org/title/814.

Report of Proceedings in Congress. 1787. The Avalon Project, Yale Law School. February 21. http://avalon.law.yale.edu/18th_century/const04.asp.

Reynolds, William R. Jr. 2012. *Andrew Pickens: South Carolina Patriot in the Revolutionary War*. Jefferson: McFarland & Company.

Richter, Julie. 1999. "Slavery in John Blair's Public and Personal Lives in 1751." *The Colonial Williamsburg Interpreter* 20 (Fall): 1–8.

Roe v. Wade. 1973. 410 U.S. 113. Oyez. http://www.oyez.org/ cases/1970-1979/1971/1971_70_18.

Roper v. Simmons. 2005. (03-633) 543 U. S. 551 (2005) 112 S. W. 3d 397, affirmed. Cornell University Law School. https://www.law.cornell.edu/ supct/html/03-633.ZO.html.

Safire, William. 1997. *Lend Me Your Ears: Great Speeches in History*. New York: W. W. Norton & Co.

Schweikart, Larry. 2008. *48 Liberal Lies about American History: (that You Probably Learned in School)*. New York: Sentinel.

Seper, Jerry, and Matthew Cella. 2010. "Signs in Arizona Warn of Smuggler Dangers." *Washington Times*, August 31. http://www.washingtontimes. com/news/2010/aug/31/signs-in-arizona-warn-of-smuggler- dangers/?page=all.

"1790 Election Law." 2007. New Jersey Women's History. December 7. http:// www.njwomenshistory.org/Period_2/qualvoters.htm.

"Signers of the Declaration of Independence." n.d. Independence Hall Association. Accessed November 21, 2014. http://www.ushistory.org/ declaration/signers/hewes.html.

Stoll, Ira. 2008. *Samuel Adams: A Life*. New York: Free Press.

"10 Outrageous Facts About the Income Tax." 2003. Cato Institute. April 15. http://www.cato.org/publications/commentary/10-outrageous-facts- about-income-tax.

United States of America v. John Pozsgai, Gizella Pozsgai, Mercer Wrecking & Recycling Corporation, J. Vinch & Sons, Inc., John Pozsgai and

Gizella Pozsgai, Appellants. 1993. 999 F.2d 719 (3d Cir. 1993). Justia US Law. http://law.justia.com/cases/federal/appellate-courts/F2/999/719/309100/.

US Code Title 26. n.d. Legal Information Institute, Cornell University Law School. Accessed June 5, 2015. https://www.law.cornell.edu/uscode/text/26/7208.

US Congress. 1789. The Judiciary Act. Constitution Society. http://www.constitution.org/uslaw/judiciary_1789.htm.

US Congress. 1808. An Act to Prohibit the Importation of Slaves into any Port or Place within the Jurisdiction of the United States, from and after the First Day of January, in the Year of Our Lord One Thousand Eight Hundred and Eight. The Avalon Project, Yale Law School. http://avalon.law.yale.edu/19th_century/sl004.asp.

US Department of Agriculture. Forest Service. n.d. *Frank Church River of No Return Wilderness.* Accessed April 21, 2016. http://www.fs.usda.gov/detail/scnf/specialplaces/?cid=stelprdb5360033.

US Department of Justice. Bureau of Alcohol, Tobacco, Firearms and Explosives. n.d. *ATF Guidebook—Importation & Verification of Firearms, Ammunition, and Implements of War.* Accessed September 4, 2014. http://www.atf.gov/files/firearms/guides/importation-verification/download/firearms-imporation-verification-guidebook--complete.pdf.

US Internal Revenue Service. 2013. "National Taxpayer Advocate Delivers Annual Report to Congress; Focuses on Tax Reform, IRS Funding and Identity Theft." https://www.irs.gov/uac/Newsroom/National-Taxpayer-Advocate-Delivers-2012-Annual-Report-to-Congress.

US Social Security Administration. 2012. "Request for Quote for Ammunition." SSA-RFQ-12-1851. https://www.fbo.gov/index?s=opportunity&mode=form&id=6c39a2a9f00a10187a1432388a3301e5&tab=core&_cview=0&fb_source=message.

USA.gov. n.d. "A–Z Index of U.S. Government Departments and Agencies." Accessed July 23, 2014. https://www.usa.gov/federal-agencies/a.

Usher, Roland G. Jr. 1951. "Royal Navy Impressment during the American Revolution." *The Mississippi Valley Historical Review* 37, no. 4 (March): 673–88.

Vaughn, David J. 1997. *Give Me Liberty: The Uncompromising Statesmanship of Patrick Henry*. Nashville: Cumberland House Publishing.

The Virginia Declaration of Rights. 1776. Constitution Society. May 15. http://constitution.org/bcp/virg_dor.htm.

Wahl, Jenny B. "Slavery in the United States." Economics History Services. Accessed September 20, 2011. https://eh.net/encyclopedia/slavery-in-the-united-states/.

Warren, Mercy Otis. 1805. *History of the Rise, Progress and Termination of the American Revolution*. 2 vols. Edited by Lester H. Cohen. Indianapolis: Liberty Fund, 1989.

"Watts Rebellion (Los Angeles, 1965)." n.d. The Martin Luther King, Jr. Research and Education Institute, Stanford University. Accessed October 10, 2014. http://mlk-kpp01.stanford.edu/index.php/encyclopedia/encyclopedia/enc_watts_rebellion_los_angeles_1965/.

West, Thomas G. 1992. "Was the American Founding Unjust? The Case of Slavery." *Principles* (Spring/Summer): 1–12.

Wickard v. Filburn. 1942. 317 U.S. 111. Oyez.org. https://supreme.justia.com/cases/federal/us/317/111/.

Wilson, James. 1790. *Of the Natural Rights of Individuals*. TeachingAmericanHistory.org. Ashbrook Center, Ashland University. http://teachingamericanhistory.org/library/document/of-the-natural-rights-of-individuals/#26.

Winthrop, John. 1630. *A Model of Christian Charity*. The Winthrop Society. http://winthropsociety.com/doc_charity.php.

Zong, Jie, and Jeanne Batalova. 2017. *Frequently Requested Statistics on Immigrants and Immigration in the United States*. Washington, DC: Migration Policy Institute. http://www.migrationpolicy.org/article/frequently-requested-statistics-immigrants-and-immigration-united-states.

About the Author

Michael S. Law has focused much of his life's research on the Founding Era and the Founders of the US. He has a bachelor's in political science from Boise State University and a master's degree in political science from American Public University emphasizing US history and government. He continues to personally study from the writings of the Founders and their history, remaining focused on the Founding principles. He applies his political expertise locally, including involvement in local government through serving on his local school board. He has been married for twenty-four years to his wife, Kaori, and has three children.

End Notes

Chapter 1 The Course of Human Events

1   Paul Finkelman, 1994, "Thomas Jefferson and Antislavery: The Myth Goes On," abstract, *The Virginia Magazine of History and Biography* 102, no. 2 (April): 207.

2   The Magna Carta, 1215, Constitution Society, http://constitution.org/eng/magnacar.htm.

3   Ibid., emphasis added.

4   Ibid.

5   Ibid.

6   Ibid.

7   William Bradford, 1856, *History of Plymouth Plantation* (Boston: Massachusetts Historical Society), 10.

8   Ibid., 12.

9   Ibid., 29.

10   Ibid., 30.

11   Ibid., 69–74.

12   Ibid., 89.

13   Ibid., 89–90.

14   John Winthrop, 1630, *A Model of Christian Charity*, The Winthrop
      Society, http://winthropsociety.com/doc_charity.php.

15   David Ramsay, 1789, *The History of the American Revolution*, 2 vols., ed.
      Lester H. Cohen (Indianapolis: Liberty Fund, 1990), vol. 1, 23, http://
      oll.libertyfund.org/title/814.

16   Ibid., 24.

17   James I, 1606, The First Charter of Virginia (The Avalon Project, Yale
      Law School), April 10, http://avalon.law.yale.edu/17th_century/va01.
      asp.

18   Ramsay, *The History of the American Revolution*, vol. 1, 27.

19   Fundamental Orders, 1639 (The Avalon Project, Yale Law School),
      January 14, http://avalon.law.yale.edu/17th_century/order.asp.

20   Charles II, 1662, Charter of Connecticut (The Avalon Project, Yale Law
      School), http://avalon.law.yale.edu/17th_century/ct03.asp.

21   Ramsay, *The History of the American Revolution*, vol. 1, 28.

22   Charles II, 1663, Charter of Carolina (The Avalon Project, Yale Law
      School), March 24, http://avalon.law.yale.edu/17th_century/nc01.asp.

23   Ramsay, *The History of the American Revolution*, vol. 1, 29.

24   English Bill of Rights: An Act Declaring the Rights and Liberties of the
      Subject and Settling the Succession of the Crown, 1689 (The Avalon
      Project, Yale Law School), http://avalon.law.yale.edu/17th_century/
      england.asp.

25   Marcus Tullius Cicero, 52, *De Republica*, Constitution Society, http://
      constitution.org/rom/republica0.htm.

26   John Locke, 1690, *The Second Treatise of Civil Government*, Constitution
      Society, sec. 4, 6, http://constitution.org/jl/2ndtr02.htm.

27   Ibid.

28   Thomas Hobbes, 1651, "Of the Natural Condition of Mankind as
      Concerning Their Felicity and Misery," in *Leviathan*, Constitution
      Society, http://constitution.org/th/leviatha.htm.

29   Locke, *The Second Treatise of Civil Government*, sec. 17, 18.

Chapter 2 Unalienable Rights and the Proper Role of Government

30 Edmund S. Morgan, 1975, *American Freedom, American Slavery* (New York City: W. W. Norton & Co.), 4.

31 Ibid., 375–76.

32 Fairfax County Resolves, 1774, http://constitution.org/bcp/fairfax_res. htm.

33 Jay A. Parry, Andrew M. Allison, and W. Cleon Skousen, 2009, *The Real George Washington: The True Story of America's Most Indispensable Man* (Malta: National Center for Constitutional Studies), 789.

34 Ibid.

35 Edward A. Johnson, 1890, *A School History of the Negro Race in America, from 1619 to 1890, with a Short Introduction as to the Origin of the Race; Also a Short Sketch of Liberia* (Raleigh: Edwards & Broughton), http:// docsouth.unc.edu/church/johnson/johnson.html.

36 Ibid.

37 W. O. Blake, 1857, *The African Slave Trade and the Political History of Slavery in the United States*, http://books.google.com/ books?id=UgwZAAAA YAAJ&printsec=frontcover&dq=w.o.+blake+the+history+of+slavery&hl= en&ei=WzB4TqWLE4XisQKx28HADQ&sa=X&oi=book_result&ct= result&resnum=1&ved=0CC0Q6AEwAA#v=onepage&q&f=false.

38 John P. Kaminski, ed., 1995, *A Necessary Evil? Slavery and the Debate over the Constitution* (Madison, WI: Madison House), 15.

39 Dumas Malone, 1981, *Jefferson and His Time: The Sage of Monticello* (Boston: Little Brown and Company), 319.

40 Benjamin Franklin, 1839, *The Works of Benjamin Franklin,* vol. VIII, ed. Jared Sparks (Boston: Tappan, Whittemore, and Mason), 42.

41 Emberson Edward Proper, 1900, *Colonial Immigration Laws: A Study of the Regulation of Immigration by the English Colonies in America*, Studies in History, Economics and Public Law (New York: The Columbia University Press), 28–29. http://archive.org/stream/ colonialimmigrat00proprich#page/28/mode/2up.

42   Thomas Jefferson, as cited by Andrew M. Allison, 1983, *The Real Thomas Jefferson: The True Story of America's Philosopher of Freedom*, 2nd ed., vol. 1, American Classic Series (Malta: National Center for Constitutional Studies,), 628.

43   Hamilton Pierson, 1971, *Jefferson at Monticello; The Private Life of Thomas Jefferson* (Freeport: Books for Libraries Press).

44   Jefferson, as cited by Allison, *The Real Thomas Jefferson*, 630.

45   US Congress, 1808, An Act to Prohibit the Importation of Slaves into any Port or Place within the Jurisdiction of the United States, from and after the First Day of January, in the Year of Our Lord One Thousand Eight Hundred and Eight (The Avalon Project, Yale Law School), http://avalon.law.yale.edu/19th_century/sl004.asp.

46   John Quincy Adams, 1837, *An Oration Delivered before the Inhabitants of the Town of Newburyport at Their Request on the Sixty-first Anniversary of the Declaration of Independence* (Newburyport: Charles Whipple), July 4, 50.

47   Abraham Lincoln, 1858, "Speech at Lewistown, Illinois," August 17, in the *Collected Works of Abraham Lincoln*, 1809–1865, ed. Roy P. Basler, vol. 2 (New Brunswick: Rutgers University Press, 1953).

48   James Madison, 1788, "The Powers Conferred by the Constitution Further Considered," Federalist No. 42 in *Federalist Papers*, January 22, Constitution Society, http://constitution.org/fed/federa42.htm.

49   Larry Schweikart, 2008, *48 Liberal Lies about American History: (that You Probably Learned in School)* (New York: Sentinel), 116.

50   Johnson, *A School History of the Negro Race in America*.

51   John Hancock, 1865, *The Great Question for the People!: Essays on the Elective Franchise; or, Who Has the Right to Vote?* (Philadelphia: Merrihew & Son), 21.

52   Ibid., 22–23.

53   Ibid., 24.

54   John Adams, 1776, "From John Adams to James Sullivan" (National Archives, Founders Online), May 26, https://founders.archives.gov/documents/Adams/06-04-02-0091.

55   James Madison, 1787, *The Debates in the Federal Convention of 1787*,
      August 8, Constitution Society, http://constitution.org/dfc/dfc_0808.
      htm.

56   Luther Martin, 1787, "Luther Martin's Letter," in Jonathan Elliot, 1836,
      *The Debates in the Several State Conventions on the Adoption of the Federal
      Constitution as Recommended by the General Convention at Philadelphia in
      1787 Together with the Journal of the Federal Convention, Luther Martin's
      Letter, Yates's Minutes, Congressional Opinions, Virginia and Kentucky
      Resolutions of '98–99, and Other Illustrations of the Constitution*, 5 vols.,
      2nd ed., Liberty Fund, http://files.libertyfund.org/files/1905/1314.01_
      Bk.pdf.

57   Thomas G. West, 1992, "Was the American Founding Unjust? The Case
      of Slavery," *Principles* (Spring/Summer):,5.

58   Ibid.

59   Edward C. Papenfuse et. al, eds., 2002, *A Biographical Dictionary of the
      Maryland Legislature 1635–1789*, Archives of Maryland Online, http://
      aomol.net/megafile/msa/speccol/sc2900/sc2908/000001/000426/html/
      am426--486.html.

60   Ibid, http://msa.maryland.gov/megafile/msa/speccol/sc2900/
      sc2908/0000
      01/000426/html/am426--589.html.

61   Francis Nash, 1903, *Hillsboro: Colonial and Revolutionary* (Raleigh:
      Edwards & Broughton), 92, http://books.google.com/
      books?id=YF0dAAAAMAAJ&pg=PA1&lpg=PA1&dq=francis+nash+
      hillsboro+colonial+and+revolutionary&source=bl&ots=9ef1wvLiYh&
      sig=s3INENFayYrS8XZLi74Ffo-Jj-8&hl=en&ei=K8t6Tqf0DMKIsQK
      fzs29Aw&sa=X&oi=book_result&ct=result&resnum=2&sqi=2&ved=
      0CCEQ6AEwAQ#v=onepage&q=william%20few&f=false.

62   William Few, 1804, "Slavery in the Early Republic," Digital History,
      http://www.digitalhistory.uh.edu/documents/documents_
      p2.cfm?doc=359.

63   Jenny B. Wahl, n.d., "Slavery in the United States," Economics History
      Services, accessed September 20, 2011, eh.net/encyclopedia/article/wahl.
      slavery.us.

64   Julie Richter, 1999, "Slavery in John Blair's Public and Personal Lives in
      1751," *The Colonial Williamsburg Interpreter* 20 (Fall): 1–8.

65   America's Founding Fathers—Delegates to the Constitutional
      Convention, n.d., accessed September 22, 2011, http://www.archives.
      gov/exhibits/charters/constitution_founding_fathers_virginia.html#Blair.

66   David Barton, 2008, "As a Reformer," in *Benjamin Rush: Signer of the
      Declaration of Independence*, 1st ed. (Aledo: Wallbuilders Press), 133.

67   Andrew M. Allison, W. Cleon Skousen, and M. Richard Maxfield, 2009,
      The Real Benjamin Franklin (Malta: National Center for Constitutional
      Studies), 482.

68   Ira Stoll, 2008, *Samuel Adams: A Life* (New York: Free Press), 55.

69   Ibid., 234.

70   Locke, *The Second Treatise of Civil Government*, sec. 135, emphasis added.

71   William Blackstone, 1803, *Commentaries on the Laws of England*, ed.
      George Tucker (Philadelphia), http://www.constitution.org/tb/tb-1102.
      htm.

72   Thomas Jefferson, 1811, "Jefferson to Benjamin Rush,"
      Library of Congress, http://memory.loc.gov/cgi-bin/
      ampage?collId=mtj1&fileName=mtj1page045.db&recNum=55.

73   Locke, *The Second Treatise of Civil Government*, sec. 124.

74   George Mason, 1776, The Virginia Declaration of Rights (Constitution
      Society), May 15, emphasis added, http://constitution.org/bcp/virg_dor.
      htm.

75   John Adams, 1954, *Political Writings of John Adams*, ed. George A.
      Peek Jr., American Heritage Series (New York: Liberal Arts Press), 96,
      emphasis added.

76   John Adams, 1856, *The Works of John Adams, Second President of the
      United States: With a Life of the Author, Notes and Illustrations, by His
      Grandson Charles Francis Adams*, vol. 6 (Boston: Little, Brown and Co.).

77   Stoll, *Samuel Adams*, 48.

78   Jefferson, as cited by Allison, *The Real Thomas Jefferson*, 595.

79   Locke, *The Second Treatise of Civil Government*, sec. 123.

80   Ibid., emphasis added.

81   Ibid.

82   Ibid., 149, emphasis added.

83   Ibid., 155.

84   Ibid., 199.

85   Ibid., 221, 222, emphasis added.

86   Ibid., 225.

87   Jefferson, as cited by Allison, *The Real Thomas Jefferson*, 458.

88   Locke, *The Second Treatise of Civil Government*, sec. 223.

89   Ibid., 230.

90   Ibid., 225.

91   Ibid., 230.

Chapter 3 The Charges: Abuses of Executive Power

92   Stephen E. Lucas, 1989, *The Stylistic Artistry of the Declaration of Independence*, National Archives, https://www.archives.gov/founding-docs/stylistic-artistry-of-the-declaration.

93   Thomas Paine, 1776, *Common Sense* (Philadelphia), http://constitution.org/tp/comsense.htm.

94   Franklin, *The Works of Benjamin Franklin,* vol. VIII, 42.

95   Stoll, *Samuel Adams*, 55.

96   Parliament, Great Britain, 1766, The Declaratory Act (The Avalon Project, Yale Law School), March 18, http://avalon.law.yale.edu/18th_century/declaratory_act_1766.asp.

97   Sarah Kliff, 2013, "Charts: How Roe v. Wade Changed Abortion Rights," *Washington Post*, January 22, http://www.washingtonpost.com/blogs/wonkblog/wp/2013/01/22/charts-how-roe-v-wade-changed-abortion-rights/.

98   James Wilson, 1790, *Of the Natural Rights of Individuals*, TeachingAmericanHistory.org. (Ashbrook Center, Ashland University),

http://teachingamericanhistory.org/library/document/of-the-natural-rights-of-individuals/#26.

99   See, for example, French geneticist Jerome LeJeune who said before the US Congress: "To accept the fact that after fertilization has taken place a new human has come into being is no longer a matter of taste or opinion. The human nature of the human being from conception to old age is not a metaphysical contention, it is plain experimental evidence" (Jerome LeJeune, as cited in *The Human Life Bill—S. 158, Report Together with Additional and Minority Views to the Committee on the Judiciary, United States Senate, Made by Its Subcommittee on Separation of Powers*, 97th Congress, 1st session, 1981, 9. Also see Francis J. Beckwith, 1993, *Politically Correct Death: Answering Arguments for Abortion Rights* (Grand Rapids: Baker Books), chap. 3.

100   Arizona State Legislature, 2010, House Bill 2162, http://www.azleg.gov//FormatDocument.asp?inDoc=/legtext/49leg/2r/bills/hb2162c.htm&Session_ID=93.

101   *CBS News*, 2010, "Feds Sue to Block Arizona Immigration Law," July 6, http://www.cbsnews.com/stories/2010/07/06/politics/main6651468.shtml.

102   Ramsay, *The History of the American Revolution*, vol. 1, 42.

103   Parliament, Great Britain, 1764, The Currency Act (The Avalon Project, Yale Law School), April 19, http://avalon.law.yale.edu/18th_century/curency_act_1764.asp.

104   Thomas Jefferson, 1774, *A Summary View of the Rights of British America*, The Avalon Project, Yale Law School, http://avalon.law.yale.edu/18th_century/jeffsumm.asp#back10.

105   James I, 1620, Charter of New England (The Avalon Project, Yale Law School), http://avalon.law.yale.edu/17th_century/mass01.asp.

106   Stoll, *Samuel Adams*, 46, 48.

107   Circular Letter to the Governors in America, 1768 (The Avalon Project, Yale Law School), April 21, emphasis added, http://avalon.law.yale.edu/18th_century/circ_let_gov_1768.asp.

108   George III, 1763, *The Royal Proclamation*, The Avalon Project, Yale Law School, October 7, http://avalon.law.yale.edu/18th_century/proc1763. asp.

109   Parliament, Great Britain, 1774, The Massachusetts Government Act (The Avalon Project, Yale Law School), May 20, emphasis added, http:// avalon.law.yale.edu/18th_century/mass_gov_act.asp.

110   Ibid.

111   Jefferson, *A Summary View of the Rights of British America*, emphasis added.

112   Mercy Otis Warren, 1805, *History of the Rise, Progress and Termination of the American Revolution*, 2 vols., ed. Lester H. Cohen (Indianapolis: Liberty Fund, 1989), vol. 1, 42.

113   Ibid., 72.

114   Ramsay, *The History of the American Revolution*, vol. 1, 73.

115   David J. Vaughn, 1997, *Give Me Liberty: The Uncompromising Statesmanship of Patrick Henry* (Nashville: Cumberland House Publishing), 65–66.

116   Parliament, The Massachusetts Government Act.

117   Ramsay, *The History of the American Revolution*. vol. 1, 73.

118   Parliament, Great Britain, 1767, The New York Suspending Act, TeachingAmericanHistory.org, (Ashbrook Center, Ashland University), July 20, http://teachingamericanhistory.org/library/document/the-new-york-suspending-act/.

119   Jefferson, *A Summary View of the Rights of British America*.

120   Barack Hussein Obama, 2009, Executive Order 13503 (White House), February 24, https://www.gpo.gov/fdsys/pkg/FR-2009-02-24/pdf/E9-4068.pdf.

121   George W. Bush, 2001, Executive Order: President's Commission to Strengthen Social Security (White House), May 2, http://georgewbush-whitehouse.archives.gov/news/releases/2001/05/20010502-5.html.

122   Locke, *The Second Treatise of Civil Government*, sec. 134.

123   Ramsay, *The History of the American Revolution*, vol. 1, 64.

124 Edmund S. Morgan and Helen M. Morgan, 1995, *The Stamp Act Crisis: Prologue to Revolution* (Chapel Hill: University of North Carolina Press), 108.

125 Proper, *Colonial Immigration Laws*, 61, 65.

126 Allison et al, *The Real Benjamin Franklin*, 94.

127 Australian Government, n.d., "Convicts and the British Colonies in Australia," accessed April 6, 2016, http://www.australia.gov.au/about-australia/australian-story/convicts-and-the-british-colonies.

128 *Navigation Acts*, n.d., Digital History, emphasis added, accessed January 9, 2014, http://www.digitalhistory.uh.edu/disp_textbook. cfm?smtID=3&psid=4102.

129 Allison et al, *The Real Benjamin Franklin*, 354.

130 Jens Manuel Krogstad, Jeffrey S. Passell, and D'Vera Cohn, 2016, "5 Facts about Illegal Immigration in the U.S.," Pew Research Center, November 3, http://www.pewresearch.org/fact-tank/2015/11/19/5-facts-about-illegal-immigration-in-the-u-s/.

131 Tony Lee, 2013, "Jerry Brown Signs Bill Making CA Sanctuary State for Most Illegals," *Breitbart*, October 6, http://www.breitbart.com/big-government/2013/10/06/ca-gov-signs-bill-making-ca-sanctuary-state-for-most-illegals/.

132 Jerry Markon, 2015, "Senior Obama Officials Have Warned of Challenges in Screening Refugees from Syria," *Washington Post*, November 17, https://www.washingtonpost.com/news/federal-eye/wp/2015/11/17/senior-obama-officials-have-warned-of-challenges-in-screening-refugees-from-syria/.

133 North Carolina Court History of Interest, n.d., accessed June 13, 2014, http://www.nccourts.org/County/Orange/Interest.asp.

134 Herman Husband, n.d., *An Impartial Relation of the First Rise and Cause of the Recent Differences in Publick Affairs, in the Progress of the So Much Talked of Regulation in North Carolina*, Learn NC, accessed June 13, 2014, http://www.learnnc.org/lp/editions/nchist-revolution/4939.

135 Francis L. Hawks, 1853, "Battle of the Alamance and War of the Regulation," in *Revolutionary History of North Carolina, in Three Lectures,*

by Francis L. Hawks, David L. Swain, and William A. Graham, with William D. Cooke, compiler (Raleigh: William D. Cooke; New York: G. P. Putnam and Co), 14.

136   Ibid., 36.

137   In two recent US Supreme Court cases, *Roper v. Simmons* and *Lawrence v. Texas*, the Supreme Court made part of its decision in both cases based on foreign courts and foreign authorities. This is in violation of the Constitution which requires that the Constitution and laws made in pursuance thereof are the supreme law of the land. Foreign authorities, laws, or court decisions have no relevance in the US. These two recent decisions violate Article VI of the Constitution. The justices' violation of their oath requires that Congress impeach and try them, though the outcome is never pre-determined. More on these two cases will be discussed in chapter 4.

138   Parliament, The Massachusetts Government Act.

139   Parliament, Great Britain, 1767, The Townsend Act (The Avalon Project, Yale Law School), November 20, emphasis added, http://avalon.law.yale. edu/18th_century/townsend_act_1767.asp.

140   "History of the Federal Judiciary," n.d., Federal Judicial Center, accessed April 8, 2016, http://www.fjc.gov/history/home.nsf/page/judges_ impeachments.html; and "November 30, 1804: Senate Prepares for Impeachment Trial," n.d., United States Senate, https://www.senate.gov/ artandhistory/history/minute/Senate_Tries_Justice.htm.

141   Lucas, *The Stylistic Artistry of the Declaration of Independence*.

142   Parliament, Great Britain, 1765, The Quartering Act (The Avalon Project, Yale Law School), May 15, emphasis added, http://avalon.law. yale.edu/18th_century/quartering_act_165.asp.

143   Parliament, Great Britain, 1774, The Quartering Act (The Avalon Project), June 2, http://avalon.law.yale.edu/18th_century/quartering_ act_1774.asp.

144   Parliament, Great Britain, 1764, The Sugar Act (The Avalon Project, Yale Law School), avalon.law.yale.edu/18th_century/sugar_act_1764.asp.

145   Ibid.

146 Ibid.

147 Parliament, Great Britain, 1765, The Stamp Act (The Avalon Project, Yale Law School), March 22, http://avalon.law.yale.edu/18th_century/stamp_act_1765.asp.

148 Ibid., emphasis added.

149 Vaughn, *Give Me Liberty*, 51–53.

150 United States of America v. John Pozsgai, Gizella Pozsgai, Mercer Wrecking & Recycling Corporation, J. Vinch & Sons, Inc., John Pozsgai and Gizella Pozsgai, Appellants, 1993, 999 F.2d 719 (3d Cir.), Justia US Law, http://law.justia.com/cases/federal/appellate-courts/F2/999/719/309100/.

151 Ibid.

152 Wickard v. Filburn, 1942, 317 U.S. 111, Oyez.org, accessed July 23, 2014, https://supreme.justia.com/cases/federal/us/317/111/.

153 USA.gov, n.d, "A–Z Index of U.S. Government Departments and Agencies," accessed July 23, 2014, https://www.usa.gov/federal-agencies/a.

154 James Madison, n.d., "Selected Quotes of James Madison," Constitution Society, accessed May 22, 2015, http://www.constitution.org/jm/jm_quotes.htm.

155 Jeanine Cali, 2013, "Frequent Reference Question: How Many Federal Laws Are There?" Library of Congress, March 12, https://blogs.loc.gov/law/2013/03/frequent-reference-question-how-many-federal-laws-are-there/.

156 Locke, *The Second Treatise of Civil Government*, sec. 141, emphasis added.

157 US Internal Revenue Service, 2013, "National Taxpayer Advocate Delivers Annual Report to Congress; Focuses on Tax Reform, IRS Funding and Identity Theft," https://www.irs.gov/uac/Newsroom/National-Taxpayer-Advocate-Delivers-2012-Annual-Report-to-Congress.

158 Jefferson, *A Summary View of the Rights of British America*, emphasis added.

159 US Social Security Administration, 2012, "Request for Quote for Ammunition," SSA-RFQ-12-1851, https://www.fbo.gov/index?s=

opportunity&mode=form&id=6c39a2a9f00a10187a1432388a3301e5
&tab=core&_cview=0&fb_source=message.

160 National Oceanic and Atmospheric Administration,
     n.d., "13—Ammunition and Shooting Targets,"
     accessed April 14, 2016, https://www.fbo.gov/
     index?s=opportunity&mode=form&tab=core&id=4370194550dd10f4a
     ae476069e17eb85&_cview=1.

161 Associated Press, 2013, "Homeland Security Aims to Buy 1.6 Billion
     Rounds of Ammo," *Denver Post*, February 14, http://www.denverpost.
     com/nationworld/ci_22594279/homeland-security-aims-buy-1-6-
     billion-rounds.

162 Leonard Devin, 2014, "Why Is the Post Office Buying Bullets?"
     Bloomberg Businessweek, April 21, http://www.bloomberg.com/news/
     articles/2014-04-21/why-is-the-post-office-buying-bullets.

Chapter 4 The Charges: Abuses of Legislative Power

163 James I, The First Charter of Virginia.

164 James I, The Second Charter of Virginia.

165 James I, Charter of New England.

166 Government of New Haven Colony, 1643 (The Avalon Project, Yale
     Law School), October 27/November 6, http://avalon.law.yale.edu/17th_
     century/ct02.asp.

167 Charles II, Charter of Connecticut.

168 Commission of John Cutt, 1680 (The Avalon Project, Yale Law School),
     http://avalon.law.yale.edu/17th_century/nh08.asp.

169 Penn, William, 1701, Charter of Delaware (The Avalon Project, Yale Law
     School), http://avalon.law.yale.edu/18th_century/de01.asp.

170 George II, 1732, Charter of Georgia (The Avalon Project, Yale Law
     School), http://avalon.law.yale.edu/18th_century/ga01.asp.

171 Charles II, 1663, Charter of Carolina (The Avalon Project, Yale Law
     School), March 24, http://avalon.law.yale.edu/17th_century/nc01.asp.

172 Charles I, 1632, The Charter of Maryland (The Avalon Project, Yale Law School), emphasis added, http://avalon.law.yale.edu/17th_century/ma01.asp.

173 Ibid.

174 Parliament, The Declaratory Act, emphasis added.

175 George III, 1775, *King George III's Address to Parliament*, Library of Congress, October 27, http://www.loc.gov/teachers/classroommaterials/presentationsandactivities/presentations/timeline/amrev/shots/address.html.

176 Lawrence et al v. Texas, 2003, No. 02-102, FindLaw, http://caselaw.lp.findlaw.com/scripts/getcase.pl?court=US&vol=000&invol=02-102#opinion1.

177 Anthony Kennedy, 2005, Roper v. Simmons, (03-633) 543 U.S. 551 (2005) 112 S. W. 3d 397, affirmed (Cornell University Law School), https://www.law.cornell.edu/supct/html/03-633.ZO.html.

178 David McCullough, 2001, *John Adams* (New York: Simon & Schuster).

179 Jefferson, *A Summary View of the Rights of British America*.

180 Parliament, Great Britain, 1774, The Administration of Justice Act (The Avalon Project, Yale Law School), May 20, http://avalon.law.yale.edu/18th_century/admin_of_justice_act.asp.

181 Parliament, The Massachusetts Government Act.

182 Cleveland Board of Education v. Loudermill, 1985, 470 U.S. 532, (Oyez, IIT Chicago-Kent College of Law), http://www.oyez.org/cases/1980-1989/1984/1984_83_1362.

183 *Navigation Acts*.

184 Parliament, Great Britain, 1774, The Boston Port Act (The Avalon Project, Yale Law School), May 31, http://avalon.law.yale.edu/18th_century/boston_port_act.asp.

185 Stoll, *Samuel Adams*, 120.

186 Tim Boersma and Charles K. Ebinger, 2014, "Lift the Ban on U.S. Oil Exports," Brookings Institute, http://www.brookings.edu/research/papers/2014/01/lift-ban-us-oil-exports-boersma-ebinger.

187 US Department of Justice, Bureau of Alcohol, Tobacco, Firearms and Explosives, n.d.. *ATF Guidebook—Importation & Verification of Firearms, Ammunition, and Implements of War*, accessed September 4, 2014, http://www.atf.gov/files/firearms/guides/importation-verification/download/firearms-imporation-verification-guidebook--complete.pdf.

188 Locke, *The Second Treatise of Civil Government*, sec. 138.

189 Samuel Adams, 1772, *The Rights of the Colonists*, November 20, http://www.constitution.org/bcp/right_col.htm.

190 Jefferson, as cited by Allison, *The Real Thomas Jefferson*, 504.

191 Parliament, The Sugar Act.

192 Parliament, The Massachusetts Government Act.

193 Parliament, The Sugar Act.

194 Parliament, The Administration of Justice Act.

195 First Continental Congress, 1774, Declaration and Resolves on Colonial Rights of the First Continental Congress, Constitution Society, October 14, http://www.constitution.org/bcp/colright.htm. The initials N.C.D. stand for *nemine contradicente,* which means "unanimous delegation support."

196 United States of America v. John Pozsgai.

197 Parliament, Great Britian, 1774, The Quebec Act: An Act for Making More Effectual Provision for the Government of the Province of Quebec in North America (The Avalon Project, Yale Law School), October 7, http://avalon.law.yale.edu/18th_century/quebec_act_1774.asp.

198 George III, *The Royal Proclamation*.

199 The Quebec Act.

200 Later those lands became part of the United States and were called the Northwest Territories.

201 Jay O'Laughlin, 2011, "Fact Sheet #8: Federal Land as a Percentage of Total State Land Area," College of Natural Resources Policy Analysis Group, University of Idaho, http://www.idahoforests.org/img/pdf/CQHSNFPAG-factsheet.pdf.

202 US Department of Agriculture, Forest Service, n.d., *Frank Church River of No Return Wilderness*, accessed April 21, 2016, http://www.fs.usda.gov/ detail/scnf/specialplaces/?cid=stelprdb5360033.

203 Quoctrung Bui and Margot Sanger-Katz, 2016, "Why the Government Owns so Much Land in the West," *New York Times*, January 5, http:// www.nytimes.com/2016/01/06/upshot/why-the-government-owns-so- much-land-in-the-west.html?_r=0.

204 Parliament, The Massachusetts Government Act.

205 Parliament, The Declaratory Act, emphasis added.

206 Constitutional Convention of Idaho, 1890, Constitution of the State of Idaho, http://legislature.idaho.gov/idstat/IC/ArtIIISect28.htm.

207 Idaho Secretary of State, n.d., "November 7, 2006 General Election Results," accessed September 12, 2014, http://www.sos.idaho.gov/elect/ RESULTS/2006/general/tot_stwd.htm.

208 Latta et al v. Otter et al, 2014, No. 1:13-cv-00482, http://www.plainsite. org/dockets/uoehxt8w/idaho-district-court/latta-et-al-v-otter-et-al/. See PDF under entry 101.

209 Parliament, The Declaratory Act.

Chapter 5 The Charges: Abuses of War Power

210 George III, 1775, *Royal Proclamation of Rebellion*, Digital History, August 23, http://www.digitalhistory.uh.edu/disp_textbook. cfm?smtID=3&psid=41055.

211 George III, *King George III's Address to Parliament*.

212 "British Royal Proclamations Relating to America, 1603–1783," n.d., Archive.org, accessed September 18, 2014, http://www.archive.org/ stream/royalproclamations12brigrich/royalproclamations12brigrich_ djvu.txt.

213 Jie Zong and Jeanne Batalova, 2017, *Frequently Requested Statistics on Immigrants and Immigration in the United States* (Washington, DC: Migration Policy Institute), http://www.migrationpolicy.org/article/

frequently-requested-statistics-immigrants-and-immigration-united-states.

214 Warren, *History of the Rise, Progress and Termination of the American Revolution*, vol. 1, 120.

215 Ibid., 133.

216 Ibid., 134.

217 Ibid.

218 Ramsay, *The History of the American Revolution*, vol. 1, 165.

219 "Watts Rebellion (Los Angeles, 1965)," n.d., The King Center, accessed October 10, 2014, http://mlk-kpp01.stanford.edu/index.php/encyclopedia/encyclopedia/enc_watts_rebellion_los_angeles_1965/.

220 Jerry Seper and Matthew Cella, 2010, "Signs in Arizona Warn of Smuggler Dangers," *Washington Times*, August 31, http://www.washingtontimes.com/news/2010/aug/31/signs-in-arizona-warn-of-smuggler-dangers/?page=all.

221 Lord John Emerich Edward Dalberg Acton, n.d., "Lord Acton Quote Archive," Acton Institute for the Study of Religion and Liberty, accessed October 13, 2014, http://www.acton.org/research/lord-acton-quote-archive.

222 Warren, *History of the Rise, Progress and Termination of the American Revolution*, vol.1, 191.

223 "Hessians," n.d., Mountvernon.org, accessed October 10, 2014, http://www.mountvernon.org/research-collections/digital-encyclopedia/article/hessians/.

224 Lord Acton, "Lord Acton Quote Archive."

225 "British Royal Proclamations Relating to America, 1603–1783," Archive.org.

226 Roland G. Usher Jr., 1951, "Royal Navy Impressment during the American Revolution," *The Mississippi Valley Historical Review* 37, no. 4 (March): 673–88.

227 Ramsay, *The History of the American Revolution*, vol. 1, 167.

228 Ramsay, *The History of the American Revolution*, vol. 1, 167–68.

229 Ibid., 182–85.

230 Jefferson, as cited by Allison, *The Real Thomas Jefferson*, 482–83.
231 William R. Reynolds Jr., 2012, *Andrew Pickens: South Carolina Patriot in the Revolutionary War* (Jefferson: McFarland & Co.), 63.
232 Franklin, *The Works of Benjamin Franklin,* vol. VIII, 42.
233 Blake, *The African Slave Trade.*
234 Malone, *Jefferson and His Time*, 319.
235 Jefferson, as cited by Allison, *The Real Thomas Jefferson*, 630.
236 US Congress, An Act to Prohibit the Importation of Slaves.
237 Johnson, *A School History of the Negro Race in* America.

Chapter 6 Reconciliation Attempts

238 Parliament, The Declaratory Act.
239 "Olive Branch Petition," 1775, Digital History, July 8, http://www.digitalhistory.uh.edu/disp_textbook.cfm?smtID=3&psid=3881.
240 Ibid.
241 Ibid.
242 Allison et al, "In England Again: Fighting the Stamp Act," in *The Real Benjamin Franklin.*
243 Ibid., 160.
244 Ibid., 161.
245 Ibid.
246 Stoll, *Samuel Adams*, 41.
247 Edmund Burke, 1999, *Select Works of Edmund Burke*, Payne edition, vol. 1 (Indianapolis: Online Liberty Fund), emphasis added, http://oll.libertyfund.org/titles/burke-select-works-of-edmund-burke-vol-1--5.

Chapter 7 Separation and the Appeal to Heaven

248 Locke, *The Second Treatise of Civil Government*, sec. 199.
249 Ibid.
250 Allison et al, The Real Benjamin Franklin, 202.

251 "Signers of the Declaration of Independence," n.d., Independence Hall Association, accessed November 21, 2014, http://www.ushistory.org/ declaration/signers/hewes.html.

252 B. J. Lossing, 1866, *Biographical Sketches of the Signers of the Declaration of American Independence* (Philadelphia: Davis, Porter and Co), 73.

253 Ibid., 236–37.

254 "Signers of the Declaration of Independence," Independence Hall Association.

255 Lossing, *Biographical Sketches of the Signers of the Declaration of American Independence*, 89.

256 "Signers of the Declaration of Independence," Independence Hall Association.

257 Lossing, *Biographical Sketches of the Signers of the Declaration of American Independence*, 96–97.

258 Thomas Alonzo Dill, 1983, *Carter Braxton, Virginia Signer: A Conservative in Revolt* (Lanham: University Press of America), 103.

259 Ibid., 104.

260 Lossing, *Biographical Sketches of the Signers of the Declaration of American Independence*, 76.

261 Ibid., 217–18.

262 Ibid.

263 "Signers of the Declaration of Independence," Independence Hall Association.

264 Ibid.

265 Lossing, *Biographical Sketches of the Signers of the Declaration of American Independence*, 207.

266 Ibid., 70.

267 Ibid., 80.

268 Ibid., 213–14.

269 Ibid., 64–65.

270 Ibid., 190–92.

271 William Safire, 1997, *Lend Me Your Ears: Great Speeches in History* (New York: W. W. Norton & Co.), 171.

Morgan James
Speakers Group

www.TheMorganJamesSpeakersGroup.com

We connect Morgan James published
authors with live and online events
and audiences whom will benefit
from their expertise.

CPSIA information can be obtained
at www.ICGtesting.com
Printed in the USA
BVHW07s1521200618
519524BV00011B/780/P

9 781683 505853